Veteran
Volunteer

Veteran Volunteer

Memoir of the Trenches, Tanks and Captivity 1914–1919

Frank Vans Agnew

*'I expect to get my fill of thrills in command of a Tank, which I shall name
The Old and Bold, and try and live up to.'*

Edited and introduced by *Jamie Vans* and *Peter Widdowson*

Pen & Sword
MILITARY

First published in Great Britain in 2014 by
Pen & Sword Military
an imprint of
Pen & Sword Books Ltd
47 Church Street
Barnsley
South Yorkshire
S70 2AS

Copyright © Jamie Vans 2014

ISBN 978 1 78346 277 3

Typeset in Ehrhardt by
Mac Style, Bridlington, East Yorkshire
Printed and bound in the UK by CPI Group (UK) Ltd, Croydon,
CRO 4YY

Pen & Sword Books Ltd incorporates the imprints of Pen & Sword
Archaeology, Atlas, Aviation, Battleground, Discovery, Family History,
History, Maritime, Military, Naval, Politics, Railways, Select,
Social History, Transport, True Crime, and Claymore Press,
Frontline Books, Leo Cooper, Praetorian Press, Remember When,
Seaforth Publishing and Wharncliffe.

For a complete list of Pen & Sword titles please contact
PEN & SWORD BOOKS LIMITED
47 Church Street, Barnsley, South Yorkshire, S70 2AS, England
E-mail: enquiries@pen-and-sword.co.uk
Website: www.pen-and-sword.co.uk

Contents

Foreword

Captain Vans Agnew left to his family a full account of his time on the Western Front and as a Prisoner of War (PoW) in Germany, in the form of diaries, letters and memoirs. He had clearly always intended to publish an edited version of them and it seems probable that only his unusually busy life and the lack of a settled home could have prevented him from approaching a publisher with the typescript from which the following extracts are drawn. He had reached the stage, at least, of making a list of publishers and their special interests. If any such approach was made, though, no record survives of it.

Although I have been the owner of this archive since 1966, I have put off until recently the job of editing the work and making it available to the wider readership for which it was always intended. I owe a considerable debt to Professor Peter Widdowson (who sadly died in 2009) who collaborated on the first steps of selection and configuration of the material and whose enthusiasm and knowledge helped me to see its importance and to appreciate what a remarkable character my great uncle was.

Frank was forty-six when he travelled from America in 1914 to fight the Germans, but in order to get into the 2nd King Edward's Horse, a regiment recruited from overseas volunteers, he claimed to be forty. 'I can call to mind vividly the day that he came to me whilst my regiment was training in England and begged me to accept him as a trooper in the ranks. I was so much struck at the time by his spirit that I immediately took him into the regiment even though his age appeared to be against him. I never regretted for one moment taking this decision,' his commanding officer[1] wrote in a letter in 1918. 'No man under my command did harder, more active or braver service than your brother.'

Posted to the front in May 1915, Frank was soon trained as a bomb-thrower, which got him into the thick of the action, but not enough to satisfy him. He was quickly promoted and in August proudly accepted a commission which led to a period of training in Ireland. He returned to France in December 1915 for further training in machine guns and acted as an observer of the

Battle of the Somme where he first saw tanks in action. Another spell of training in the use of the Vickers machine-gun followed but, to his disgust, this was interrupted by a posting of several months as Divisional Cavalry, guarding the headquarters of General Haig at Montreuil-sur-Mer.

In January 1917 he was finally able to get himself a transfer to the Tank Corps and as a tank commander was wounded at Messines, 'the model show of the whole war' as he described it, in an action for which he was awarded the Military Cross. He saw further action at Third Ypres, 'not surprising that B Battalion was butchered that day' and at Cambrai where he commanded No.5 section. After a successful attack on 21 November, heavy fighting followed on the 23rd and the tank Frank was in was disabled. He and several of the crew were wounded and were forced to give themselves up as prisoners.

Frank was sent initially to Münster where his wounds were treated by a 'dud' doctor. Luckily, he was soon transferred to hospital in Hanover and thence successively to prison camps at Karlsruhe, Heidelberg and Fürstenberg. His account of this time is rich with details, including photographs and memorabilia, of how the prisoners passed their time (tennis, musical theatre and escaping were among the entertainments they made for themselves). Extraordinarily he was able to obtain, in Germany, first an atlas showing the various theatres of war and later a set of maps which he joined together to make a sheet about seven feet square on which he plotted the progress of the war – with increasing contentment, especially when the Germans announced that they were retreating 'according to plan'.

On and off, he had hopes that his age and wounded arm would persuade the Germans to allow him into internment in Holland or Switzerland but he was one of the unlucky ones despite the recommendation of the medical board. Frank was convinced that being in the Tank Corps made him a villain in the eyes of the German doctor who made the final decision and who persisted in refusing his application.

He was stuck in this succession of German camps until after the Armistice, then volunteered to go to Copenhagen to help in the repatriation of British troops; 'it seems a shame not to come back to spend Christmas with you but you know how it is, and you would do the same yourself,' he wrote to his sister. He finally made it back to England in January 1919 and left for the USA in October. A 50-year-old survivor of some of the fiercest actions on the Western Front, Frank described the war variously as 'disgusting' and 'hideous' but also, as it neared its end, as 'a grand war'.

During his military service he wrote most regularly to his sister Ida who lived in London and with whom he spent his leaves. She acted as the main point of contact for family and friends on both sides of the Atlantic, passing on news to and from Frank and organizing parcels of food and other necessities, first to Belgium and France and later, more importantly, to the German camps in which he was held prisoner. She also, crucially, kept all his letters to her, no doubt at his request.

The memoirs stand out among contemporary accounts for his attitude to the war which was a very personal mix of the crudely 'gung-ho' and thoughtful assessment of its historical context, particularly his intense desire to see the United States join the war. I am sure it was with that outcome in mind that he sent articles for publication in *Scribner's Magazine* in New York and wrote his most vituperative letters to friends and relatives in the USA.

At times, he loathed Germans and hurled vile insults at them in his letters; at others, he admired the courage of the soldiers in the opposite trenches, describing them at various times as a 'mangy, yelping mongrel' and as 'good fighting material'. Reasonably enough he blamed Germany's leaders for causing the war and British and Allied generals and staff officers for its mismanagement. He had no time for those who fought from a safe 30-mile distance, whom he described as 'gilded beings' with halos (and did not mean that kindly) and he despised all those whom he considered to be cowards or defeatists.

He made his feelings plain when he wrote, in a paper he entitled *Things that ought to be remembered:* 'After the war, we were presented with several well known and much read accounts of the War, dished up as novels, in which the neurotic, temperamental and sentimental authors had the hardihood to publish their experiences. These were no worse than those [of] thousands of other men, but their authors managed to convey to a large section of the public, both at home and in enemy countries, that their version portrayed the general feelings of the members of the British Army.' Whether Frank expressed the 'general feelings' of the British Army either must remain an open question.

Frank Vans Agnew was born in India in 1868, third son of the sixth son of a family of Galloway landowners. As the third Vans Agnew at school in England he was called Tertius; this, in the family at least, was corrupted to Tosh and to some he would always be Tosh.

Like many younger sons Tertius had to find a way to make a living and emigrated to America at the age of sixteen with his brothers Bertie, Alec

(Minor) and Ernest (Quartus). Frank, Bertie and Ernest qualified as vets at the Ontario Veterinary College in Canada, Frank in 1895. He seems to have worked for some time in Minnesota and Georgia before moving to Florida where his elder brother Alec was a lawyer.

In Florida, the family story goes, he planted orange trees and waited to make his fortune in the citrus fruit business and there he met Edward Nelson Fell, a mining engineer, and his family, who were later to play an important part in Frank's life.

Frank was always keen on horses; he owned or trained a number of horses in the 1890s and one, Kitty V.A., he proudly recorded, covered the half mile in 53.25 seconds with 85lbs up and was unbeaten in three years' racing.

In 1898 he enlisted as a farrier in Roosevelt's Rough Riders, a regiment of volunteer cavalry organized by Theodore Roosevelt to fight in the Spanish-American War, though Frank saw no action himself.

Two years later he was working for Nelson Fell at the Athabasca gold mine in British Columbia where he qualified as an assayer. In 1902–3 Fell took over a copper mine at Spassky in the Kirghiz steppes (now Kazakhstan) where he and Frank worked for some six years. Frank's letters from this period written to Nelson Fell's two daughters convey some of the pleasure he found in the vast emptiness of the steppes and the freedom of the life he led there.

The Fells returned to Florida, and Frank too. Perhaps he tried seriously to settle down; his job as Postmaster of Kissimmee and the accolade of 'premier peach-grower' of the area rather suggests that he planned a more conventional life. This however was to be interrupted by the war.

Notes on the Text

The majority of the text consists of a mix of material from three sources: Frank Vans Agnew's diary, letters by him and a smaller number of letters by other writers. In order to make reading a more comfortable experience, we have inserted a number of headings, removed many abbreviations and altered dates and ranks to a consistent format. We have made minor alterations to the text to avoid repetition and to clarify passages where we were confident of what Frank intended.

We have added a small number of words or phrases in brackets where these were necessary to make sense of the text but where an element of guesswork was required as to Frank's intentions, and we have made minor cuts within letters and diary entries which are not indicated.

Where possible we have included short footnotes on people mentioned and added further notes where we felt these would enhance the text. These are a combination of Frank's notes and of our own research from a number of sources, notably:

Forces War Records, www.forces-war-records.co.uk
Military Genealogy, www.military-genealogy.com
Ancestry, www.ancestry.com
Verrinder I, *Tank Action in the Great War,* Pen & Sword, 2009

Diary entries are simply headed with the date.

Letters are headed in bold type with the **addressee, the location of the author and the date**, with the name of the author where this is not Frank himself.

Words (in parentheses) were written by Frank either at the time of writing or as an addition when he was preparing the text for publication.

Notes [in brackets] are those of the editors.

Sentences in CAPITALS are those blotted out by the German censor in Fürstenberg PoW camp.

Some spelling anomalies which appear to have been unintended have been corrected, but American spellings and those which seem to be intentional and characteristic of Frank's writing have been allowed to stand.

Notes on the editors

Jamie Vans is the great-nephew of Captain Frank Vans Agnew, the owner of the family archive and self-appointed family historian and genealogist. I am grateful to Peter Widdowson, Ian Verrinder whose book about B Battalion has been essential reading and who kindly answered all the additional questions I put to him, and to my wife, Judy, for her help and encouragement.

The late Peter Widdowson was Professor of Literature at the University of Gloucestershire and the writer/editor of a number of scholarly works including *Thomas Hardy: Selected Poetry and Non-Fictional Prose* (Macmillan, 1997). His PhD thesis (1969) was on the poetry and painting of the First World War.

Notes on the units in which Frank served

King Edward's Horse (The King's Overseas Dominions Regiment) was a cavalry regiment of the British Army, formed in 1901, which saw service in the Boer War and the First World War. A second regiment, 2nd King Edward's Horse, was raised in 1914.

These extracts from a poem written by a trooper in the 2nd King Edward's Horse, give a flavour of the ethos of the regiment; the fact that Frank kept the poem suggests that he endorsed the writer's views.

From the far off lands beyond the seas
They came as a matter of course,
Some they came from love of the game,
Or manhood's cheque to endorse;
And because they were King's Colonials,
Joined the 2nd King Edward's Horse…

Strathcona's Horse and the R.C.D's[2]
Together with us on Parade,
Were known on the Army List as the First
Canadian Mounted Brigade;

And although I ses it as shouldn't, perhaps,
A jolly fine bunch they made.

We had lived our lives in the saddle,
In the saddle we'd hoped to go;
But cavalry weren't needed, cos—
Well, I expect you know
The fighting was all in the trenches,
And the game is confoundedly slow.

We left our horses behind us,
We fired the bandolier,
And we padded the hoof through Flanders
To the village of Festubert;
And we went into action a thousand strong,
With Seely our Brigadier.

I can't do the high falutin, I haven't got much to tell,
We've been in many a hot time since,
But that was a taste of Hell,
With day and night the shriek and the crash
Of the high explosive shell...

The Tank Corps was formed as the Heavy Branch Machine Gun Corps (HBMGC) and became the Tank Corps in July 1917.

Tanks were used for the first time in action on the battlefield of the Somme on 15 September 1916. That November the eight companies were expanded to battalions carrying the letter designations A to H with three companies in each.

In the winter of 1916 crew training was carried out and officers instructed their own sections in map reading and sketching, visual training, revolver and pigeon handling. Following this intensive training B Battalion received its first Mark IV tanks on 18 May 1917 and at 12 noon on 7 June 1917 went into action for the first time, attacking ground east of the Messines–Wytschaete Ridge.

Chapter 1

To the Front, May–October 1915

Letters to Ida[1]

From Maresfield Park, Oakfield, Sussex, 29 April 1915

We got the news from the Colonel[2] *at about 2pm today and I wired you as soon as possible. The Colonel said we would leave for the front – Flanders, the real front – on Saturday, but we go without our beloved horses. Dismounted, foot-sloggers, bang into trenches, I suppose. But everyone is very pleased. My feelings are those of ferocious glee. I had begun to despair. As cavalrymen we were dodos, out of date relics of wars far past where small handfuls of men scuffled together. This is a new war, absolutely.*

I will wire any definite news I may learn but do not feel badly if you miss seeing me off. Leave takings really mean nothing. I can add nothing now but will wire as soon as I can. Goodnight.

Yours always, Frank.

(At Strazeele)

In Belgium on active service, Base Army Post Office, 11am, 8 May 1915

We left the camp I sent the post cards from the day before yesterday, travelled all night by train in horse-boxes, then were billeted in a big farm. Today we moved away to another big farm. Our brigade is still intact and the Canadians are with us in other farms nearby. The sound of the big guns is to be heard all day and night and the sky at night in their direction was lit up by their flashes. About 7pm last night the motor hospital vans passed near us on the way to the rail. A long line of searchlights. It is all very wonderful and we are greatly honored to be where we are.

These farms produce eggs and milk and butter and crisp, long rolls, so we do ourselves well, and the weather is perfect.

(Meteren, near Bailleul)

In France, 11 May 1915

Two letters from you the day before yesterday evening and one more yesterday evening. Also the respirators and goggles and morphine.

Your list of things to be sent weekly and bi-weekly seems to me to fill the bill completely, but I will be able to tell you of possible alterations later.

We have moved on to another big farm where, under ideal weather conditions, we are really enjoying ourselves. Today the big guns in the distance are much more quiet. That steady continuous pounding, day and night has stopped; but we get less news here than we got at home from the papers. Yesterday evening several aeroplanes passed along, high up, and with my glasses I could distinctly see the shells bursting around them, apparently with no harm. As they were our machines we were delighted.

I am keeping my small diary which will be more interesting than these letters. To keep within the bounds of the censorship is a drag on letter writing, for one does not want to say anything not allowed and one does not know quite how far to go.

Eggs, milk and butter we can buy at the farms around, and red and white vin ordinaire, *also a most pernicious form of beer. Coffee is the best of all. Bathing is just possible in small ponds around, and you go more to change from dirt to cleanliness than for much pleasure. We do not know how long we shall stay here but everyone hopes we shall get to grips before long. After all these months of waiting there is only a normal state of eagerness.*

At 4pm, 100 cigarettes, in two sealed tins, just arrived. Ever so many thanks.

(Towards Locon)

In France, Sunday, 16 May 1915

We have moved on again since I last wrote, moved on twice in fact, and are waiting all packed and ready to move on again as soon as a division of troops have done marching by. I wish I could tell you where we are and all details because this must be dull reading. Our march from the last farm I wrote you was a very hard one, from 8.45pm till nearly 8am Saturday morning. The distance was somewhere between fifteen and twenty miles, and the pace was terrific. We carried no knapsack or blanket, which went by wagon, but we carried everything else, amounting to about 60lbs in weight. The halts

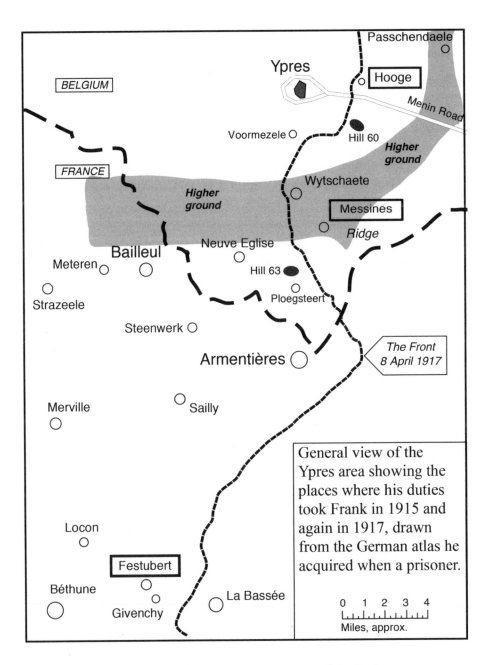

The Front
8 April 1917

General view of the
Ypres area showing the
places where his duties
took Frank in 1915 and
again in 1917, drawn
from the German atlas he
acquired when a prisoner.

0   1   2   3   4
Miles, approx.

*were few and far between and by the time we stopped for food everyone was
about at his last gasp. But next morning we were all up and about, somewhat
footsore and stiff and sleepy but very much alive. It is surprising what a good
wash and shave and a breakfast will do. We rested all day, doing not much*

else, and at 7pm our whole brigade marched off again to the place I write from now, a distance of nearly six miles. As we were the rear guard of a long column it meant that the pace was very fast for us, but we must be getting into better condition for we did not seem to mind it at all. Ten o'clock saw us all stretched out in good clean oat straw in the inevitable big barn, in a village. At night, marching, we can see the big rocket flare lights at the front quite plainly. They float like electric arcs in the air for a surprisingly long while. There is some scattered gunfire, big gun ejaculations, but no steady conversations. This morning an airship is in sight, evidently a French one from its strange shape.

The rope trailing is longer than I have shown[3] with about seven lumps on it, like this. This seems to act like an anchor and keeps the nose to the wind. Then, I suppose, if the engines run slowly, they can keep the affair up into the wind and keep it about in the same place all the time. It is near the front and hangs in the air as an observation balloon.

We expect to move again this afternoon.

Diary entries

Monday, 17 May (Rainy and very grey)

At 5am quick orders came to fall in, in a few minutes, to march off. Just had time to swallow some hot tea. Before 6am the whole brigade was on the move. Marched due south and a trifle west to Gommesheim, with full 90lb packs, in steady rain, then marched east and north to Locon, about eleven miles altogether. Stood in the rain about an hour outside Locon. All very cold and wet and hungry, but most cheerful. Arrived in Locon at 12am and got coffee and food. Billeted in a big forge. Big fight going on about three miles off. Guns rattle windows. Town crammed with troops. Regulars, Indians, artillery, etc. Several bands of German prisoners were marched by. Hundreds captured. Some wounded. Miserable, bestial types. Marched at dusk to a billet a mile away. A horrible, dirty farm.

Tuesday, 18 May (Rain all day)

Parcel came and 100 cigs. Did nothing but lie up all day in this very filthy farm, where troops have been billeted steadily for months. Mud and dirty straw and crowded quarters. Our whole brigade is close around and the entire Canadian contingent near. The guns at the front have been very quiet owing to the hazy and cloudy day. We are in the first line of reserves and may be called on at any time. Heard that we had 4,000 casualties today, but that we have made some progress. In afternoon we had a lecture on bomb throwing and making, and we practised with jam-pots. Not so easy to throw properly, and very ticklish things to prepare too, seems to me. Troops pass frequently on the way to and back from the front. Indian cavalry, Royal Horse Artillery (RHA), ammunition trains. All quite drab and dishevelled.

Wednesday, 19 May (Rain and mist until evening)
Still cold, wet and miserable weather. Impossible to do anything but wait. We were told today that the fighting going on to our immediate front is around Festubert, and that our mounted brigade is in the Canadian Division of the First Army. Also that we are in the first reserves. Apparently, our troops are gaining trenches slowly, and keeping the German in his place. No gun firing was heard all day today or yesterday, except occasional bangs reported to be 15-inch guns of ours trying to wreck a bridge the other side of Lille. Heard from Ida, Mrs M.[4] and from Kate[5] this evening. Marched away at 11pm to other billets three miles away.

To Ida (at Locon; saw the Prince of Wales here)

Wednesday, 19 May 1915
(Canadian YMCA. Do not mention your rank, battalion, brigade, or the names of places; expected operations, movements or numbers of troops; casualties, previous to publication of official lists, or make specific reference to the moral or physical condition of troops. O.D. Irwin, Secretary)

Since I last wrote we have had a trying time. I went on guard last Sunday night and gathered very little sleep and, at 4.30am, there came the order to march off at once. As we (the guard) had already lighted the cooks' fires, we had tea ready and after a cup of boiling-hot we pulled out. Soon it began to rain and the rain stayed with us practically all day. We marched about eleven miles and, what with halts long and short, we did not arrive at the town we were aiming for until about 12am. All this time we were carrying the full pack, over 90lb in weight, and we were wet and cold and mortal hungry, but most surprisingly cheerful. The men singing songs as the big guns sounded nearer and nearer. Very few men even fell out. These were a few of the sick and the sore-footed. We were billeted in a big forge and soon we fed and were busy cleaning water-soaked rifles as we did not know but what we might go right on into the thick of it. The town was literally full of troops. Regulars, Indians, artillery, transport in a never-ending, shifting stream. All the while the guns banged and whacked away and rattled the windows. At one place, with my glasses, I saw shells bursting. Several bands of German prisoners were marched by under guard: miserable-looking men, some wounded and bandaged, all muddy and all yellow with lyddite fumes. Their physique was not bad on the whole but their type of face was evil. I was told they were Bavarians and Saxons. One officer showed, with his Iron Cross of course. About 6pm we marched off again, a little over a mile, to a really dirty farm, where troops have been billeted for months, I should think, and here we are yet. The rain has hardly stopped, and the place is an eyesore.

Yesterday afternoon the bomb-throwers were called out for a lesson and a lecture. It seems to be quite a ticklish business needing care and accuracy, and the actual throwing will require practice to be able to do it properly. A badly thrown bomb may kill one's own men remarkably easily, and in the hands of inexperienced men I should call them good allies for the Germans.

Do not please send any more of the white cloth for cleaning rifles. White cloth is too dangerous here owing to its colour. The first parcel from the Army and Navy came yesterday, also 100 cigarettes, and the two paper-bound books. All mightily and gratefully appreciated. I just jumped into the thin socks for I do so loathe the thick ones. Since the rain started and kept up so steadily the guns have let up their racket. I suppose, in such cloudy and hazy weather, the range is hard to locate. We are still under orders to be ready to move into the scrimmage at any time. In the meantime we lie up, under cover, on the straw, and are not too uncomfortable, except the unfortunates on duties such as 'guards'.

Thursday, 20 May (Cloudy but fine with some sun. Fine on the whole)
Marched last night, full packs, back through Locon to farm billets about one mile SW of that town. Whole brigade was moved. Guns at front were getting busy again, and there was much aeroplane activity all day. All around us and over us they fly, now and then coming down low to drop messages and back to the front, high up. La Bassée Canal is quite close. Bathed and swam in it. Last winter it was red with blood and choked with bodies. Béthune is in sight, down the canal, west. Saw *Daily Mail* of 19th today. Apparently the main British fighting is going on to our immediate front. As day wore on the gunfire grew worse and worse.

Friday, 21 May (Fine on the whole – some spots of rain)
Package from Ida, tin things. Wrote her.

Fighting went on at the front all night to considerable extent. Went on a route march to Béthune in morning, only two miles west along La Bassée Canal. Many barges there and passed big hospital Red Cross barge pulled by army tug. Béthune has been shelled but saw no traces. Seems to be full of our troops. French people are very friendly and enthusiastic. Heard from two Canadian-Scotch that the Canadians lost heavily yesterday again, capturing trenches that the Devons and Coldstreams had failed to get. At 7pm our guns at front began a continuous roar and later it was terrific. It was not possible to sleep. One could hear the rifles pop in the lulls, steady stream of pops. Star-shells shooting up all along the front and the never-ending hammering of the batteries at work.

To Ida (near Festubert)

In France, 9.30am, Friday, 21 May 1915
Since my last letter, I think it was Wednesday, we have left behind us the rainy weather and the cold and that very dirty farm and have come about three miles to another inevitable farm, where the natives are clean and kindly disposed and there is no mud.

We are nearer now than ever to the big guns, and it cannot be long before we shall be right underneath them. We marched to this place on Wednesday night arriving at this billet about 1am yesterday. I never saw so many aeroplanes. They hum around all day and seem to have the field to themselves. No hostile machine appears to chase them and no shells are fired at them. I got up at dawn today to watch two of them sailing along very high over the fighting lines, circling and turning back and forth unmolested. Sometimes one will come down from the front very fast and when close to the ground (2 or 300 feet) will drop something which is no doubt news and maps, and then return to duty up aloft. All last night the guns kicked up a dickens of a row. The flashes of bursting shells were like fireflies flickering along a lakeshore in Florida and the rocket star-shells flared high up, all to the accompaniment of the bang of the guns.

Saturday, 22 May (Fine, sunny and cool)
Spent morning and afternoon in preparing to go to trenches tonight. Had a bath in La Bassée Canal, and general clean up. Were issued an army respirator – a big pad of cotton waste, well soaked in a solution strong in soda, wrapped in a sort of coarse black muslin. Filled water bottles with

boiled water, got 300 rounds of ball and extra rations, and started off at 8.30pm. Walked about six miles south-east through Festubert. This is a one-time prosperous village, now smashed up. As the regiment neared the reserve trenches, one and a half miles on, was heavily shelled. Much delay and we sat by the road while big shells dropped near enough to scatter mud on us. Went through reserves to the front line trench. Most forward trench on whole British front. Great honour!

Sunday, 23 May (Big thunderstorm in night with rain. Rest of day very fine)
Spent very strange and uncomfortable night, standing to arms all the time. The storm wet us badly, and made much mud. Cold too! Was a lookout nearly all night. Heard our adjutant and another man wounded coming in on the road. Shelled us heavily in early morning, but very few casualties. Quiet until about 4pm when they poured shell into us. I was next Dickson-Hill[6] and Meiklejon[7]. Shell came through parapet and smashed up Dickson-Hill and Sherris[8], grazed me, and gave Meiklejon a scalp wound. Dickson-Hill died in a few minutes. Left leg shattered and right hand gone. For an hour they hammered us and we had to take it.

Four other men in my troop (of thirty-eight) killed: Hunt[9], Aurbach[10], Scallon[11], Alexander[12]. Same shell killed all four. Six wounded, Willis[13], Meiklejon, Brandon[14], O'Hea[15], Devertieu[16]. After the bombardment, sent in the wounded. After dark, buried the dead. A dreadful job. At 9pm we were relieved by B Squadron, and we went to reserve trenches.

Monday, 24 May (Fine weather. Sunny and warm)
Shaved today under bombardment. Had fairly quiet night but hardly any sleep, having to stand to arms as the Canadian infantry was attacking a trench to our right and we were supports. At 4am they began to shell the reserve and front trenches, and the devilish bombardment lasted practically all day long. Our artillery finally won and silenced them. Back and forth at each other and at us, bang, bang, bang. It is hard to sit still and be able to do nothing. Very nerve racking. Lieutenant Grosvenor[17] and two sergeants were buried once and we got them out safely and repaired the trench. They were unhurt. We must have over fifty casualties all by shellfire. To get water one dodges shells and a sniper to go to a small stream. Strathconas have killed two snipers today. In evening went to Festubert to get rations. Got back by 9pm. At 10pm the whole regiment took over the front trench again, and again I had no wink of sleep – almost none since Friday.

Tuesday, 25 May (Fine, clear and sunny)
It was broad daylight before we were finally assigned our positions in the front trench, and we heard the Canadian attack about 11.30am. Short and rapid burst of fire. About every two hours we were heavily shelled by Jack Johnsons and had a few casualties, but the dugouts we had made helped matters. Spent most of the time in them. About 4.30pm I took a sack full of water bottles to a stream behind and dodged the inevitable snipers. Just after I returned there was another Canadian attack to our right and all the bomb throwers were called out. The devils were being bombed along this trench. Our party had to go a mile, or more, in one trench in a desperate hurry with a tremendous fire all around. When we reached the scene, could see the Germans in a trench quite close. I carried a box of bombs up to the nearest point to the Germans and had to crawl to it, for the air was alive with lead. Then they showed us how to bomb and I had the pleasure of landing a lot among lumps of Germans. Finally, had to stop, played out, and helped to dress wounded, etc. great many of our dead about. We lost three killed and two wounded of our party of nine bomb-throwers, and one more went crazy that evening.

Wednesday, 26 May (Fine, cool and sunny)
At 3.30am, dawn, we were hastily called out, our troop only, and ordered to climb over our parapet and occupy a trench just made by the Royal Engineers (RE) ahead, towards the enemy. We all sailed over, under Lieutenant Grosvenor, and rushed on headlong, expecting a fusillade. None came but we had to cross several boggy deep streams and many of the men went up to their necks. All got very wet. We occupied this new trench all day, expecting to get wiped out by shrapnel any moment. But the Germans had not seen us or knew nothing of the trench because they never shelled us at all. About 2am we were relieved by the Cameron Highlanders and slipped off back to billets. Before we went out, a flarelight went up, they saw us and here came the shrapnel. About twenty of us were hit, and some RE were killed. We marched till dawn to our old billets at Long Cornet, arriving nearly dead.

Thursday, 27 May (Fine, but cold and northeast wind)
Although it was full dawn we went to sleep and slept all the morning nearly. Everybody very stiff and sore. Bathed in stream of ice-cold water. In afternoon saw the doctor who iodined my (first) small wound, and then I walked to Béthune on pass to try to get a hot bath. Failed, but got a grand

meal, steaks, potatoes, soup, etc. and ice-creams, coffee and cakes. Changed all underclothes and threw old ones away. Found letters and parcels and papers. Went to bed early and slept and slept. We had been four days and five nights practically with no sleep except scraps here and there, and under strong strain from continuous bombardments. Never a wash either to speak of.

Two Letters to Ida (Festubert) [To avoid repetition these two letters have been combined.]

In France, Friday, 28 May and Sunday, 30 May 1915

I hastily sent you a service post card on our return from the trenches yesterday morning to say that I was well, because you will see that I am returned as 'wounded'. But my wound is only a scratch on the arm and I did not show it to the doctor until our return to these billets yesterday. It is ridiculous to return me as 'wounded' as it might give you all sorts of wrong ideas, but there it is and all beyond my stopping.

We marched from our billets at 5.30pm Saturday the 22nd, about six miles towards the heavy gun firing, passing through a good sized village (Festubert) which had been shelled thoroughly. Some houses were hardly hurt and others all round were in ruins. The church was absolutely wrecked and shells had torn up the graves, but a great life-size crucifix of the Saviour high in the air, was quite untouched. I noted shell holes in stiff soil four feet deep, about nine feet across at the bottom and nearer fifteen feet across at its upper circumference. These are made by 'coal-boxes'. When they go through the air, high over you, on their way to some spot a mile or so away they sound exactly like a freight car moving slowly on the rails.

Leaving the village on a straight, hard road to the trenches our regiment was shelled repeatedly. There seemed to be some hitch going on, with frequent halts wherein we sat by the roadside, or grovelled in a ditch, according to the various temperaments of the men, and the shells exploded every now and then near enough to scatter mud and stones on us. This in the dark is very uncanny. Before we left the road our adjutant was wounded and another man or two.

We arrived at the support trenches and went on to the front line trenches, after much stooping and falling flat when star-shells lighted up the sky and, with a heavy pack and 500 rounds of ball, I was nearly dead. Very uneven, shell-torn ground, barbed wire and bad tempers all around. It must have been about midnight when we were finally assigned places in the trench and when the (8th Canadian) infantry we were relieving had gone. They were only too glad to get out and told us gruesome tales of ninety-nine casualties that day. The truth is that this was a German trench, recently captured, and of course what had been its back parapet was now our front parapet, and back parapets are not built very strongly because there is no need for strength in them. All trenches just here are made and built up of sand bags, for you come to water pretty soon if you dig much. So you see that this particular trench offered no great resistance to shells coming against our front, being really a sort of man-trap.

Before dawn a nuisance of a thunderstorm passed over and wet us quite distinctly and then it was cold. We stood to arms practically all night, feeling very raw and ill at ease. Soon after dawn we were quite heavily shelled with HE (high explosives). It comes from afar with a moaning whistling sound, nearer and nearer and still nearer and nearer and louder and louder, Whangg!! somewhere near you and often pieces of dirt fall on you. This shell makes a hole in the ground – not as big as the 'coal-box' but over half as big. Up and down the trench these shells played, driving one every now and then to the support trench behind. Generally from left to right. You can do nothing but crouch low where the sacks at the base offer a greater thickness to attack, and grin and bear it. That is the trouble, you have no answer, and must take it all and return nothing.

No-one near me was damaged by that shelling. The sun came out strong and we were soon warm. Meals were eaten and guards kept and forty winks also, here and there, until about 4.30pm Sunday the 23rd, when we got our fatal shelling, the shells coming right through our front parapet and killing poor old Dickson-Hill and the five other men in our troop, and wounding Meiklejon and five others of ours.

At the same time, almost, another shell burst in our trench in the next traverse to mine, about forty feet away, and killed four men. All this happened last Sunday afternoon.

They shelled us for over two hours that time and a shell would come for us about every three minutes I should judge. After dark we buried the men in shell holes with some digging besides, right behind the trench. Four in one grave and two in another. About 10pm we were relieved by 3 Squadron of ours, and we went back, stooping and falling flat, etc. to the support trenches, about 400 yards in the rear. There we had no sleep to speak of, for an attack of ours was in progress on our right and we were standing to arms as supports if needed.

We buried Dickson-Hill right behind our trench in a shell hole and under shellfire, and I am sending his wife his diary and all the letters I could find in his kit. Cannot you go to see her? He suffered nothing because he was terribly smashed up and lived less than ten minutes. We gave him morphine but I do not think he was conscious after the first minute. Meiklejon went to hospital at once and I have not seen him since, but tell Mrs Meiklejon that his was a scalp wound only and not to be the least worried about him. He went off to the dressing station quite cheerfully himself after we had bandaged him up in the trench and the bleeding had stopped entirely.

At 4.30am the 24th [Monday] they began to shell us again, both trenches, and the devilish bombardment kept up practically all day long. This support trench was a much more substantial affair though and one felt safer. All the same there were quite a few casualties and Lieutenant Grosvenor and two sergeants were buried in sandbags in their dugout from a shell landing in the wall itself. Very luckily none of them were hurt when we got them out. All day long till evening the racket went on and the shells came all around us. We were sprinkled with mud and dust and bits of shell repeatedly. To get water you went to a stream about 250 yards off and dodged snipers and shells.

Our guns finally seemed to silence the enemy and then kept it up alone. At dusk I was one of a ration party of about forty men to go to the village I mentioned for food supplies down that same hard road. On returning, very soon, we went back to the front trenches and again one got no sleep at all. As soon as possible we dug ourselves in behind the rear parapet (which was the strongest) making dugouts, leaving only the men on lookout in the man-trap proper. This was the 25th [Tuesday]. We heard our men, of another regiment to our left, attack about 1.30am and we heard after that they got the German trench. These dugouts saved us a lot of casualties for they shelled us for a while about every two hours, all day. One made tea and boiled water in the open, behind our trench, with one ear open for the particular moan and whine which meant you, and joked and lived a normal existence as it seemed. Quite a few wounded today and one or two killed.

It is a one-sided game, with the odds with the artillery. You sit and hold a trench, being the ninepins while the guns roll the ball at you. You can do nothing but swear softly. No Germans actually attacked our trench, but they tried to do so on each side of us. But on Tuesday afternoon about 3.30pm I got a little of my own back on them. I had just returned with a sack full of water-bottles from a stream near-by behind our trench, where you dodge snipers, when the call suddenly came for 'Bomb throwers to the front' and the rifles and machine guns started a terrific popping. I was in shirt sleeves, and just slammed on my ammunition equipment and skedaddled off with my rifle up the trench towards the racket.

After a long time, crouching and running and crawling I got to where I could see our men throwing bombs into the Germans. You could hear nothing for the noise; it seemed as if every German rifle, Maxim, and big gun was turned on that spot. Their shrapnel was going 'Brrangg' overhead and their shells going 'Whangg' all about. I took a few shots at the devils with my rifle, by way of resting and getting my breath, and then I got hold of a box of bombs and started to crawl and drag it up there. The box was very heavy and, to my delight, another young chap, a Strathcona (Lord Strathcona's Horse), came and helped me. We dragged and humped it along, over bumps and across shell holes and over our dead, until we got to the extreme point where the Germans were retreating up their trench and being bombed by our men unmercifully. There I found my own sergeant[18] of our bomb-throwing-squad, to my great relief, and he was as merry as a grig.

I had never thrown a live bomb in my life but soon found out, as it is quite a simple affair and they were lovely bombs for working. You could see a clump of German bayonets huddled like sheep, over their parapet top, and you chucked a bomb into it and prayed for the explosion. When it came the bayonets wavered and wobbled and then disappeared. If the bomb did not explode you waited and backed up because those plucky Germans lighted it again and threw it back. And so on and so on. I know I got three bombs into them fairly and squarely and heard them explode and saw the bayonets flop down. We finally got to a place at a turn in the trench, an angle, and our own Tommies were firing directly across us, excitedly of course, and they killed about twelve of our men there, two of them being of my squad and within a few feet of me, and two more were wounded.

I was by that time about played out and the bombs were all exhausted, so we sat down to wait for more, and when they came I could not get up for I had cramp in both of my legs and had to be rubbed and rubbed. That must have been about 8pm; but I could drag around so I dressed two wounded men and helped to fill sand bags and pass them along, until 10pm I should judge. About 10.30pm the only officer present told us the thing was over for the time and no more could be done, and we crawled back, as the rifles and Maxims and shrapnel and Jack Johnsons were just as busy all the time. The sergeant and I got back to our own trench after 11pm and I was more than tired. Never had I been so played out in my whole life. We lost five killed, two wounded, and another who went off his head later, out of our bomb throwing squad of nine. And I had not a scratch, just a bump on the breastbone from something kicked up by a Jack Johnson. It was a bad thing for the Germans but we lost a lot of good men there.

Our troop was thirty-eight strong but now only twenty-six are left. We were in the foremost British trench of the British front here and our troop had the post of honour. So we ought not to mind anything.

You know how rumours fly about. Well it is troop and regimental talk that Sergeant Morris has been recommended for the VC. I hope he gets it, but glory be, I never saw him throw a bomb and he never gave me any orders. No-one gave us any orders. There were the Germans in the trench and we threw all the bombs we could at them, and that is all there was to it. Out of our party of nine bomb throwers, including the sergeant, three were killed dead where they stood (two of them I could have touched as they fell), two more were wounded, and another young chap, a big fine fellow, came to me with cramp in the thick of it just when I had cramp also, and I rubbed him as he lay and swore. This young chap then seemed to get back safely to his own trench but temporarily lost his reason and wandered off into trouble, a shell, I suppose, and had a hand blown off. So that leaves only three of us intact. The sergeant, Walrond[19] and myself. And jolly lucky, too!

I was so dog-tired when I returned about 11pm that I crawled to a dugout and went to sleep all standing for a couple of hours. Heavy shelling on top of us continuously, as the Germans were very much worked up over our attacks, and kept their artillery busy. At dawn of the 26th (Wednesday) we were ordered (our troop only, under Lieutenant Grosvenor) to climb out over our front parapet and occupy an empty trench, just made after nightfall by the RE. We sailed over the parapet expecting a lively fusillade and rushed headlong ahead. As it happened there was mist enough to hide us completely. The trench was three or four hundred yards ahead where we struck it and we had to cross three streams. It was just possible to jump them with a good jump but many of the men plumped right into their waists and even to their necks, slap into boggy mud below, and had to be pulled out. We passed our dead out there in no man's land, and one German, all being unburied and lying there for days or weeks. Pretty bad!

This new trench was not very deep so we dug. And the more we dug the more water came in, and we had a very wet affair after a while. Being an open trench, if the Germans had seen us, we would have been wiped out by shrapnel. But they did not as we were protected by high grass a good deal.

Anyway, we spent a quiet restful day there, because the enemy shelled over and behind us into the trench we had left, and we could watch the aeroplanes at work quite serenely. Just after dark, squads and parties of RE came along to dig more trenches and later another whole regiment (Canadian Camerons) relieved us.

We left the trench and walked in the dark up above, dropping to the flare lights the Germans kept nervously sending up. We were only about 400 yards from their trench, full of rifles and Maxims. But at a turn where the trench struck the road, known as 'Suicide turn', when we were well bunched up, the Germans, who had the exact range, sent up a light, saw something and let fly 'Brangg' with shrapnel. Luckily it burst too high or it would have been bad. As it was there were about twenty casualties for there were a lot of men of other regiments there. I had just time to fall flat, but with no luck in the shape of finding a hole or cover. I was on the flat, bald, hard ground. The stuff pattered round me but as usual I had not a scratch. We gathered the wounded and hurried away from that unholy place, down the road to billets and straw and peace from shells, and sleep, and letters and parcels and a wash.

We went into the trenches on Saturday night, last, and came out yesterday, Thursday, morning just before dawn. Four days and five nights practically without sleep, and being shelled by Jack Johnsons more or less the whole time.

We got to our old billets (Long Cornet) at dawn of the 27th, tired, tired, tired out.

Goodbye, Your loving brother Frank.

Friday, 28 May (Fine but much too cool)
Spent the day in cleaning up generally and getting lists of equipment lost in action. I had thrown away my rifle and bayonet when bomb-throwing, also I lost my mess tin, shovel, waterproof sheet and other small things. In afternoon the brigade paraded before General Alderson[20] of the Canadian Division who praised us. Afterwards, Major Murray[21] paraded the squadron and congratulated us all warmly. He said if he could pick out anyone it was the bomb-throwers, who had shown 'extraordinary bravery'. My chest measurement is now forty-nine inches. Then the squadron gave three cheers for the bombers. Imagine!

Saturday, 29 May (Fine and sunny, cold NE wind)
All our squadron went to Béthune in morning to get a hot bath. The baths appeared to be in a big school building. Twenty or thirty hot sprays and

a few long baths. Afterwards we were allowed liberty for an hour or two. Spent mine in getting English papers, slippers, and in drinking coffee and eating little French cakes and things. Town is full of our men and officers and French soldiers. Quite a few Indian cavalrymen. Had a talk with one who knew some English. He came from Jullundur. In the town square is a very quaint church and some very old buildings, but the town elsewhere is not very interesting as far as I have seen. Germans shelled the observation balloon all afternoon in front of us – uselessly.

To Ida (Long Cornet near Festubert)

In France, May 29, 1915
Please send enclosed letter to Mrs Dickson-Hill. I do not know her address. It is just a description of how the old chap met his death and how we buried him under fire, and about the funeral service and firing salute two days later, also under fire. Details of that sort will please her and his children will want to know when they get older. We are resting in a very nice billet – the one we left just before going to the trenches. Today the squadron marched to the nearest town and had a hot spray bath, which was needed although we had streams and the canal near-by, also much used. The packages of razor blades, vaseline, tooth paste and lovely rifle cloth came yesterday, including coffee and a letter from you enclosing letter from Florida, which was a photograph of one of my faithful band there.
    With much love from
    Your brother, Frank.

I might just add that Aurbach was killed almost at the same time as Dickson-Hill and as you met Mrs Aurbach at Maresfield Park you might like to write to her, if you know her address.
    Yesterday the brigade paraded before Alderson the general of our division, who seemed to think that we might not go back to the trenches for some time, if at all. All depending on the pressure on the line at the front. But I feel pretty sure that we will go back, at any time. I have got to the point that 'taffy' I can taste a mile away and this is no time for taffy.
    If men are needed they will call upon us.
    Am delighted to hear how well you are getting on with motor work and I must say that you deserve great praise.

Monday, 7 June (Fine and sunny and hot)
Heard from Ida. Physical drill in early misty morning and rifle inspection, etc. Had a most delightful swim in La Bassée Canal with a lot of the men. Under shellfire. La Bassée is only four miles away north-east. About 3.30pm we had a hasty order to stand by with respirators as the wind was from the German trenches and gas was expected. Of course nothing happened. At 8pm we hurriedly packed up and marched away to within one and a half miles of Givenchy, which place seemed to be burning merrily. Marched along the canal mostly. Went about two miles till we were quite close to the fighting lines, then turned off to the right into a wood, where we slept under the trees and in the tangle, expecting shrapnel to find us at any moment. Had only a waterproof sheet (no coat or blankets) but slept as well as the cold and the row from the guns would allow. Not so badly either!

Tuesday, 8 June (Fine morning, afternoon wet with thunderstorm)
When sun rose, all soon were warm and happy. Big gnats and mosquitoes had bothered some of the men badly. Some men dug dugouts and holes in the ground, and covered them with branches still thinking of shrapnel. Working from dawn feverishly. All the scared ones did and we know them now quite plainly. This wood is almost an island in a marsh where the water is deep and well stocked with fish. Other islands appear in it and the marsh is quite large. Our battery is very busy firing over us. One especially nearly deafening us. The report each time is a physical shock and pain. Now and then bits from our shells fly loose and crash about in our wood. Shoddy shell bands I suppose. In afternoon came a thunderstorm and rain. The French guns keep up a steady and terrible hammering to our right. That big fire is not Givenchy but a bridge at La Bassée set on fire by the French.

Wednesday, 9 June (Fine in morning and rain in afternoon and evening)
Letter from Ida. Last night at 12.30am we tumbled out to carry ladders to reserve trenches, two ladders ten feet long, rifle and ball cartridge equipment. Long communication trench narrow and deep, much sniping and firing. Our guide lost his way in the trenches and we laid those blessed ladders down finally at dawn. Shoulders black and blue. Twenty of us spent the day in peace among the trees and shade and flecks of sunlight. Some cannonade over our heads and deafening reports. At 7pm we marched back to Beuvry to a farm quite near our last billet here. It rained all evening, and drizzle. Made a shelter for two outside from our waterproof sheets, got dry

straw and slept well. Tremendous thunderstorm and rain at night which our shelter negotiated very successfully. Most of the men in dugouts drowned out.

Letters to Ida (Givenchy)

In France, 6pm, Thursday, 17 June 1915
Dearest I,

Such a grand budget of letters from you today, just when we had returned from being 'first reserves' to a big attack. The attack being quite successful and three lines of German trenches to the credit of our men.

Our farm billet, since Tuesday, is the same one we came to on June 5th, and it is as near to the firing line as is decently possible. Since our stay here before, the Huns have shelled the very farm house, putting one shell through the roof, wounding several men and nearly slaying a lot of really fine Flemish milk cows. Beautiful, great, well bred looking, velvety, dark liver brown beasts. Then in the village, 200 yards away, within a few yards of the house where two women and a baby in arms were killed when we were here last, a shell came into the street, killed three artillery horses, one man and wounded about eight more. That was pure chance as they were driving through.

Tuesday the 15th, shortly after our arrival, at 5pm, our guns started an appalling bombardment on the German trenches. At 5.58pm, a mine of ours was blown up. I saw it go. A great cloud of dust, 200, maybe 300 feet high, containing Huns in great numbers, I hope. Soon the attack began. A perfect blur of rifle pops and the wicked, woodpecker-hammer of machine guns; our guns, in the meantime still spraying the ground ahead with lead. It was not long before the wounded began to draggle down, along the canal. A most cheerful if battered lot. The ones able to walk plug along somehow. Ambulance motors bring the worst and others come along in ammunition limbers and in any other conveyance. The bombardment lasted till after midnight, and, as many of the batteries, big fellows, were close to us, you can imagine the din. The German guns did nothing except hammer at our trenches and not much of that, evidently relying more upon bombs and many machine guns. At dawn, all was quiet and supremely peaceful and I wrote you of that in my last. But, yesterday afternoon, the 16th, about 4pm again our guns began in earnest, hammering and pounding. You could see the great splashes of smoke and dust plunge up in the distance, sometimes a cloud of red when a building is blown to bits, and here and there up in the air the white puffs of shrapnel, like puffballs and just as deadly. As I write, they are dropping 'coal-boxes' about 300 yards to my left, trying to find two batteries of ours in a wood, every minute or less there is a terrific crash over there. We have just finished a game of cricket and it went on quite regardless of these bangs near-by.

Then we were hurried up, as first supports, if needed, and going up we met the same pitiful, because so cheery, stream of wounded, and it looked as if we were to come to grips ourselves. But, the attack of ours was so very successful that in two hours time we were ordered back to our same billet. Today the German guns have been dropping coal-boxes on both sides of us and behind us, in their desire to find our troublesome batteries.

Our front seems to be resting today and the French, to our right, this evening, are popping it to them. Such a succession of booms and 'bumps' and growls of thunder in the distance. The Hun is not getting much rest.

My bi-weekly parcel which contains the shirt and under-things has not come. In fact I have only had one of them since the beginning. Therefore, and in fatal consequence, I am in distressful need of a change. The shirt I had last seemed to be thin enough, for the nights are, to me, very cold. The idea of a thinner and cotton shirt fills me with horror. I suppose it must be summer time because everyone seems to agree that it is, but to my idea it is still late spring and I am patiently awaiting summer. The nights here now are like cold winter ones in Florida. Maybe one blanket and a greatcoat have something to do with it.

Goodnight. I read your last long letter with a great interest, and I wish I could give my mind to it more out here.

Your loving brother, Frank.

In France (Givenchy, in the Duck Bill Trench)

6pm, Sunday, 20 June 1915
Dear I,

I am writing this letter in the front firing trench with the Huns 250 yards away to the eastward, Our 'vis-à-vis' are Saxons and seem to be peaceable folk, but they have just begun their 'evening hate'. I have most discreetly retired to my burrow. It is too small to be a 'dugout', as it just allows me inside if I tuck my knees in, but as I want to write, I find my knees in just the right position. As if in rage at what I have just written a shell has just burst close enough to spatter me with dry bits of clay. Now the shelling has passed me and is going down the line to the right. They always shell from our left to our right.

I wrote to you last on Friday. That evening, our regiment marched off to support trenches where they are now, but Sergeant Morris and I were told to stay behind, as bombers. The only two from our troop, for this reason: the bomb throwing section of our regiment and of the brigade is going to be properly organized now. They have begun with ten men from each regiment, a sergeant from each regiment and an officer in charge of all. We met and slept in another billet a few hundred yards away (Friday night). Saturday (yesterday) we spent the morning with dissertations on bombs, time fuse and percussion and gascons[22], and in throwing both dummy and live bombs. At 3pm, four of us from each regiment, with Sergeant Morris in charge under the officer (of whom the less said the better), marched up to the front firing trench, where we are now. We are split up into three parties, one at each end of the regiment holding this sector of trench and one in the centre. Our party is in the centre and we have a fine collection of bombs all ready for instant use in a dugout magazine. Our party is made up of Sergeant Morris, old regular cavalryman, 21st Lancers, who wears the two South African war medals and the Omdurman, for he was in that famous charge there; a man who has just come from the Andes for the war, where he has been engineering; another young chap from the Argentine where he has been on a big stock ranch, both of these being gentlemen and very fine types, and myself. The regiment whom we are with (Strathconas) persist in calling us the 'Suicide Club' and are very merry about it. To be a bomber seems to be a most intimate introduction to anyone wearing khaki, with offers of tea, cigarettes and particular delicacies. So you see how well I am looked after.

Apparently, whenever the brigade needs a bomb-throwing display it will call on us. The rest of the bomb-throwers stayed behind to receive more instruction and practice, but I have heard, pretty safely, that we are to be relieved tomorrow by some of them who may be considered proficient enough. So far our time has been that of comparative indolence, but the time will come when we shall have to, once again, blot out the Hun at close quarters and forget everything else. It will be much more satisfactory now that we are well organized and better instructed and equipped. The rest of our regiment is just behind in support trenches, and I paid them a visit today while filling our water demijohn, and heard that they had had no casualties so far but that one of the other squadrons had not been so lucky. I do not like being separated from my troop and hope it will not be for long. This is a life of surprises and one must expect nothing else, I suppose.

A friend from the troop is coming up tonight with our letters and I will give him this letter to take back.

Shelling has all stopped. 'Evening hate' is over and it is getting dark and, what I call, 'beastly cold'.

From your loving brother, Frank.

Wednesday, 23 June (Fine on the whole – some rain last night)
Spent another purely wasted day, doing much, none of which was intelligent or practical. Sincerely hope we shall go to the front trenches tomorrow, to get away from this foolishness.

Thursday, 24 June (Fine and warmer)
Pottered about, doing some things over again. Both officers always late for every parade. A few shells dropped not far south of us today, searching for a battery of big ones of ours, in a wood over there.

At 5pm we thankfully marched off, by a roundabout route to Béthune, arriving there about 8pm. We were then deserted by our officers who told us to wait for the regiment and to rejoin our respective troops and squadrons. Through one of our sergeants, we found our billets in about an hour. C Squadron is in a rambling tile factory, not at all a comfortable billet. Foster[23] and I found a good place where hay and oats are kept. The regiment arrived about 10pm. Rained at night, hard.

Friday, 25 June (Cloudy, grey, warm and raining hard)
Got parcel of shirts, etc. Most unpleasant day. Very wet. This factory is infested with excellent clay for tiles and the rain softened it inches deep. In afternoon a lot of us went into the town (we are on the edge only) for a bath. Could only get a cold shower and enjoyed that. Then some tea and cakes. Not leaving here until tomorrow. Shall not be sorry to leave this place. Wrote Ida. Pay day today. Usual ten francs.

Saturday, 26 June (Turned fine again, north-west wind and grand)
Got letter from Ida (ten francs) and Mrs Carr and Gardiner[24]. Rained hard in night but cleared in morning. Clay dried fast. Germans shelled our observation balloon at mid-day. Seemed to be heavy artillery at it for the shells burst high and near balloon, showing black clouds of smoke. Made

the balloon come down. It was slowly lowered. Received parcel of books from Ida at 9.20pm. We marched off north, parallel with the trench line through Locon to a village near Bailleul. Up in our old stamping ground. Marched till 3.30am. Most of the men nearly played out. Some did. Rained on us at intervals. A 14-mile march at a very fast pace. A cruel performance, seemingly unnecessary. Billeted at dawn at a very fine and prosperous and clean farm. Made a shelter in the orchard.

Letters to Ida (near Merville)

In France, Monday, 28 June 1915
Dear I,

I wrote to you last on Friday when we were in the clay tile factory. Ankle deep. Some books from you came and saved the situation. Rained much in the night but cleared in the morning. On Saturday evening (night really) we marched away north, parallel to the trench lines. Leaving at 9.30pm we did not stop until about 3.30am. Fifteen miles we must have walked, carrying those desperate packs! I never saw the men so badly broken up before. Very few fell out but the great majority were absolutely dead beat. I suppose some guiding hand (apart from Providence) directs these affairs and it is, probably, proud of its directing powers, but it may be sure that in civil life, engineering or mining, such guiding incompetence would be swiftly dealt with. A manager has to show better than this to hold his place with a board of directors. Why men should be run off their legs, almost, when there is no need at all of haste is incomprehensible. Let anyone try to carry over 90lb dead weight for fifteen miles much faster than he wants to walk! Personally, I seem to manage it without any serious trouble to myself, for my whole life has been a training for just this sort of thing, while many of these men have not had that chance. So I am able to discuss it from both points of view.

Luckily, our farm billet was the nicest place we have tried yet. Such a quaint old thatched house and buildings, and crops the very richest and thickest. But it rained, off and on, and was grey and damp. In the evening, yesterday, we marched off again, a very dubious and dotty lot, about five miles to our old stamping grounds of six weeks ago (Meteren), being billeted in the same farm house as before. Here we are, and quite comfortable. Friends all about who welcome us, and plenty of good coffee, eggs, milk, butter, and beer for those who like this queer stuff. We shall probably leave this afternoon and march about eight miles or so to the trenches of this district.

These trenches (Plug Street) are, perhaps, the most famous of the whole of our line, and I am quite keen to see them. Moving so much we get few posts and it is also hard to send letters away. All is well, though, in spite of the weather. Goodbye dear.

(Neuve Eglise)

In Belgium, Tuesday, 29 June 1915
Dear I,

We left our nice friendly farmhouse at 4.15pm yesterday and marched in the same ruthless, brainless manner a matter of about eleven miles to this heavily shelled and battered village, less than two miles from the most famous trenches of this whole front. Talk about riding willing horses to death! Almost five hours, with six minutes rest at one go, and we arrived about 9pm with no earthly reason to hurry at all. Stony, uneven road; much heavily cobbled. Such limping and shuffling and language! But there it is!

We are where poor Geoff Bowlby[25] was killed on May the 16th and I hope I may get the chance to drop a bomb or two in his honour among the men who got him. It seems to be understood by all that we move up into the trenches tonight, so if you do not hear from me that will be the reason.

K[26] wrote me, the letter finding me yesterday evening, having seen me down as 'wounded'. I feel a desperate fraud but it was none of my doing. Post goes at once, so goodbye.

In Belgium, Sunday, 11 July 1915
We are back in the village we recently left to go to the front trenches. A number of children and women, some of whom we knew, have been wounded and battered about. The front trenches allotted to us lie at the point of an apex, a salient, allowing a good amount of German cross-firing to take place; this, and a multitude of snipers make life highly exciting. Bullets come, almost from any direction, both spent ones and the vicious snappy kind. We left the trenches at dawn of the 7th, Wednesday last, after four days and six nights up there. From the trenches we went to the reserve dugouts, which are just outside the long communication trench leading to the firing line, and we stayed there four days till we came here last night. We shall stay four days, and then go up to the front trenches to begin the round again. The reserve dugouts are just badger-holes into which you crawl on your hands and knees. They are literally holes in the ground for two men at a time. You cannot sit

up in them at all upright and they are roofed with sand bags on poles, with earth on top, ending up with a layer of grass. As they are dug irregularly and show mole-like mounds, the whole affair is like a prairie-dog town on a big scale; men sitting at their holes, popping in or popping out. All day, bullets lop over at odd intervals, and only one man was actually hit here, and that was through the ankle. When you go to wash at a farmhouse close by, you have to follow a hedge closely and risk a bullet each time you cross the road. During our four days in the front trenches we had about fifteen casualties, two being killed, and all sniper and stray bullet work.

The night before last, the brigade bombers, about forty of us, went up to the front trench, where it is nearest the Hun, in readiness and bristling with bombs. The idea being that the Hun has made a sap to our trench and has mined it, and when he blows it up, he will make a big hole, a crater. It is our job to make that crater, with bombs, too hot a place for him. So we lay behind the trench, where we were thought by our officer to be safe, all night till dawn. Lay under a pollarded willow in wet grass. A heavy mist obscured everything and dripped like rain from that confumigated willow. Most of the men had not even overcoats, none of us had waterproof sheets, and the cold damp went right through. Personally, as I am positive that Germans never explode mines at night, I went to sleep, and in that way forgot my troubles. Our trench is, of course, evacuated along that stretch, except for one lookout, who was amusingly sarcastic about his future. Coming back at dawn down the communication trench, we met our general with one orderly, striding along not in the trench but up above on the flat. He is much admired by all the men, being quite fearless and cool and a hard worker.

Yesterday evening, about 6pm at the prairie-dog town we saw one of our aeroplanes a long way east of us and over the German lines. They were sending shell after shell up at him. We saw one shell go very close to him, and soon the machine began to travel lower and lower while it aimed steadily for home. As it passed over the German trenches all their rifles blazed away at it and things looked bad. But it came on very slowly and steadily, a big biplane. It passed through the zone of rifle fire and was safe, except for a fall in landing, coming lower and lower with engine stopped, just silently gliding in, straight and true, no flurry. It passed about two or three hundred yards to our south and would have landed in our big field if we had not been there. About that time cross-bullets from German lines, fired at it from the sides of the apex, began to fizz among us and the prairie-dogs dived below, but I did manage to see the machine just top a row of poplars to our south-west boundary of the field, and settle safely and quietly in a field beyond. Great sigh of relief all round. Very soon the German big guns began to search for the luckless machine, and they got the range correctly for the distance but fired too much to the north, by several hundred yards. Shell after shell they fired. Great high explosive shrapnel that burst beautifully about forty feet in the air and left a cloud of smoke. Till dark they sent these great whistling shells over us. We found afterwards that the pilot had been shot in leg and shoulder when high up over the Germans and that, after he had pluckily made his landing, they pulled the machine along and saved that too. It was a wonderful sight and never to be forgotten.

Wednesday, 14 July (Fine in morning, rained hard all afternoon and night)
Going to firing-line trenches tonight. Left at 8pm for front trenches in the pouring rain and high north-west wind. Had our full equipment and 150 rounds of ball, each. Went up and along the long and narrow communication trench, after three-mile tramp to it. Clay soil, slippery as ice, wet and dreadful. Was 12pm before we reached our posts in firing line, and raining as hard as ever. Everyone soaked and weighing heavy with clay all over one. At 12.30am I had to go out as 'listening patrol corporal' over the parapet to a row of willows ahead, had to crawl through three lots of barbed wire, going and returning. Crouched out there among the flares and big rats. Rain poured, wind blew, pitch dark, wet through and unspeakably dirty, hungry and thirsty. Came in at 2am, break of dawn.

Thursday, July 15th (Half rain, half sun)
Letter from Willie[27], and from Ida and Micky. Stood to till 3.30am after coming in from listening patrol. Made some tea then, and ate bread and cheese. Famished! Went to sleep at 5am. Then Mr Heath[28] found me and claimed me as a bomber. Got his way and I had to leave my troop and go. Mr Heath told me to post all bombers along our line of trench, twenty-two of them from every squadron. Took me till 6pm. Then had to report to him with three men. Found out his plan as follows. We were all, Mr Heath and four of us, to go out and try to bring in a German prisoner alive. Each of us had bombs in our pockets and a revolver. We crawled from 9pm to 1am. Crossed the river close to Snipers' Farm. Heard Huns tapping stakes for wires and talking, and a whistle close to us. Came back with no luck. It is a foolish game.

Friday, 16 July (Rain and wind and cold)
Slept till 10am. Very wet and cold and damp. Everything slimy with greasy clay. Walking about, even in daytime, is a treat, at night it is torture. Wrote to Ida and Willie. Rested and kept out of sight. In the twilight, C Squadron moved out to support dugouts near Ration Farm. We bombers stayed. So I and Foster, Walrond and Carey[29] took the big dugout the C Squadron sergeants used. Much more roomy and dry, can cook inside in a brazier with wood. Wood is valuable, more so than gold. Our rations come regularly. No complaining about want of food. Tea, bacon, sugar, jam, bread and some fresh beef and potatoes. We stand to with troops from 9am to 10pm and from 2am to 5.30am.

To W. [Olivia Fell, nicknamed Willie] (Plug Street)

In Belgium, 16 July 1915

No time for more than a few lines. Am writing from the firing trenches. Your letter reached me when I woke up this morning at 9am. I had been out, scouting round in no man's land from 9pm to 1am and some friend laid the letter on my pillow.

Am enclosing some grass picked out there within 100 yards of the Hun trench. Picked it myself and know there is no mistake.

I have been offered a commission in our regiment and, of course, said I would be proud to accept one. So I suppose I will soon go back to England for a short time and then back here again as an officer. Good luck, isn't it!

The weather is very wet here now and the mud and clay are appalling. One's clothes are doubled in weight.

The Hun is going to try for Calais again, they say, but he is not going to get there. He can run no steam roller over us as he did over the Russians lately, and if he tries hard enough the war will end quicker than ever.

Meiklejon has been wounded again and is back in England. It was a nasty rifle wound in leg but no bones broken and in a few months he should be well.

That was a cheering letter of yours and sank into me to a safe depth.

I hope to be able to tell you stories forever when this disgusting war is over. It is a hideous war. Last night I stepped on a dead thing out there in the dark. A poor unburied victim, and the rats in no man's land are legion. They are happy. They and the Kaiser and his military clique.

Personally, I am well and contented and enjoying all the best of it and skipping the rest.

Goodbye.

Yours always, Tertius.

Thursday, 22 July (Fairly strong south wind, cold)
Budget of letters from Ida, Kate and Johnny[30]. Peaceful day again. Foster and I will not like to leave our nice dugout where we have made ourselves quite comfortable. Received regimental orders to join our troops again when the regiment marches back to Neuve Eglise billets this evening. So my eleven bombers will leave me and we are all pleased, as each man's troop means so much to him. At 7pm the regiment marched back to the village to the same farmhouse, where my section (No.4) and No.1 Section live. Very friendly people. Arrived about 9.30pm. Storming and raining in squalls. Mosquitoes quite plentiful. Flies a pest all the daytime. Wasps also.

Friday, 23 July (Cold and stormy)
Peaceful day. Shook down, slept late, washed well and generally cleaned up and rested. Enjoyed fresh bread, eggs, butter, milk and good coffee. The church is nearly gone at last. The whole place is burned out, roof has fallen in and only part of the spire left. Every day the Huns throw more shells at it and around and about our ears. But no one seems to get hurt.

Saturday, 24 July (Windy, sunny and showery)
The Squadron marched to Bailleul (known usually among the men as 'Balloo'), to get a hot bath. A good two hours' walk. Saw any quantity of troops, guns, transports, ambulances on the way. Had leave in Balloo until 3pm, so had my fine boots re-soled while I waited. Old French cobbler with his two sons. One of the sons lost a foot at Berry-au-Bac and there he was, back at home and busy. Marched back at 5pm. The Huns shelled us about 10pm after we had turned in. Did not get up.

Sunday, 1 August (Lovely day)
Letters from Ida, Gardiner and Margaret and papers. Officially reported a few days ago that Sergeant Morris (see May 25) has been awarded the DCM. Am very much pleased! At 3.30am I went back to reserves with No.2 Troop, and joined my own troop there. German aeroplane driven off at 6am by a battery near us, flew home! Late evening we marched off to camp under some trees to be more out of sight.

Monday, 2 August (Showery and squally. Cold)
Slept in a ditch paved with dry wheat straw, and covered over with branches and straw and waterproof sheet. Under thick pollarded willows. At night,

bullets whiz around low down. Carried galvanized iron and slabs of timber for dugouts up to the 'supports' and dug and shovelled till 12.30pm. After lunch took a stroll (out of bounds) to a hill behind and got fine view of German lines and Messines behind them. In the evening the Huns shelled Headquarters Farm, 300 yards from us, and put ten shells right into it. Finally set it on fire. Great scattering of hospital and headquarters staff. Mr Lucas[31] was wounded and a B man lost half an ear. Trumpet Major of Strathconas had right arm shattered and another of their men hurt.

Tuesday, 3 August (Same as yesterday)
Quiet morning. Took another stroll in afternoon. Huns began to shell a deserted farm over our bivouac, hunting a battery. Sent over a number of big shells, but failed to find battery. Various 'fatigues' went on which all seemed to miss me. At 5pm the regiment marched back, by a very devious route to Neuve Eglise, to our old and familiar billets in various farm houses. Arrived just before dark when it rained steadily into the night. A new draft of about forty men from home had come. This included a number of fellows who had been through the recent campaign in South West Africa.

Wednesday, 4 August (Still showery but not so windy)
Had a decent, long, undisturbed, comfortable and dry sleep. Good clean oat straw in plenty. They still thresh here with a flail. Followed [by] an open bath in mild rain in a meadow. Clean change too! Getting fresh bread, eggs, butter, etc. better yet, the latest English papers. Two new men of the draft came to my section. Both went through the South West Africa campaign and are splendid chaps. This makes the third draft we have had: about 150 men in all, to cover up our casualties.

Saturday, 28 August (Rain and shine and uncertain)
Foot drill in morning. Troop under Lieutenant Heesman[32] who is very good in his drill. At 6.30pm whole regiment fell in for a night fatigue. Went to Plug Street Wood, Hyde Park Corner and up Hill 63 to a trench there. Mended a traverse which a shell had caved in, with six of my section. Had to build it afresh; 2 x 4 stakes, net wire and 2 x 8 boards formed breast, with dirt and sandbags behind. Had to wire stakes to a central stake behind also. Worked to 1.15am, marched to camp. About a ten-mile walk there and back. Great view, in dark, of the front lines from this hill. Flare lights trace the line of trenches for miles. Some firing and a few bullets pretty close to us at times.

Monday, 6 September
Expected to go out on fatigue but did not. Too wet and muddy I suppose. A Squadron went out, later, to Hill 63, and must have showed themselves, because Huns sent over eight whiz-bangs, one after another, and wounded six men, one of which is serious, the rest being nasty ones.

Wednesday, 8 September (Perfect day)
Paraded in morning before General Seely[33] for his inspection of our 'smoke helmet' and the new 'tube helmet'. We now carry both. Both are flannel hoods, long enough to tuck inside your tunic. The 'smoke helmet' is grey blue flannel, with two oblong eye holes. This mica easily cracks and is then a death trap. The 'tube helmet' is grey blue flannel, with round glass eye holes and a tube inside to insert in mouth and breath through. Both hoods are soaked in a carbonate solution and in the tube are chemicals to counteract the gas. This 'tube helmet' is declared to be an absolute safeguard.

Thursday, 9 September (Perfect weather and windy)
Shooting practice at the little range near-by. From the trench to 6-inch bull's eye, thirty yards off. Fifteen rounds rapid. Load ten, begin shooting then reload five. From whistle to whistle, one minute. This is fine practice and one must load and shoot as fast as possible to finish. At 5.30pm squadron marched off to Hill 63 for night's digging. Told off to dig and deepen an observation post for the General (Alderson). Had to finish job before we left. Trench was along a hedge and ground full of roots. Then had to cut green tufts and cover all traces of dirt thrown up. Took us till 4am (dawn) working hard and then we had four miles to walk home. Nearly twelve hours up and doing. Everyone very tired and disgusted.

Tuesday, 14 September (Inclined to rain)
Received orders to get ready to leave for London in the morning to report for our commissions.

Sunday, 19 September (Grand day)
Still waiting impatiently. Put in for passes for Havre. Started at 2pm. Had to wear a belt. Took train, packed with the human race. From the Hotel de Ville Station we walked around, and sampled the many restful cafés and watched the Sunday crowds. Everyone was out. Swarms of dishevelled French soldiers, mostly Territorials, I should judge, and older men. Some smart

regulars, Turcos, Algerians and other riff-raff. Equal swarms of our men from all regiments. All very friendly. People much interested in Hallowe's and Helpman's bare knees and my lace-up boots. Great pointing and smiles and talk of trenches. Back by 9pm.

Monday, 20 September (Perfect weather)
No news. We might be pensioned off till the duration of the war. Who knows! No one pays any attention to us, officially. We go on no parades, do no fatigues, and are left absolutely to our own devices. Other big fatigue parties are busy. Some leave early, to the docks at Havre and come back in evening. Others do all the duties in Camp. Cleaning up and sanitation. Queer mixture of new drafts and wounded and now-cured veterans. Man in my tent, old regular RE has been wounded three times, and buried alive in mines twice. Still dapper. Hopes, in five years, to retire, time expired, pension. Going back to front, full of hope.

Saturday, 25 September (Fine day. NW wind)
Were told about 11am that we were to go today. We fell in and marched off to the train, delighted.

Chapter 2

Training and Guard Duty,
October 1915–August 1916

[From October, Frank underwent a period of training in Ireland, rejoining the battalion in December 1915; further training in the use of the Vickers machine-gun followed, but to his disgust this was interrupted by a spell of several months as Divisional Cavalry guarding the headquarters of General Haig at Montreuil-sur-Mer.]

Letters to Ida

In Belgium, Friday, 7 Jan 1916
This letter is going by a brother officer on leave, Lieutenant Pearson, so I can say about what I please. The regiment is at Aldershot Camp in huts, close to Neuve Eglise, three miles behind the front line of trenches, and we go up with our working parties, at night only, to Hill 63 and the trenches in front of Plug Street Wood, up the Messines road and the Rossignol road which run right to the German trenches. This Messines road is a great point for trouble, also Hill 63, and, of course, Plug Street Wood needs no advertising. Bailleul is our nearest town of size, where civilization really commences, and it is about three miles away. The Huns dropped 160 shells the other day around Hill 63 and Plug Street as a reminder that they are full of life with, luckily, no damage.

The news is all confirmed and official about the 2nd KEH becoming Divisional Cavalry in a few days and I am completely disgusted. If I am allowed to finish my machine-gun course I see a chance to leave the cavalry and see something of the real war with the help of the Maxims or Colts, and I expect to be allowed to finish. This course will keep me three weeks longer, 9am to 5pm every day, Sundays included. I may call upon H.J.[1] to help me to find another regiment where I can be a machine gunner instead of a cavalry policeman posing as a trench warrior. The real fact being that the cavalry police never go near enough to hear the sound of a gun in a trench.

You might send me, please, each week a tin of oatcake and a good cheese. This will help any mess I may be with. Do not send any cigarettes for I can get them much cheaper here and the same ones exactly. No time to continue!

In France, 16 January 1916

Yesterday we moved back from the front and we are now close to headquarters, billeted in a village.

Our job is to be cavalry. To act as bodyguard to the headquarters' staff, I believe. Highly honorary but a futile profession. Any day now, though, I go to a course of Maxim gun instruction and I propose to follow my nose when I am qualified.

At present I am O.C. Gun Section (Machine Gun), and yesterday brought the section to this place. We entrained with the rest of the regiment, after a march of a few miles, at 11am. All of us travelled in horse-trucks, officers and all.

About 2pm we detrained and marched five miles to this village. With my usual luck I struck a grand billet. Two of us are together, Pearson and I. He is the real O.C. Gun Section, I being only his understudy. As he is on leave I shall look out for him. We have a big sitting room, intensely French, with mural oil paintings, stuffed birds and distorted plaster frescoes dotted about and tiled floor. A bedroom each, quite void of any hint of washing, full of mirrors. Funny old farm people, very polite and hospitable. They have three sons serving, one being a prisoner in Germany. The old lady says 'He is hungry; ah yes, I know.'

It would do England good to have the same conditions for a while and, as for Ireland!

Bessie has sent me twenty-four Banbury cakes and, remember, she is from near Banbury, and Mrs Micky sent me a cake of a richness indescribable.

My news will be very uninteresting for some time but I cannot help it. Later, perhaps, I can liven it up.

Chapter 3

At the Battle of the Somme, August–November 1916

Letters to Miss F.[1] (The Somme Battle at Hébuterne)

In France, 11 August 1916
I am back in harness and doing real work again. Since I last wrote we have left Belgium and the Salient and are now just behind the Big Push to the south in a very excited portion of the scrimmage.

We rode through in four and a half days in very blazing hot weather with dust on the roads unbelievable. I had to break away on the journey to a hospital to have two teeth hauled out, for I had half [again] as much face as normally for the sun to burn and, as I was Billeting Officer for the regiment on the trip and busy in the saddle from early to late, it was beyond a joke after a day or so of torture. But that is past and finished and I am again as fit as possible. I am now in charge of an 'observing station', for the Corps (mind you) just behind the front lines on a ridge. This gives one a view of it all with a good telescope and my Zeiss glasses. I have a corporal and four men with me and we keep incessant watch night and day.

There is a deep dugout where the men can go in a bad strafe and be pretty safe from any ordinary 'crump', but as long as we can keep the Hun from spotting our station we are safe enough. As soon as, or if, they ever spot us we shall be fairly smothered in no time, so we are pretty careful you may be sure. By day we can see more, of course, and we are in touch on the 'phone always, but the sight at night is stupendous. I reported seeing a lot of little 'smokes' in a wood about four miles behind the Hun, as if men were camped there and cooking, and, in about three hours, our 'heavies' began on that wood, which was soon a cloud of dust and branches and chaos. It was worth all my troubles and privation to see that wood go up skywards through glasses. At night there is a firework display quite unimaginable coupled with the dreadful noise of guns and terrific shell bursts. This is a duel of heavy guns, monsters, prehistoric beasts, dinosaurs, Siberian elephants of metal.

You occasionally hear the patter of rifles and the clatter of machine guns or the bursts of bombs, but the big guns hold the floor. The music is drowned by the big drums.

I am out now for a day or two in the nearest village behind for a rest and I go back on Sunday the 13th. This village is a tumbledown wreck and is shelled every now and then, but I have a deep funk-hole cellar if it is needed. Batteries all around and their noise is almost worse than ever. But I thoroughly enjoy it for the Hun is being given some of his own medicine in large doses, freely and gratis.

We were five days on duty in the OP (Observation Post) and five days out on rest (?) at Sailly-au-Bois. And we much preferred the O Pip to the village.

(Sailly-au-Bois)

In France, 9pm, 24 August 1916

I shall be very pleased to get out of this village. My mind is quite made up. I shall kiss my hand to this village as it fades away.

A short while ago I had two wounded men in my cellar, there were three more outside, quite near, too bad to move, and there were four dead lying in a heap alongside them. The effects of two shells that might just as well have got me and my men. The Hun strafed us properly today, at the usual time, and plastered the village from end to end.

They dropped all about my billet and the house across the road got another one. Its roof sits on the rest of it in the way that a man's hat looks when it is bashed in over his eyes. The poor chaps who got caught were on their way to the front lines on the road through the village. They all lay down along the hedge but the shell dropped right into them. Even steel helmets were smashed and ripped. I and my men got to them first and rescued those able to be moved to our cellar. A doctor, Royal Army Medical Corps (RAMC), arrived almost at once and bandaged the badly wounded, while I gave them some whisky I had, which bucked them up amazingly. The four dead were stone dead from the first. Earlier in the evening before dark, I went out digging shell-noses, for exercise as much as anything and, coming home, the Hun seemed to follow us up with 5.9 crumps. By dint of dropping – you really don't drop – you hurl yourself down till it hurts – we avoided the flying bits which pass over you most distinctly and got back to the billet just in time to get the rest of the entertainment the Hun had prepared. Tomorrow evening, D.V.[2], I relieve Lieutenant Monk[3] and his men, at the Observation Post, and very glad, too.

It is much safer. In a day or two I rejoin the regiment, I believe. This is one of the worst OPs in the line, because even to reach it from this village you have to run the gauntlet of the Hun fire at our batteries which are between the village and the front lines. As soon as you reach the trench it is all right, but there is a mile of open ground where you feel a mile high. As a trooper it was different, no responsibilities, but if you even have only a corporal and four men and a servant, the feeling is very different. I shall be most pleased if I get them away unhurt. Any bravado foolishness they might have had at the start has quite gone. They are now very thoughtful and have an eagle eye for cover. But even if the Hun does strafe us, you may be sure that we strafe him more by ten times and his losses must be heavy indeed.

P.S. I get no letters, no papers, nothing out here, and begin to feel marooned.

Letters to Ida (Sailly-au-Bois)

In France, 5 September 1916

We are having miserable weather. Heavy rains and cold north-west winds but as Hun prisoners are going through our camp every day, everyone is cheerful. Batches of 500 and 700 and so on. They average up a very poor specimen. Not because they are dirty and dishevelled but in physique and intelligence. Flat and narrow chests, many spectacles, undersized and with degenerate faces.

The only two officers in one batch were most ordinary looking grocers. But they seem contented and pleased with their lot and show no proud disdain. Not a single neck is arched, rather the reverse. All through the rain and cold and shine and misery the attacks have gone on, by day or night. Weather does not exist in this war, light and dark do not exist, only Time and War.

The French are doing wonderfully well to the immediate south of us. We hear the 75s hammering away like pneumatic riveters. Last night you never heard such a row! Rain pattering on the canvas and explosives on the Hun. From behind us everlasting columns of men march doggedly through the shiny clay to the front, and the tired columns come back from trenches. Some columns of men and transport and guns seem to be miles long. You hear pipes squealing and drums and fifes at all times. We are the most advanced cavalry regiment behind the heart of the Big Push. Our patrols are all under shellfire and we get the Hun prisoner direct from his captor in the trench. And the Tommy is as cheerful as ever. As time passes he gets fitter and fitter for his job, more capable and clever at it, keener and quicker. Send me the August Scribner [4] *please. I have the July.*

P.S. This is 'Tommy' writing paper, all I can get. He likes his lines well ruled.

(In The Happy Valley near Bray)

In France, 11 September 1916

Since I last wrote I have been in a Hun prisoners' camp and helping another officer of ours. Today we have nearly 200 Huns in the cage and we take them to railhead in about an hour. More come along almost every day. This present lot interests me more than the usual because I saw many of them coming in across no man's land last Saturday evening during the great fight wherein the 'crown of the ridge' was captured, according to English papers. I was up there observing for the Corps and saw everything. You need two observers at least, for the guns make such a noise that it keeps one at the 'phone and the other to look and bellow what he sees to his partner, who bellows it on to the Corps. We were just in front of the massed batteries and the row must be heard to be believed. It is a never-to-be-forgotten sight to see a big, perfectly planned and highly successful attack under these conditions.

The area to be captured is carefully laid down, that much and no more. Then the ground is consolidated against counter-attacks. The old reckless way of going as far as possible and not being able to hold on caused more losses than the original attack. It was a fine evening and no man's land was very clearly seen, except when obscured by smoke from shells. I have no words to express my feelings for the men who face the monster shells now being used freely on both sides. It is monumental and grand and must be seen to be imagined. Since then, we and the French have been very busy and the Hun is getting no rest or time to take breath.

(Near Albert)

In France, 22 September 1916

It is some days since I have written, but the first few days were in the thick of things and the last few have seen me more or less on the damaged list. I had a tremendous spill going at full and stretched-out gallop slap into a trench hidden in long grass. I was right on the tail of a fox, not twenty yards away. My horse was lamed and so was I. We run foxes and hares down without dogs. Just naturally run them down till they can run no more.

I was observing in the last big fight and saw a great deal of it. At dawn of the 15th I saw the debut of the 'Tanks', against the unspeakable Hun. They squashed their way forward up the slope and over the crest of the ridge and disappeared silently like rhinos, and straight for the enemy. We observed operations from the ruins of the church in the village (Ginchy) which was the occasion of the big fight on September 9th.

Of course we kept our telephone back about 300 yards and the rest of our men and the pigeons, because the village, being the crown of the ridge was under heavy shellfire, but Monk and I crawled out from time to time, if there seemed to be a lull, and saw all we could and hastily crawled back. All that day we had 'phone trouble on account of shells breaking our cable and we used up all our pigeons. Ours was a particularly interesting bit to watch because just to our right front was that infernal 'quadrilateral', which held our men up and enfiladed them, and in early evening some of our chaps had to retire to a trench farther back and close to us. They came streaming back, running hard, and every now and then they were blotted from view by shrapnel and bursting crumps. Then you saw the ground strewn with bodies, men crawling on hands and knees and others still running on. Later reserves came up and tried to get through the barrage which was intense. A solid wall of bursting explosive and bits of metal in the air. Some got through and many did not. Then French battalions came to our help (from Leuze Wood, we join up there) and they suffered in that same spot in the same way. I could see solid patches of sky blue dotting the ground. That was the only place that held up our line and triumphal advance. To watch men run straight ahead into almost certain death is a woeful sight. I saw batteries moved up, further, under shellfire, guns and hundreds of horses, going at a slow trot or walk, for the RHA traditions are nothing in this war. The popgun, with which they galloped into action, is not used here.

Prisoners passed by in great batches and any number of wounded. I spoke with Asquith's[5] son just before he died and turned him over on his left side at his request. He was bullet shot through upper part of left lung and bled internally.

It was an amazing day, perfect weather, a lovely summer day. I saw one of our aeroplanes plunge headlong and I saw a German balloon go up in flames. Our batteries roared and bellowed worse than ever. The ground rocked with it.

I saw our two horse ambulances go right up in heavy shellfire after our wounded, and the motors were nearby, but I take off my hat to the RAMC and stretcher-bearers. They see men downed by shellfire and calmly walk or run into it, to tend to them and get them out. This is slow and tedious work and it is a marvel that any come from that fiery furnace unburnt. I saw during the day the dear old blundering tanks barging about, grunting and snuffling like giant pigs. 'Get out of my way or I'll squash you flat.' I hope and expect to see and help in the next big jamboree and I will let you know.

To Miss F. (Near Albert)

In France, 2 October 1916

Your last long letter found me up to my neck in things here, and here I am, choosing a very wet and cold and rain and wind-swept day to write to you from my iceberg of a tent. Outside, the long lines of wretched horses stand and shiver in the storm. I will not repeat my experiences to you. They are better hot from the anvil. The Big Push keeps on irresistibly and the Hun is squeaking like the pig he is. We have got the secret now and we will never let up. The Hun is being killed in droves; he is given no rest; he is worried and he is hustled; he is half-starved in his lines, and he is very demoralized. I have seen batches of Huns coming through our lines with no escort of any kind, asking anxiously the way to the nearest prisoners' cage, and the grinning Tommies pointing out the way and watching them shamble off in a desperate hurry. The war is not nearly over, but we have won it already, hands down!

Every night their aeroplanes bomb our camps if the weather is decent. Bang! Bang! All about, the searchlights frantically search and the archies shoot madly at the stars. I used to get up and watch it all but now we just turn over, if we wake up, and go to sleep. They are not nearly as worrisome as mosquitoes in your tent or dugout, but they certainly kill a lot of horses and cause a few other casualties. The poor horses in the lines catch it badly. Of course our 'planes are doing the same thing and, as there are no women and children or civilians here, it is legitimate warfare and no one is objecting. If the Hun only knew that, owing to Zepp raids over in England, for every life he kills there – women and kiddies – he is paying a dozen over here, of able-bodied, dog-bodied, butcher-booted Fritzes. Many Tommies, very many, bayonet the 'kamerad'-whiners and murmur 'Zepp' to him before the big sleep gets him.

By the help of our multitude of guns and shells, and our good Staff work, our casualties are not excessive – nothing like the Hun slaughter. All the same it is terrific fighting and a man is but a straw in a cyclone. By good luck he may win through but the odds are against him. Men you lunch with one day are below ground, if lucky, next day. The word 'missing' is a gruesome word, usually meaning that the recipient was the centre of a monstrous crump and is literally missing.

After my six months of trench work last year it is most interesting to be doing and seeing other phases of this war. Traffic control, with batteries all around nearly blowing you out of the saddle, wrestling with streams of traffic all in a hurry; escorting prisoners to railroad, searching them and seeing the doctor patch them up (the real wounded, of course, go to the hospital, but there are always sore feet and rheumatism and sores among them, and others, shell-shocked, have a habit of fainting dead away at any time); also dispatch riding among the shells.

Letters to Ida (all near Albert)

In France, 15 October 1916

I am busier than ever just now. Behold me acting-adjutant of the regiment while the adjutant is home on special leave. This is 'some honor' for a 2nd Loot, in the presence of others of higher rank and experience. It is a thankless sort of job but interesting.

The only sorry I have is that this will make it harder for me to transfer to Machine Gun Corps for next year's show, but that bridge is not yet in sight.

You do seem to have had water troubles, too, of your own. Our cause of water trouble here is the German airbomb or shell descending (with a splash) into tanks or pipes, for all our water has to be piped miles across this devastated country, and when you have 20,000 horses watering at one set of troughs every day the importance of it is manifest. The engineers, in this colossal and amazing war, should get their full share of praise. Aerodromes, rows of great canvas over wooden ribbed hangers spring up around us like mushrooms for speed. Roads of liquid mud become widened and macadamized by black magic. Broad, full gauged, 90lb per foot steel railroads follow the fighting front methodically over ground a mass of shell holes, and little narrow gauge pony rail tracks are frequent everywhere. All this is done amidst a moving multitude of men, motors, and horsed vehicles which must be kept going. Not to speak of the various annoyances they are subjected to by the Hun in the distance. Everything has to be brought a long way to do anything with because this lovely bit of country had been turned into a death smelling, towzelled wilderness.

No signs of leave yet. Only 'special leave' for those who have the most urgent reasons. At this rate I shall be lucky to get off before Christmas, and then I will look into my needs for new togs.

Any papers you can send will be most welcome. Your Daily Telegraph *sent on every day would fill what is almost a void here. The postage will be appalling though! We are lucky to get the continental edition of* Daily Mail *at irregular intervals.*

Any books you can wheedle or demand from your friends also will be read by dozens of officers and men here after I have had precedence. Books or papers. There is a winter ahead to be spent by us probably in dugouts and tents in this locality, and books keep you warm by making you forget the cold and wet and discomfort.

The question of fuel, wood or coal, is going to be impossible here on account of the transport of more important things, and I expect to live in my sheepskin-lined trench coat. Yes, and sleep in it too. When it comes to cold I am all beyond conscience or cleanliness.

The guns boom steadily, at times madly, but always they boom, and at night the frantic agitations of the Hun searchlights in the sky are a source of great amusement to us. The agitated antics of that beam of light cause joyous bursts of laughter from our men. You never saw such hurried and flustered searching, and you can imagine the bombs biffing around the searcher. One of our night-hawks the other day dived down a beam of light and put the Hun searchlight crew to scandalous flight with his machine gun, leaving the beam alight, then our thoughtful airman wheeled, returned very low and dropped a bomb on the light itself, fairly blew it out!

It is getting woeful cold already, and it is raw and wet and windy. One never sees a fire or a stove and when, in a few days, we move up to a new place nearer trouble, we shall whistle for warmth till we get re-arranged in tents and dugouts. I am going to dig down three feet inside my tent and put a small stove inside with the [flue] running out through the ground at the side. Properly ditched outside this will be quite snug, and then I shall pilfer wood and coal shamelessly.

6pm, 16 October 1916

Have been riding fast and steady all day preparing arrangements for the protection of the searchlights about here against Hun aeroplanes.

Our regiment is to do the protecting and I am confident that some of our fellows will bring a Hun crashing down. All last night there was the most terrific bombardment I ever heard or saw. Today we learn that the Hun attacked heavily, twice, and was heavily repulsed. Just out in front of us. The more he attacks the better and the quicker the end of him will come. We can handle him with ease now and no one worries a moment. Today it turned clear and fine and very cold, the sky populated with aeroplanes and spotted with shrapnel puffs. Saw two Huns over, being relentlessly strafed.

To Miss F. (The Somme Battle, near Albert)

In France, 17 October 1916

I am enlarging my set of army experiences by acting as adjutant to the regiment in the place of the real one, who is away on two weeks special leave. This is a distinct and notorious compliment, and I realize that I am in the full beam of the regimental limelight. The adjutant is usually the most hated man in the regiment (the present one – on leave – is most decidedly so), and I took up his mantle with my eyes open. I have modelled my behaviour on the lines of a tank, slow, unassuming, tactful and direct. The absentee adjutant modelled his on the rhino. He charged madly about at things he could not see or hear in a most untactful manner and always caused angry feelings in his wake. Being adjutant, mess president and training signallers is quite enough all the same. Before long I hope to get my second star and become a lieutenant, which will mean that I shall have gone over the heads of six or eight of my fellow 2nd lieuts, who preferred staying at home long after I had returned to the front. Most of them got married in the meantime over there, so they should not mind. It is dangerous for a bachelor to be in uniform at home now. They almost knock you down and marry you, I am told. I shall hide behind my fighting suffragette-sister's skirts [Ida], when our leave re-opens. I fear it will be Xmas before I shall be able to get off, if leave is re-opened by then.

The Hun has massed a desperate lot of men and big guns in front of us here, and our progress is slower at the moment, but we are killing them in a most satisfactory manner. Methodical slaughter in grim earnest is the plan.

Soon we move camp nearer to the front (Montauban), as near as it is safe to camp horses on open lines, and in the midst of all the hurly-burly just behind the fighting. Big 12- and 15-inch guns and batteries showing their ugly snouts on all sides, and the never ceasing stream of interesting traffic flowing in great road-rivers to and from the front. Traffic here, on nearly all roads, travels under the strictest regulations in one direction only and the routes are planned to go in circles along the front to bases behind. You can hustle along a lot of traffic in this way in spite of weather and Hun shells. Our chief excitement is at night time, with the Hun aeroplanes. They are much braver at night than by day; they come over very high and drop bombs on our camps every night unless the weather is too bad. It is legitimate and no one feels grieved about it but, if they came over oftener by day, we would respect them more.

They kill a lot of horses. Two bombs killed sixty-odd and wounded seventy-odd in one camp near us. We have had five killed and eight wounded a week ago in our camp. Yesterday two bombs dropped into us on the edge of camp and in soft ground and not doing us a particle of harm. None of our men have been hurt because they lie on the ground to sleep and a bomb would have to fall directly on a man to blot him out. The poor horse stands up like a barrel on stilts and catches all the flying bits in his pin-cushion.

The weather has been wholly (or is it wholely) vile of late. Equinoctial spasms. In the open, on a high plateau, with good wind space, life in a tent or rabbit-hutch of a 'bivvy' with Duties (with a big D) to perform, is about one per cent as uncomfortable as it would be in a front line trench, so we do not complain in the least, having had our own bitter experiences of much worse times. A life of rooms, fires, (Great Scott!) table cloths, chairs, food not rations, and sheets seems like a long past dream, but I am rather fond of it than otherwise.

Letters to Ida (Near Albert)

In France, 4 November 1916

We are still wallowing in rain and bottomless mud. Day after day and night by night it rains. Grey, thick, woolly clouds race overhead all day long. It is a choicely foul climate, with no redeeming features! The human race is the most illogical of all the things alive on this earth. Of course, I have little or no news. It is impossible to do anything. If you have succeeded in keeping your temper, much less your health, you have really done a good deal.

My efforts have been in the direction of making our mess quarters more comfortable, and despite the weather we now have a sweet small abode made up of ammunition boxes, sand bags (full of wet clay) and two tarpaulins. A stove and a hanging lamp give light and enough warmth when it is possible to get oil or coal. The effect has been so popular that tonight the colonel, for the first time in my knowledge, is coming to dine with us, and we are preparing him quite a decent spread. The conditions of storm in the Channel affect us in the way of post, papers, etc., and we get practically nothing. Infantry regiments get their desperate bit of work in front trenches, four days or a week at most, and then they go back to billets to lick their wounds and sores, but we have been two months under conditions of supreme discomfort which should be put to our credit in the weight book. I do not count bombs at night – that our men seem to rather enjoy – but just wet and mud and grovelling around in dugouts and bivvies.

(Near Albert)

In France, 8 November 1916

The weather is the war just now. It is not Huns now, it is weather to fight. For the past full month it has been nothing but rain, gales of wind, storm succeeding storm, one after the other, southerly, westerly and north-westerly, day and night. Occasional half hours or so of respite and then at it again hammer and tongs. And still going on as I write, blowing and squaking and streaming wet. Cold as charity, of course, and fuel as scarce as pig fat in Germany.

Now and then, at night, the stars come out keen and bright and the wind drops, but at dawn flying scuds of clouds appear low down and the old dance commences. The night before last was just such a night and two infernal Zepps paid us a visit. They dropped a lot of bombs of great power, four or five close to our camp, close enough to nearly knock tents down and to loosen all tent pegs with the blast of air, although the nearest bomb was over a mile away. I will not say what they did but they raised the mischief in the French lines next to us, and the fuss lasted from 11pm to dawn and more. The sky was bright over there and all sorts of explosions occurred and the air was alive with bursting shells, search lights, machine guns and whirling aeroplanes.

It was a great sight and sometimes I had to laugh. The world had gone mad, it seemed, mad beyond any efforts of fiction. The stuff those Zepps dropped produced greater shocks than 12-inch gun shells. Given fine weather we may expect them often, I suppose, until our chaps wake up and strafe one or two as you have done at home.

(Near Albert)

In France, 13 November 1916
Life pursues the even tenor of its way quite regardless of the Hun and all his machinations. I have been very busy building winter stables for our horses. Shacks made of a wooden skeleton covered with tarred felting and other makeshifts. This has kept me in camp and our excitement is provided by the Hun at night time. He gives several performances at irregular hours to keep us properly keyed up to a fine and bursting state of health. Every fine and moderately fine night he considers the proper time to administer to us doses of joyous excitement. It is true that he has torn holes through my saddle and ruined my bridle by dropping a bomb near my tent the other night, but his feat, in my opinion, was offset by the fact that he failed to wake me up. There was pandemonium that night all round and I finally had gone to sleep in spite of it.

The question of leave fluctuates from day to day. Rumours abound but, officially, our corps is giving no leave yet at all, and no hope for the future. It is not possible to live without hope for me, so I am still bearing up and able to build horseshacks and follow a Hun in the air at night with my glasses.

(Near Albert)

In France, Sunday, 26 November 1916
Owing to this never ending rain and mud there is no news to speak of. Leave for our corps is opening in a respectable red-tape way very soon and I can, to a certainty, I think, say that I shall leave here on, or nearly on, 19 December. We get ten days from boat to boat which is a blessing because, formerly, your train adventures in France, which delayed you up to four days, got you into scrapes with your long-suffering colonel's liver. I am due second on the list for leave but two other married sorrowfuls want to go at once and I prefer a quiet Xmas. I have ordered new riding breeches, to be kept till I arrive, and the rest of my kit will pass muster. Am sending the Xmas cards to be forwarded quickly [to America] please and then they should arrive in good time.

If I feel insecure about leave, I shall jump in about 12 December instead of a week later. You never can fathom the spasms in the official mind and to celebrate the battle of Crécy they may quite easily stop all leave again.

It is pouring, poured all night, poured all yesterday and will pour all tomorrow and tomorrow night and for a week to come. The place is a shaking quagmire upon a high plateau. Am glad to say that all the horses under my charge are comfortably under a tight roof and out of the wind. Wish they were all that way.

(Near Albert)

In France, 27 November 1916

Have settled my leave at last. I leave on 12 December, and I get ten clear days, from boat to boat. That means that I shall spend my Xmas, like last year, on some ice-house of a train between the coast of France and the front, but leave is leave and the rest is too far away to worry about.

Weather a shade worse. Ice now, mixed with mud and water and the debris of the wranglings of two large and infuriated armies. It rains a few minutes, then it freezes and your tent crackles in the wind. Then more rain and so on. Coal is all slack and soaking wet. Everyone's fires smoke. My tent literally hangs with festoons of soot three to six inches long! No one else has such a lovely collection.

'Dirty but warm' is my motto and I cannot always do full justice to the latter part. My white kitten is of my opinion also. Big strafe of our guns going on all yesterday and today, all of very heavy calibre. The Hun cannot be happy, exactly.

Chapter 4

With the Tanks in Action,
December 1916–November 1917

To Ida (Near Albert)

Back from leave! In Camp, 21 December 1916
Today I sent in my written request to the colonel to be transferred to the Tank Service, and he told me he would let me know tomorrow. Quite kind and sorrowful the old chap was.

I recently met a colonel of Tanks who put me in the way of how to join them and practically assured me a captaincy in three months after joining them, as he said they wanted older men to put over the youngsters. He also told me that my colonel could not stop me, could stop no officer who wanted to join Tanks. If Colonel Cradock refuses me I shall take the matter above his head to the Corps Headquarters.

I got back on Sunday last (17th) in afternoon, spending one night in Boulogne and one in Amiens. Found the camp in worse mud and water than ever and the blessed guns as busy as ever. Then it froze hard for a couple of days until today when it thawed and rained more and the mud is back again.

Tonight it blows a half gale. My tent I found all dug out and sand-bagged, and a nice open fireplace in the clay wall, with coal too, and I am quite snug. T., my groom[1], has done a splendid job in my absence. Very pleased, he is, to hear about his wife and family, first hand. Great preparations for Christmas going on and everyone busy. I was on a Field General Court Martial today, all morning, and gave a waster his deserts.

In Camp, 23 December 1916
All is well. My papers have gone, forwarded with a glowing recommendation from the colonel and I expect at any time to be sent away to some place near here to learn all about the life and habits of that strange beast of prehistoric origin, whose diet is live Huns, preferably mashed.

This is Christmas Eve, and tomorrow I shall have to overeat, I suppose. One always does on Christmas Day, and I have long realized that it is quite inevitable. It does little but rain and blow, walking about here is like wading the marshes in Florida after duck and snipe, only the footing here is clay and horrible.

But there is a good time coming, in a few months, unless that spineless cactus, Wilson, makes peace.

To Mr G.[2] (Sautricourt behind St. Pol)

In France, Some Place, 30 December 1916

Just a few lines to tell you that I am transferring from Cavalry to the Tank service very soon. I hope to go in a few days to some training place to learn the good and bad habits of a tank and then I shall be ready when the real shooting season opens in the spring. By shooting 'peace' into a Hun's thick hide with big and small guns of all kinds, long enough, we may reasonably hope to end this war satisfactorily in about two years and what is left of us will feebly shout 'Hip-hip 'ooray!' The measly blighters know just what is coming to them next summer and they are fairly panting for peace. They'll get peace some day but they will take what is given to them, be glad to get it and be surprised that they get anything at all.

On Xmas day, the Hun prisoners we look after lined up and gave us an exhibition of the goose-step and sang 'God Save the King' with gusto. We asked them to sing us the 'Hymn of Hate' but they begged off and said they were ashamed of it. But they all knew it. They are a lot of bullet-headed, heavy-looking burglars, fat and happy now.

I expect to get my fill of thrills in command of a tank, which I shall name 'The Old and Bold', and try and live up to.

To Mr and Mrs P.A.V.A.[3] (near Albert)

In France, Some Place, 3 January 1917

This is to be the Year! This year we smash 'em! The trouble [for the Germans] is going to be to break the [British] Bulldog's grip. The Bulldog has got his grip and he is holding on all this winter with jaws locked, eyes shut and joy in his soul.

I am transferring to Tanks. My final papers are all through and passed and approved and I am waiting for orders to report to some training place where I shall learn to make tanks eat out of my hand. The service is only for volunteers, no-one is detailed to tanks against his will. That is why it is such a success.

It is going to be a wild burst this summer and I hope to be in at the kill. Heavens, but how I loathe a German. The sight of a German prisoner, and they swarm around here, flushes and congests my being and I wallow helplessly in a stormy trough of seas of rage. Sharks and crabs of the sea, buzzards and carrion crows of the air, hyenas and jackals of the land – all being disgusting Vermin!

If I really set out to describe them, adjectively, I should riot forth into lovely medical terms which alone can give the warthogs their due. So I will refrain, but I assure you I can!

To mow the Hun maggots down, all with their flappers up on high, and whining 'Kamerad,' is the present indelible aim of my existence. A tank is the best means by which to get in among them close up and there is frequent possibility of squashing them into a shape only slightly less repulsive than the normal one. So, as I said before, I am joining 'Tanks'.

I came back from ten days leave just a week before Xmas, and it was a jolly ten days spent with Ida and her wounded Canadians. She opens house to them from 12am to 6pm, gives them tea and cake and sandwiches, all they want, and provides every Canadian daily paper procurable, all the magazines, and a lot of English weekly illustrateds and books. And they come, armless, legless, bandaged in all ways, smiling and perfect in manners. Her rooms are unaltered, nothing packed away, and they feel absolutely at home with her. They tell her about their fights, all historic names now, and she mothers them all. Nothing keeps her away and she goes nowhere, Sundays and all, between those hours. Drunken Tommies and Jackies are bought to her at any hour. She gives them the run of the house, hot bath, pajamas, the visitors' bedroom, meals and good cheerful talk, and in a few days they return sober and serious and ashamed and tell her all about it, and they write to her from ships and trenches. She has just the right way with them because there is no pose about it and they know it at once. Remember, too, that she is absolutely alone at night in her house. But she is as fearless as can be and that is all that is necessary. G⁴ comes every afternoon to help her, and it is a treat to see her collecting the crutches for them, helping them on with their coats, chatting cheerfully, and every now and then bursting forth into a particularly hearty laugh. They are a great pair and the men appreciate their ways.

Mrs M. was staying with Ida all my leave and we theatred and gallivanted everywhere. She is superintending women workers at an Admiralty cordite works and is as delightful as ever.

Letters to Ida (Near Albert)

In camp, 7 January 1917

I am still in the same place awaiting orders impatiently to report to some circus where tanks disport themselves. Two more of our officers have put in for tanks and the colonel looks at me quite sideways at present.

I have just returned from a long trip inland (near Amiens), riding, where I was sent to report on certain villages from the point of view of billeting arrangements. I went and returned well inside the specified time limit and the colonel has been complimentary about my report, so that is another dangerous corner well turned. The only alteration the colonel made was to put a frame in blue pencil around the title names of the villages in my rough, very rough, sketches of same. You know they have to do something but I hardly expected anything so trifling. It was not even amusing, not even Art.

Both my horses came back fresh and fit and I had no hitches. Weather was fair and it is a grand way to see country.

It gave me some idea too of the state of France after two and a half years of desperate war. Many French villages are built of a skeleton of timbering with spaces filled with a plaster of clay and straw, the outside of which they whitewash. Normally they look very well, clean and durable, but they are, literally, whited sepulchres. They need constant repair.

Nowadays all the men of really workable age are away and the women have their hands full with the crops and other things. Therefore repairs to these structures are wanting, and numbers of them are fairly falling down. No hostile shelling there, remember, only want of repair, and the outlook for France is not good in this respect, but it may teach them not to be so economical and to build more durable buildings. As it is, they cause hardships to our men who are billeted in the flimsy nuisances.

Other things I noticed also which point to the terrific strain going on. People in England imagine they have great hardships to bear through war and are giving great sacrifices, but as compared to France they are in clover, knee deep.

And the French never complain. It is too deep for mere complaints, their feeling. As long as these disgusting human scum are desecrating their clean soil they think only on one subject.

The old lady I was billeted on showed me a light on the future. She was old and ill and bent and looked half starved, and all alone and in the gloomiest black. But she said she could not help actively and could only help by saving money for France, and she was doing that, no doubt, at the expense of her health, her strength and, probably, her life. Not unhappy either, for she was fighting and saw victory ahead for France.

I will write at once when I get news of my transmogrification (is there such a word) into a tank and tell you where to address letters. Have tried unsuccessfully so far to get that other regimental Xmas card you mentioned, but have not given up yet.

(Sautricourt, transferred to Tank Corps)

In training. France, 11 January 1917

Last night I arrived at my journey's end after the usual highly unpleasant trip. You travel out here, on railways, very slowly, and you are supposed to, and actually do, live on air, well spiced by the red-peppered and chillied remarks of your companions, who are generally much younger and less resigned to the never failing mysteries of this most interesting world.

I have reported to my CO[5] and had a talk with him, and found him so far a man to distinctly like and admire. He was a Colonel of Lancers lately. The company I am posted to is No.5, and I am told by No.5 that it is a very good one and that if I had had the terrible misfortune to be posted to No.6 my troubles would have engulfed me.

They seem a very decent lot of officers, to my first impressions. The work ahead is going to be stiff and most full of special interests, and I hope I shall be able to hold my own. It is a new place and conditions are very raw. The same huts and mud and stoves with no coal, etc., and the same loathely wet and corrosive cold.

Censorship is extremely strict here and certain words and names must never be used or mentioned, and, of course, I can say nothing about my work. The area we work in is a closed one, but there is a fairly decent town (St. Pol, behind Arras) a few miles away where one can get a hot bath and ordinary comforts in way of food and necessaries.

Tell your Canadian friends to be of good cheer and not to worry over inconclusive peace rumours.

(Sautricourt)

In France, 17 January 1917

I have taken the plunge, head first off the bank of cavalry safely into the waters of trouble and hidden adventure, and I have come to the surface above the snow and mud much happier. Hang the cavalry and their futile ways, this is the life! Strenuous training for real work not so very far ahead.

I see a vista ahead for two or three months of courses of technical training in four or five vital subjects, and then going forth to once more test your luck.

As far as I can judge, it seems to me that everything I have done in past (and apparently futile) life has been a direct and invaluable training for this amazing climax, and there must be a reason for it. Those years of going back and forth to the island, day or night, in all weathers and by oneself, in the old 'Coot'[6], are a priceless thing for me now. The old E.N.F.[7] car is now doing me a grand turn. Siberia and the Kootenays are assisting just at present, and the time will come when a Florida summer heat will be as a cold spray to what we may expect.

My address is 5th Company, B Battalion, Heavy Branch Machine Gun Corps, and it is a question of early rising and shaving by candle light in a stone cold canvas hut with the snow thick outside. Hideous weather prevails all the time. We are twenty miles behind the front line and it is a rest from the din of the big guns. Our work goes on in a closed area and the utmost secrecy is demanded. Certain words are taboo in correspondence and quite right. The day is spent in cold storage, outside or under cover, but the work is thrilling and quite overbalances the discomforts which are really intense. Sometimes I find myself laughing aloud. The whole thing is like a bit of H.G. Wells or Jules Verne and often extremely funny.

The men and officers are a fine lot on the whole and in the fighting they will all be good, because the weeding out is tragic. To be allowed to become permanent will be a feather brush in your cap. Before I joined up here I had to be examined medically again, and the doctor passed me as absolutely sound, including eyesight. Pretty good after two years and more of these frantic exertions at my ripe old age.

My only fear is that the Boche will squeal before this 2nd Lieutenant can get among him and his horde of disgusting swine because I shall never get another chance in years to come. My letter is all about myself but please overlook for I am much preoccupied and possessed by a mania and I cannot help it.

(With the Tank Corps, Sautricourt)

In training, 21 January 1917

I am suffering agonies, not inaudibly, from cold but the work is thrilling and counteracts a great deal. Get up at 7am in an ice cold damp canvas hut, on the floor of which I sleep like a log buried in damp and clammy blankets and all my spare clothes, shave by the blazing illumination of one candle, hopping about in iceberg boots, and toy with water mixed with ice. Breakfast in a place where the fire is only just lit and leave, still cold, and drive a few miles in a car affair to a place where the mysteries are taught. There to spend six hours attending lectures and demonstrations in a series of big tents which are innocent of fire and colder than the outside, the ground being six inches deep in snow, the sun never showing and the east wind always blowing. We had a written exam on Saturday and I feel confident I got along well enough, because it did not seem difficult. Tomorrow I tackle another course and hope to do as well.

Today, Sunday, I wrote out my first 'scheme' and am awaiting the result. My ideas of promotion have entirely changed. As far as I see this is a subaltern affair entirely. The higher you go the less of the real thing you see and the Army is not worth the discomforts without the real thing. So I shall contend against promotion. This place is so different to the Cavalry. Everything is humming with work and everyone is busy and cheerful.

Frequent lectures by most interesting Staff officers on various highly interesting subjects in the late evenings after ordinary work is over.

The watch broke down for no reason, in my pocket, and the main spring is broken. I may send to you soon for a wrist watch, as I expect I shall need to save time in looking at a watch and should have two watches to keep accurate time. When I find the advertisement I am after, I will send you a cheque to get me the watch I want.

War news is not bad and the Hun is certainly worried. This year, provided some infernal peace is not declared, he will get a fearful dusting, and it will last him for just about 100 years, when the instincts of the brute will boil up again, no doubt, and then he will get another dusting from our grandsons and grandnieces.

In training, 24 January 1917

I have good news. The ordeal of my first examination on the most important of my courses is over, and I came out 2nd in the list, with a total of 96 out of 100 and, as the man above me got 100 and is an old hand at the game, I feel more than pleased. This assures me the occupation I want, when the time comes, and my heart's desire.

I am on another course now and have several more in sight. When we finish we shall indeed be highly trained. The weather is still arctic but it will pass, like everything else, and we shall have other troubles later, I suppose.

In France, Sunday, 28 January 1917
It is too cold to write, almost, but I can struggle through a few lines, sitting almost inside an idiotic homemade stove that would be much warmer, poor thing, if it were wrapped up in a blanket. This cold spell has lasted now about ten days and shows no sign of abating. Clear days and clear nights, nearly cloudless, blistering frost and all sharpened and acidified by a corrosive east wind. It is all coming from the east, the Boche lines, and my theory is that the Boches are doing it.

It is merely another form of their frightfulness, sending over streams of refrigerated air from their front trenches. No doubt they are all lying in hammocks and being fanned, behind their lines.

I have finished another course satisfactorily, although no marks have been published, but you always know, and tomorrow I begin on another. This will make three courses, and these are the three principal ones. Besides this we had to send in a written scheme on a subject given us a few days ago and the adjutant told us at a lecture, informally, that my scheme was the 'goods', and that it had been sent away to headquarters to show them what B Battalion could do. He also said that he was writing a scheme on same subject but that when he read mine he tore his up. This is all very complimentary but is a mystery to me. The whole thing is just a matter of common sense and the question of details is also only common sense.

Nothing really difficult at all. I am becoming alarmed. They might want to give me promotion which I strongly do not want, after seeing how the land lies, but, of course, I may be only needlessly alarmed. This may sound like bragging but it really is not. No one, out here, brags. What is the use? Nothing is of any use but slamming the disgusting Boche. General Peyton[8] is around here but I never see him. Am kept too busy. When I finish my courses I may be put on as an instructor to others.

To Miss F. (Sautricourt)

In France, 7 February 1917

Today's papers tell me that the States have declared war on the Beast and I can imagine how pleased you all are. At last the Anglo-Saxon is arm-in-arm, shoulder-to-shoulder, back-to-back, all together, sons, brothers, cousins, the whole family, against the bloated Beast. This next summer will see him drawn and quartered, and I hope he will taste some of the frightfulness he so proudly bragged about. It is the only way to make him understand. Hack it through him with a meat axe! Anything less he will forget in the denseness of his swollen conceit. To think that those domineering square-heads should ever rule the world! No fairy tale was ever more improbable.

I have kept off the subject somehow so far, but really, this cold weather has gone too far. For three weeks it has hovered close to zero and, in a canvas hut, sleeping on the floor, your blankets in the morning are covered with white frost and there is nowhere to get warm. Coal is scarce and very bad, and there you are. It is worse than Siberia because there one could find warmth somewhere as a rule. All day is spent in the open and one is never warm.

I have passed three courses very well and am now an instructor in one of them, so I feel quite contented. Given decently warm weather, it would be pleasant enough here. When spring comes and the little dickey birds arrive, we shall move up to the front ponderously, somewhere, and proceed to talk 'Peace' to the Hun. Shoot it into him at the rate of several hundred bullets a minute from each of our guns.

To Ida (Sautricourt)

In France, Saturday, 17 February 1917

Another week gone by and seven days nearer to the end of the war. If it were not for plenty of work and certain excitements in the near future, this existence would be about impossible. The cold, I finally vanquished with a baby coal stove in my hut, which has been and is my warmest friend, and worth its weight in that futile stuff (to the present view) called gold. I have been instructing and examining all the week both officers and men in a course which will slaughter quite a few hundred (or thousand) Huns this summer, a most cheering thought indeed!

All the same I am glad the week is over and Sunday coming before a repetition.

We are going ahead fast, and completing organization and I am detailed to No.1 Section of B Battalion HBMGC. As No.1 is the best section of B Battalion, officers, NCOs and men, this is a compliment on paper and in every way, because we will not be left out of any gnashings and clashings of teeth in the enemy's first, second or third lines this coming summer. My Section OC[9] [Captain Dudgeon] is a long stockbroker and a very fine man, two or three years my senior, and he has four subalterns under him, including myself.[10] Two of these are old hands at the game and the third is a young spark who enlisted in 1914 and found himself at the front in November 1914. He has been here since, as Tommy and officer, periodically going over the top and going home to get his wounds licked aseptically. He is only about 22-years-old now and is quite unmoved by all his adventures. Some of these boys are really amazing. The men, too, are a fine lot and as keen as can be.

Weather is warmer. Snow is now slop and mud has taken charge once more. But the great thing is that it is warmer.

To Mrs P.A.V.A. (Sautricourt)

In France, 28 February 1917

Today's news of the Hun retreat (from the Arras front) is very good but it will be better yet, and I hope to be personally on their heels before very long. These black-hearted, retreating War Lords are on their way back to complete disaster and a German Revolution in the future. The French Revolution will be but a pantomime to the Hun one.

We are working like tigers, training and practising unceasingly. I have passed all of my courses most successfully and have been instructing in one of them for past two weeks (the 6-pounder Hotchkiss gun).

My wish is realized and I am doing the work and have the job I joined this Corps for. As I am well away the oldest subaltern of them all, I hold a distinctive posish! Promotion, if only one star, would take my cherished job from me so I am resisting any move in that direction.

The cold weather has passed by and signs of spring are apparent. Rooks fly about with bits of straw in their beaks and moles are getting very active under one's bed. The zero cold was a reality and plenty of snow besides. We nearly perished, and I can say that I was never so cold for so long and so often even when in Siberia. It was a case of all day and all waking night of being dismally cold. I went through it well enough but it has left me with an abnormal throat so that I can hardly speak and, when I do, all the rooks in the country stop in envious surprise.

All is well on this Western front and is going to be better. Of that you may be quite sure, and the German Bandarlog will not rule any part of this world in the future except their own greasy beer gardens and suburban capitals well decorated with strictly German imitations of what they consider to be antidotes [epitomes?] of frightfulness in Art. Monstrous, fat, lethargic, classic platitudes in stone, wood, or marble. Even their War-Lord heavy-villain business has been exposed!

To P.A.V.A. (Sautricourt)

In France, 20 March 1917

Today's news is most stimulating. The loathely ones are in a dilemma. Enemies all round and closing in and the revolution bogey ready to eat them up at home. The punishment will fit the crime properly if, after we have done with them, they proceed to foully slay each other at home; which is most agreeably probable – with Russia as an example. With this difference, the Russian is a white man and these human refuse are black as bats. A German revolution will show the world what degraded degenerates Germans can be. Back to Berlin, slinking and snarling, there they go! Most of them will never see Berlin again although they do not know it. They think a squeal for peace pitched into the proper false note will save them but they are, as usual, wrong. Their troubles are only really commencing. The British bulldog is moving up stiff-legged and growling. He has not sprung yet or grappled, and he is not beside himself with rage – as he will be later. Wait till the grapple and death lock take place. You'll hear that bulldog growling all over the earth. There is no man in the British Army who has not lost several relations or good friends, many gassed and choked to death with poison, dying for hours black in the face; no one has forgotten and everyone intends to get even to the fullest extent. There are the French, too, and the Russians, and there is the Hun, ringed in, where he cannot escape. The vengeance of the Allies is as sure as Fate.

Of course, we are very jubilant and the French people are beside themselves with joy and delight. They are immensely pleased with us now, and show it readily and fully.

To Miss F. (Sautricourt)

In France, 11 May 1917

Tomorrow we go up there to where all those big gun things are making such a noise, to overlook our scene of action and learn the lay of the country and, about the end of this month, we shall amble forth among the Unspeakable and deal them the destruction they have been asking for. Given good and dry weather we should do most exceedingly well. Everybody is in the highest spirits and full of fun.

The steady sunshine and warmth, and the new spring green and quiet winds have all helped to make the outlook a pleasure and no one is thinking of the shadier side. But I do so hate the other side, the terrible sights especially.

Before we go over we hope to get some photos taken of our lot, and, if we manage it, of course I will send you some.

The States is in earnest and will save this war for us yet, for I have no idea that it will end this year. There are too many Huns alive. But whatever happens to us, we all know that we have won the war and nothing else really matters.

I will keep you in touch just as often as I can, but it will be a whirl of work and excitement.

Letters to Ida (Tank Driving School, Wailly near Arras)

Sunday, 19 May 1917

We are back from a dress rehearsal of our real job, held over recently captured trenches. Took us about a week of excessively hard work, all day and a good bit of the nights. Next week we move off to participate in the real thing and the tug will be on. We shall be where the big bumble bees fall thickest. Our company has the reputation of being the best in the brigade and they are sending us into the worst of it, which is a distinct and well appreciated honour. If we succeed we shall have really done something and be the proudest set of men on earth.

The days are packed with work in getting ready and final touches to training. The dress rehearsal was priceless fun, punctuated with moments when your heart stopped beating. I got into big trouble once, but after half an hour's frantic exertion, I pulled out and carried on with the job on hand. It is a wonderful experience.

The socks will come in a day or two, I feel sure. I do not think I need anything except books every now and then. This is the simple life and exactly as I like it. The less you have the less trouble.

1 June, 1917

I have been very slack of late in writing but busier than ever in other ways. It is not possible for me to tell you anything definite but much has happened with us and is happening daily. My work takes me a great deal in the front line, at all hours, into observation posts, for there is much to be found out or verified. All the old and complicated sensations of being shelled maliciously are with us again and, last night, for an hour and a half, I would not have given anyone even money on my continued existence. And so it goes from day to day. Today the motor lorry I was in, with five other officers and about twenty-five men, ran through a shell barrage on a road and one man was wounded. Shells bursting all about. What tomorrow will bring forth remains to be seen. I find I mind it all less than ever, and when the dirt and bits of shattered wood fall on you from a shell burst close by, it merely seems to me a most intensely interesting phenomenon. My chief distress in life is to find my tin hat, which I leave everywhere and have to go back and find.

The Hun is using much more gas shells than before and we have to wear our gas helmets on our chests, always at the 'alert' position. This is a fearful grievance with me and I intend that it shall be repaid them with interest. It is a most undignified thing to wear on your chest. Like the thing that Japanese girls in pictures wear on their backs.

Also of interest, I have been promoted lieutenant in the Gazette *of about a week ago. I did not see it but others did and told me, so I am wearing two pips now instead of one. This does not affect my present Punch and Judy show at all, but it puts me in line for a captaincy this summer if I have luck and other poor chaps don't.*

What we are about to do in near future is going to be a toss-up either way, so it is no use even thinking about it. A man's life here is worth about as much as the proverbial grain of mustard seed and the whole place is full of the very finest of mankind. All cheerful and funny and whimsical and interesting. The sights to be seen are intensely thrilling and never ending. Weather is delightful and we live practically in the open. Got to bed at 4am today, delighted to be alive and wanting sleep, so am turning in early today.

Letter written before the Battle of Messines

BEF, 6 June 1917
(This letter is for all the brothers and sisters, of course.)
When you get this I shall have been through the mill and either all right, in hospital or blotted out, so don't worry. As soon as I can I will write to let you know the news; if I can't someone else will.

We hope to make a page of history and go into it with light hearts and great confidence.

This place is Bedlam, the lions about to be fed, the parrot house at the zoo and a few other noisy places combined. I went through gas last night, near dawn, and had no respirator (forgot it). Held my breath till I nearly burst and blew up, and made record time. Beyond a harmless whiff picked up when I exploded for air, which has made smoking less of a pleasure, no harm was done.

Goodbye. I have had a long run out here and must not complain and I have thoroughly enjoyed it and would repeat it, every bit, if it were necessary.

Chapter 5

Battle of Messines, 5–7 June 1917

At the end of May, B Battalion moved up through Hazebrouck and Bailleul and detrained at night at Steenwerk in Belgium; which town was railhead for the front line area comprising Wytschaete Ridge, Messines and Plug Street Wood.

On de-training at night, the fifty-odd tanks of B Battalion moved in single file to Giles Camp, a dense wood about a mile north-west of the village of Neuve Eglise and close to the Crucifix crossroads on the main road between Neuve Eglise and Bailleul. The single track made by the tanks was obliterated by a squadron of cavalry following at once, these being followed by several agricultural harrows drawn by artillery horses. Such precautions were always taken, as the wood was within easy reach of enemy shellfire. Within the wood, the tanks, under their camouflage nets, were quite invisible and the enemy never suspected their presence.

For the next ten days or so, tank engines were tuned up, repairs were made, officers reconnoitred no man's land and every foot of ground up to our own front lines, and preparations were made to lay tapes on the last night over the shelled trench area to our front lines, so as to guide tanks in the dark before Zero (dawn) to their actual starting points.

As it happened I had spent five months in these very trenches in 1915 and, as they were little altered, I knew them perfectly, so my colonel detailed me to guide my section of tanks into action and dispensed with the need of tapes for my section.

On Y night, June 5th, we moved the tanks through Neuve Eglise towards the front lines and our actual starting points, and hid them in a long narrow lane lined with tall shade trees. This lane was high up on a hill overlooking the valley of the Douve River, where our front trenches lay. Good camouflage saved us again all the following day, for we experienced only normal shelling.

At 9pm on Zero night (June 6th) we moved to our starting points, which were about 400 yards behind our front trenches and between La Plus Douve Farm and Stinking Farm along the banks of the Douve River. Six wooden bridges had been made for us by the REs across the small river, all well camouflaged.

On leaving the high ground and entering the valley of the Douve we entered a heavily gassed area. Both tear gas and mustard gas. From 11pm we wore gas masks and, as I did not get my tank finally parked until 2.30am, it was a trying time. The gas delayed us one or two hours for, with masks on, it was almost impossible for tank officers to guide their tanks in the dark and I happened to be one of the last of fifteen tanks in single file. At times we had to stop and choke and wheeze for long spells when gas shells fell very near. All night long our guns were nearly silent, to deceive the enemy. Scattering shots were fired every now and then. Otherwise, our batteries were fairly massed in rows, in silence.

An interesting feature of the Battle of Messines, fought by General Plumer[1] commanding the Second Army, was the number of deep mines under Wytschaete Ridge and Messines Ridge. These were 19 in number, 90 feet deep, from 500 yards behind our front lines to as far as 800 yards behind the German front lines. It had taken a year and a half to dig them and they contained a prodigious amount of explosive and, being so deep, the enemy never suspected them.

Zero was to be at 3.10am, the first peep of dawn. As my section was not going over until noon we had a fine opportunity to watch. About two minutes before Zero, all along our front, machine guns began to play and everyone stood looking at his watch and waiting for the nineteen mines to go up. Still a comparative silence and, suddenly, sheets of flame high up in the sky and an appalling roar. To me it sounded like seven explosions all in a few seconds. The ground rocked and a hedge near us nearly flattened in the blast. At the same moment every gun in our massed batteries opened up and the battle was on. At once the enemy front was a beautiful display of white and red and green rockets and star shells, despairing SOS signals to their batteries and reserves.

The New Zealanders attacked at Zero. They crossed no man's land (the rocket display diminished as the bayonets got to work) and captured the Ridge and Messines. It was not long, though, before the enemy began to shell us heavily and my section was ordered into a trench for cover. One of my crew of seven men was wounded badly in the hand. We cooked breakfast in comfort as all the gas shelling stopped at once when our attack began.

Our orders were to join the Australians at 3.40pm at the Blue Line, about a mile and a half behind Messines and the ridge, and to precede and show them over to the Green Line, the farthest objective, about a mile in advance. At the Green Line the Australians would dig in and consolidate and, when they were finished, the tanks were to return home.

At 12 noon, Major Tucker[2] of my company gave my section orders to start. We had to go two and a half miles to the Blue Line where the Australians were waiting for us, for our attack had gone like clockwork all the morning.

My Section Commander, Captain Dudgeon, was not a military man but dead game. It was an order that section commanders must precede their section of four tanks on foot until our own front trenches were crossed, and Captain Dudgeon duly did so. But, to my astonishment, he continued ahead of us on foot across no man's land, which was being heavily shelled. Being in the leading tank just behind him I called out to him and told him we needed no more help, and Captain Dudgeon made me a most polite bow in no man's land among the shells before he stood to one side to allow us to pass. Something I never shall forget.

My section was ordered to skirt Messines to the south and to go across the main highway, called Hun's Walk, to Oxygen Trench, a German stronghold. At Hun's Walk we were to meet our Australian Infantry and, at 3.40pm, the barrage would lift and we would at once, together, attack Oxygen Trench, capture it and go on a few hundred yards. This, being the final objective, would be the digging-in place, the Green Line.

Having crossed no man's land and successfully negotiated the Douve River[3] running through it, I tried to travel over the German trenches just to the south of Messines, but our morning bombardment had made such a mess of them that I saw it was impossible, although the weather was fine and dry, so I made a long detour to the south and farther down the slope of the hill, being heavily shelled all the way. After rounding the hill, the going was better and we crossed trenches full of waiting Australians. Nearing Hun's Walk, on open shell-pocked ground, I noticed right ahead of us a wounded Australian in a deep shell hole. He saw my tank coming straight for him and he did his best to crawl out of the way, not knowing I had seen him. His struggles were piteous. Near us and behind was a trench full of Australians and before I reached the shell hole I stopped and opened the rear door and called out to them that one of their men was in the shell hole just in front of the tank. Two of them instantly jumped out and came and brought this poor chap away. As they passed the tank the wounded man gave it a beaming smile. We then went straight on and ground the wounded man's equipment into the earth. Nearing Hun's Walk I looked at my watch and found I was forty minutes too early. This was serious

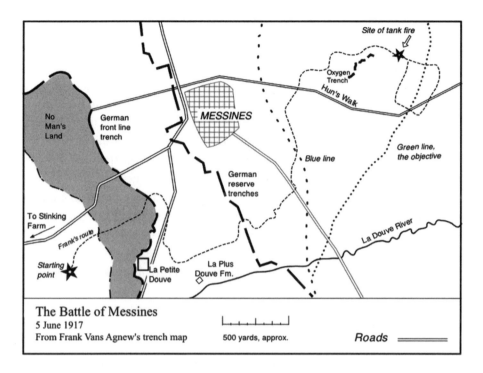

No Man's Land

German front line trench

MESSINES

Site of tank fire

Oxygen Trench

Hun's Walk

Blue line

Green line, the objective

German reserve trenches

To Stinking Farm

La Douve River

Frank's route

Starting point

La Petite Douve

La Plus Douve Fm.

The Battle of Messines
5 June 1917
From Frank Vans Agnew's trench map

500 yards, approx.

Roads ═══════

because Hun's Walk was on the skyline and the German observation balloons were still up. Luckily, I noticed a big tree on the edge of Hun's Walk which had been hit by a shell half way up, and the whole, great, shady top was bent down to the ground, so I snuggled the tank completely under the branches of this great elm tree and we rested there in great comfort and security. So secure were we that, as it was terribly hot in the tank owing to the engine and a blazing sunshine, I got out in the cool and looked over my maps and talked with several Australian officers, who came up to say how extremely pleased they were to see that the tanks were in time.

At 3.40pm our barrage, a solid curtain of smoke and shell bursts about 100 yards ahead of us, lifted and I moved out at once with the infantry. A creeping barrage then preceded us to Oxygen Trench, going very slowly, so slowly that I had to stop the tank several times or run into our own shells. The Australians walked along on each side of the tank, getting very few casualties and snap shooting at any Germans seen in the smoke ahead, just as if they were rabbit shooting.

Oxygen Trench was full of demoralized Germans (Bavarians) when we reached it. They showed small fight and either dived into dugouts or bolted back farther leaving their equipment.

The Green Line was gained and the Australians proceeded to dig in and to consolidate. Meanwhile we patrolled in front of them for a full hour to check any desire of the enemy to counter-attack the position. While doing this, I noticed two pyramidal-shaped, camouflaged structures in a wood ahead of us, and turned our 6-pounder Hotchkiss guns into them. Both structures burst into explosions. No doubt, it was a German battery position and this was their ammunition supply. Enemy shelling at this time was not serious, probably because their batteries were on the move. Being informed by Australian officers that they were well dug-in, our work was over and I started back for the long trip home – about three and a half miles of heavily shelled ground and many awkward trenches – with the advantage, however, of having our old tank-tracks as a safe guide over bad ground.

After going homewards to a point on open ground about 400 yards from the new German front lines my tank caught on fire. A camouflage net on the roof, ignited by the hot exhaust pipe, was sending showers of sparks through the cracks of the manhole in the roof and there was great danger from petrol and petrol fumes inside the overheated tank.

I ordered the crew out and we left the tank on the side which offered most protection from the enemy front lines, where machine-gun and rifle fire were very busy. Very soon, to my astonishment, and without orders, my Corporal, Tait[4], ran up the rear track of the tank on to the roof and there he was, working his Pyrene in the fullest view of the enemy. Each tank carries six Pyroxene tubes and every crew is trained in fire drill.

I ordered him down as his sacrifice up there was not necessary, in my opinion, to save the tank; he pretended not to hear me so, determined not to be outdone by my own corporal, I ran round to the exposed side of the tank and used my Pyrene there until it was exhausted. Bad Bavarian shooting was all that saved Corporal Tait and me. He was untouched and I only got a bullet in the muscles of the right forearm and a graze in the side, but other bullets missing me and striking the hard steel of the tank blew back in a fine spray of lead and casings.

Later, when at the seaside on a holiday near Paris Plage, after bathing, my friend Captain Birnie[5] picked out every day small particles just under the skin on both sides of my back.

We finally put the fire out and re-entered the tank, one of the crew having been wounded about the eye in the meantime. The extra heating of the fire had added to an already overworked and overheated engine and we could barely crawl at one mile an hour. At 8.30pm we finally limped into our original starting place, still on our own power but being also towed by another tank of my section, Lieutenant Blackwell's[6], which was nearly in as bad condition as we were.

Tragedy and amusement were mixed together in an incident on our homeward journey. I noticed a tank of my section had stopped and seemed to be in trouble so I went out of our direct way to find out the reason. I found Lieutenant Ley[7] of my section outside the tank and his sergeant stretched out on the ground. The sergeant had been badly wounded inside the tank when in heavy action and I am sorry to say he died a few days later. Ley said it was so hot in the tank that he had brought the sergeant out for air but, as the enemy shelling was not to be despised, I advised putting the sergeant back at once and getting him home as soon as possible to a doctor. This we did.

I asked Ley if he had any pigeons left and he said he had one still in the tank (out of the two every tank carries into action) which really he should have released on reaching his final objective. Ley could not find his pigeon message paper, very thin tissue paper to fold up and put inside the small aluminium cylinder which clips onto the bird's leg, so he used ordinary paper. This made a clumsy bundle but he tied it on laboriously and released the pigeon. The bird flew off with difficulty and, when in the air about 100 feet up, it proceeded to kick violently at the bundle and very soon kicked it off, flying home hilariously.

B Battalion suffered fairly severely in the Battle of Messines, but it was our first trial with tanks in actual battle. The gassing of the night just previous to Zero had been very demoralizing and many tank officers and men went into action half choked and half blinded. The day after the battle several officers and men of B Battalion were temporarily completely blinded, their eyelids inflamed by mustard gas and irritated by tear gas having swelled so much that their eyes were tightly shut and they had to be led away to ambulances. If gas enters a tank you can imagine how it would hang there tenaciously. This, added to the normal heat and fumes and noise, must be endured to be imagined.

This battle was memorable to me for two new features showing the thoroughness and thoughtfulness of General Plumer.

(1) Roads were made at intervals along the entire front of twenty miles right up to our front-line trench. These roads were covered with heavy planking about ten feet in length and laid crossways. The work was done

at night and duly covered with earth and grass before dawn. Trenches were strongly bridged and the work of the REs was thorough.

Less than an hour after Zero batteries of artillery were galloping up the road, deploying at our front lines and instantly going into action. These were closely followed by cavalry equally in a great hurry.

Unfortunately, on our fighting front it was the Australian Light Horse who gallantly galloped into almost certain death by shrapnel. There is a shallow trough between Wytschaete Ridge and Messines Ridge which was fairly paved with Australian Light Horse casualties and I doubt if any of them actually got into action. Being a clear, bright day, enemy observation balloons could spot them easily.

(2) At intervals along the entire front special new communication-trenches were dug for the evacuation of wounded only. Every corner, usually right-angled, was rounded for the easier handling of stretchers, and numerous shelves were made on which to rest them. These trenches saved much life. After being dug they were camouflaged, and the enemy shelled only the old communication trenches which he had on his maps.

It is generally conceded that the Battle of Messines was the model 'show' of the whole war from the point of view of the British Army in France and Flanders.

To Mrs P.A.V.A. (after the Battle of Messines, near Neuve Eglise)

In Belgium, June 10, 1917

Your letter found me in hospital and was most delightful company. My trouble is not much – just a bullet through the fleshy part of right forearm and a graze in the side and I am up and about and going back to my lot in a day or two. We were an active part in the great drama of the 7th and what with the bursting mine-earthquakes and the tempestuous bombardment one was lucky to be left with one's senses. I was personally very successful, reaching all my objectives and getting slap into the blue-grey devils, Bavarians, and blazing away like a dreadnaught. Oh the sights that were seen! Luck, good and bad, was with me, for my bus caught on fire in action just where the thing was thickest.

After that we carried on and as I had finished my job to the last letter we came on home and I brought the old thing back safely.

When home I had the arm dressed at the most advanced place and the bits of bullet casing in there pulled out and, as it seemed so trifling, I put on my coat and carried on as before. The next morning my brigadier came to my sleeping palace (tent), in person and indignantly asked me if it was true I was going about with a bullet in my arm and I indignantly denied it, but he Ordered me (with a capital O) to hospital to be inoculated for anti-tetanine [sic], patted my back, shook my sore arm, and said we had done the best show of our lot the whole day. This display of indiscreet joy made me at once put in the names of my corporal and another of my crew for 'immediate awards for merit', and he agreed cheerfully, so I feel sure they will be decorated with something or other.

Our game sounds so comfortable and protected but that is a myth. The Boche is afraid of us and he concentrates salvos of large crumps on us whenever he observes us. It is a mystery how any of us ever get there or get back. You feel very important because you are heralded, followed and encircled by miniature geysers of earth, smoke and biff-bangs, and your own infantry flees from you as if you bore the plague. A good many of our lot got into serious trouble and quite a few faces of chums are missing today. The day for the British Army was a veritable howling success and the Boche fought here with no spirit at all. They bolted like rabbits, throwing away rifles and equipment, some back to Berlin and some to us, hands up, and kamerading. Our casualties were very light indeed, owing to the absolutely artistic work of our artillery. There is no artillery quite as good as ours today, not even the French, and with our airmen the combination is unbeatable. These wonderful airmen! Like meteors in the sky they swoop and fly, entirely regardless of everything but the job on hand. And the observers miss nothing. When the day (der Tag) arrives, the Boche batteries are turned upside down, miles behind their lines, their trenches drowned in shell and all their wire cut and well removed or buried. Talk about 'frightfulness'. The Boche is now learning the fine points of it from us. Our men fight so cheerfully and whimsically and sarcastically. There is no vestige of hate towards the Boche, only an abiding disgust and hearty contempt. A feeling as towards a mangy, yelping mongrel, who has finally gone and got hydrophobia and must be killed to save valuable human life.

We are really most jubilant over the past three days work and everyone is smiling and happy and cracking jokes. Gramophones are whirling at top speed, bands are playing in the camps, pipes are skirling and moaning and quickening the pulse, and the dirty Hun is licking his wounds in silence over there to the East. In silence and afraid.

To Ida (near Neuve Eglise)

In Belgium, June 16, 1917

I am absolutely all right and my arm is nothing to bother about. Things heal up on me in a wonderful way always.

We are resting just behind and getting ready for more trouble wherever it is hottest. That is our programme. Not in all the time, but pushed into the warmest and most critical spots. We have been getting out our derelicts and wrecks and picking up the pieces and burying our dead and visiting our wounded and making good deficiencies of kit and equipment. Quite a few of our lot got into serious trouble and received rough treatment. My bus is well marked and shows all the signs of having been in a metallic cyclone.

In The Times *of the 14th, page 5, column 3, you will find an account by an Australian war correspondent of my doings. I was the unfortunate who caught on fire and blazed so merrily for twenty-five minutes. He timed it. I didn't. I hadn't time. Would you mind getting a number of these papers and cutting out the account and sending it to the brothers and sisters and friends. You know who I mean.*

I am told by real friends that I shall get some decoration or other for my share in that wild flare-up of a day, and my corporal's name has gone in for a DCM. If it pleases you and everybody else, I am delighted but I cannot get very excited myself. Out here you see so many things done, unrecorded and unrewarded, that are magnificent, and it seems presumption to be singled out when the others are not. It makes me sad instead of glad.

I see no chance of any home leave for weeks or months yet, although leave has opened and officers and men are going, but everyone is so far behind that my chance is slim for a long time. Therefore, I have put in for six days special leave to Paris Plage, I and my friend, Birnie. It will be a grand change in every way, and I am looking forward to it.

Chapter 6

Interval

After the Battle of Messines, B Battalion returned to Giles Camp and hid its tanks, as before, in the thick cover of the wood near Neuve Eglise. This interval was memorable for the visit of the King and the Prince of Wales, and B Battalion was honoured by being the only Tank Battalion to be inspected. My tank, a male or 6-pounder Hotchkiss-gun tank, carrying two big guns and four Lewis machine guns, and the tank commanded by Lieutenant Doyle[1], a female, carrying six Lewis machine guns, were selected by Lieutenant Colonel Hill[2] to perform before the King.

It was so arranged, most dramatically, that we should completely hide our tanks on the edge of the wood where it opened onto a fine grass field, in which trenches had been dug, wire put up and dugouts constructed. On a given silent signal, Doyle and I were to burst out of the wood and knock down, each of us, a large and very tall poplar tree placed there by Providence and throw the leafy tops into the open grass field. Then without stopping we were to make a half-circular turn and come rushing down the field, side by side, towards the King and the Prince of Wales and General Plumer and his Staff, through the heavy wire and over the trenches and dugouts which were opposite the King. We were to play fair and keep side by side, which was none too easy to do, and to make an effect of an irresistible massed attack, so to speak stirrup to stirrup.

We were to pass through much wire and then over a deep and wide trench with dugouts on each side of us, allowing us about a foot to spare to right and left. Doyle and I studied the problem the evening before and, unobtrusively, we placed a small peg for the centre of each tank.

As it happened, Doyle and I and our faithful crews made no mistakes, and our trees fell into the field with loud crackings and crashes and we grumbled and rumbled over the obstacles and then kept on, irresistibly, until we circled back into the wood again in the distance, disappearing magically.

Personally, I was too busy to see much of the Royalty, especially as a tank is not built to allow you to see much except the business strictly in hand.

Other tanks of other companies performed perfectly and B Battalion nearly blew up with pride.

Letters to Ida (near Neuve Eglise)

In Belgium, 12 July 1917
War news is reassuring and slow but sure. The Russian push is all to the good. If they keep it up, added to our small endeavors, the Boche will be in a bad way by winter. American troops may be in time and again, they may be too late to cut the Porcine throat. How the All Highest War Pig will squeal for generations to come, and root around lovingly and lonely, in his own domestic offal. It is indeed a cheerful prospect and more power to it.

(Merlimont, near Paris Plage)

In France, Monday 16 July 1917
I am down at the seaside for a week and as happy as can be. No duties, no men, only my friend Birnie and myself. We have a whole house of about twenty rooms to ourselves, 100 yards from the sea, and we get meals where we please. Our batmen look after the house and [we] sleep and roast in the red-hot sand of the dunes. On each side of us, about three miles away, are gay French watering places, and it is merely a pleasant hour's walk to either place, along the sea. Saturday and Sunday were French flag-days, Red Cross, and holidays. All the young French butterfly girls, in their most prismatic raiment were out and they take no refusals.

Birnie's kilt and his Highland carriage, neck well arched and head high, nearly cost me a fortune. They flocked to him like hens to a peacock and almost worshipped him. Hang Birnie and his kilt.

We bathe early, middle and late and it is a wonderful and complete change. There is no room for future in this marvellous present. We shall go straight from this to the hottest part of the whole front. It seems incredible. I have no other news. I am only ten years old down here.

(Bailleul)

In France, 18 July 1917
Today's papers give us the first chance to mention the King's trip out here. Until it appeared in the papers we were debarred from thinking of it. You

will be pleased to hear that I and other officers of my company were picked to perform before the King and, in the accounts I enclose, I was the 'second monster' to appear from the wood and to negotiate the wire, trench and dugout, etc. We performed with no rehearsal and no hitch occurred. The thing went perfectly and the King was actually animated in his evident excitement and pleasure, and he saw the humour of it, no doubt. Our battalion was the only one of our branch of warfare to perform in this way, and I must say we did the affair in proper and dashing style. A cinema man was busy all the time and, if you see the pictures over the wire, trench and dugout, my beast is the nearest one of the two beasts to the King, and is the one with the big guns. The other beast only is armed with machine guns. My colonel is, of course, very pleased.

(near Neuve Eglise)

In Belgium, July 21, 1917
On my return here to my own lot I was being congratulated and handshaken on all sides and, to my surprise, found out that four days ago I was awarded, officially, the Military Cross. I am more than pleased that the award is popular with my own lot, because often there is so much bad feeling about such things and it is a kind of a good confirmation besides. So I shall wear my ribbon and not feel ashamed of it, as some unfortunates are.

P.S. I hope to add a Bar to that MC before two weeks is up or know the reason why.

Letter from Theodore Roosevelt to J. Pennington Gardiner

432, Fourth Avenue, New York. 28 November 1917
My dear Gardiner:

That's simply fine! I am more pleased than I can say. Really, Agnew's record is something extraordinary. When you write him will you send him my heartiest congratulations and good wishes?

Faithfully yours, Theodore Roosevelt

(Ouderdom)

In Belgium, July 26, 1917

Will you please do a wee thing for me? My Corporal [Tait] won a Bar to his Military Medal and a Bar is indicated by a small silver rosette on his medal ribbon. This cannot cost more than a shilling or two, and he needs two of them, one for each tunic. They are, officially, so slow about it that I want you, please, to get them from the Army and Navy Stores and send them to me in a letter. He is quite keen, of course, on wearing the Bar and it is a shame to keep him waiting so long.

All is well and there is savage fighting out here all the time. Chiefly colossal artillery duels, day and night raids and air fighting. The tone of it all is savage and remorseless to a degree. A man feels very small amidst it all, a mere feather in a tornado, and very helpless and insignificant.

It is no use crying over spilt milk but the Russians are betraying us shamefully. Reining themselves and trying, unconsciously, to ruin us. The worst is that it heartens and uplifts these disgusting Boche people. The American Army will find plenty of work to do next year.

Chapter 7

The Third Battle of Ypres, 31 July 1917

T he opening, or Zero, day of this battle was 31 July and it lasted, roughly speaking, till November 1917, with the capture and consolidation of Passchendaele Ridge east of Ypres. It was a battle which cost the British Army terrific casualties for we were the attacking force, but the enemy also suffered enormously in losses of men and, still more important, in loss of morale.

The start on the opening day was a bad one for us and only the first line of objectives, instead of three lines, was taken. A few days later it was officially announced that a sergeant of ours, Sergeant Phillips, who had been captured by the enemy, or who had deserted, about a week previous to the opening day, had divulged the day of attack and much other valuable information to the enemy[1]. This meant that the German was absolutely ready and expectant.

B Battalion was on the extreme right flank of the battle front and, added to the frontal fire of artillery, came in for heavy enfilading from our right.

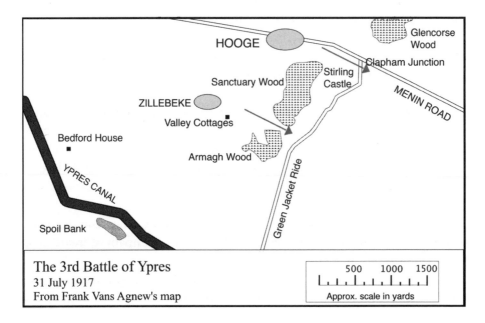

The 3rd Battle of Ypres
31 July 1917
From Frank Vans Agnew's map

Approx. scale in yards

Owing to the configuration of the ground, we had only two ways of getting to the enemy, (1) through the Hooge Gap, and (2) between Sanctuary Wood and Armagh Wood. The Hooge Gap was wider but the gap between the two woods was only about 150 yards across and this was so wet and low that it was nearly impossible to move a tank through, apart from any shelling that might be going on.

The enemy, of course, was acquainted with these two gaps and, consequently, directed all that day an appalling barrage of heavy artillery on them. A tank had to go through the gap and its barrage to get into action and, after being in action, with so many chances of being knocked out by shellfire, it had to come through the same gap and the same barrage to return home. It is not surprising that B Battalion was butchered that day. Out of the ten tanks that went into action only two returned, in a damaged condition.

To crawl through a heavy-gun barrage at a speed of less than a mile an hour is not a cheerful prospect, and it was impossible to travel faster on account of the deep mud and shell-holes which overlapped each other and were all full of water. Add to this the never ceasing downpour of new shells and their tragic results, and those not present could imagine about ten per cent of the effect.

B Battalion left Giles Camp and entrained at night for Ouderdom farther north towards Ypres. At Ouderdom there had been made a vast 'Tankodrome', and here we detrained and tucked the tanks away into great canvas and wooden single-stalls like those in stables. A high board fence enclosed the sacred area. Later we moved up by night nearer to the front, to a field near Voormezele and parked the tanks along the hedges round about. This required careful camouflage work with the nets to avoid being seen by enemy aircraft. Here we met with much annoying enemy gas at night when working and a due share of shelling. Our actual starting points for the battle were in comfortable reach of a few hours travel by night, and we had to cross the Ypres Canal, pass by Spoil Bank and onwards on a corduroy plank road to Valley Cottages, which was a ruin, amidst fields and hedges and close to Observatory Ridge, with Hill 60 to the extreme right. Valley Cottages was the actual starting point.

Orders were that No.6 Company was to go to Valley Cottages on the night of July 28–29, while my Company, (No.5) and No.4 Company, were to go to the same place on the night of July 29–30.

No.6 Company duly obeyed orders by starting off but they ran into terrific enemy shelling near Spoil Bank coupled with heavy doses of gas. The result was that a number of tanks were knocked out and the rest were so scattered and gas-demoralized that the company was practically out of action for the battle. Major Bryce[2], in command, did wonderful work personally all that night and saved what he could.

This was not cheerful news for us but the next night, we started off, quaking, to try our luck.

The two companies meant about twenty-five fighting tanks, a long, unwieldy line in single file, including my tank, which was named 'Bandit'[3].

The trouble would begin when we reached the Ypres Canal, and from there, past Spoil Bank, all along that corduroy road to Valley Cottages, we might expect the worst. Just before we reached the canal, I noticed that my engine was running hot and, upon close investigation, I found that, underneath the belly of the tank, a small petcock had been broken off by striking some obstacle in the dark and all the water in my radiator was running away. The nearest water was not far ahead in the canal, and as I did not want to use the reserve water in my tins, we travelled there safely, and proceeded to fill the radiator with water from big shell holes. The canal was a canal no more. Two years of shelling had so dammed it up that it was a morass of reeds and bull-rushes studded with shell holes. My stoppage blocked the line badly and soon came my angry colonel and major. My plight they decreed to be unavoidable and they diverted the held up line to another crossing near-by, exhorting me to hurry. Luckily my small bamboo stick just fitted the broken pipe snugly and we cut a plug from it and stopped the leak. We then hurriedly filled the radiator because it was a most unhealthy spot to loiter around. This crossing of the canal was close to Bedford House, where my cousin Captain 'Dickie' Bowlby[4] of the Scots Greys, is buried. After re-filling we hurried on and caught up the procession on the corduroy road opposite Spoil Bank. This road was made on account of the liquid mud comprising the whole country around, and it was also used by artillery limbers to and fro. When these last met a column of about twenty-five enormous tanks, they had to give us the road and you may imagine their language.

From here to Valley Cottages, enemy shells did their best to destroy that road and everything on it and our speed did not equal one mile an hour. It was an unholy shelling. An officer walked ahead of each tank to guide it, with one man of his crew with him in case of a casualty and a fall in the dark unseen, in which case the tank would unwittingly squash the casualty flat. Corporal Tait and I were together ahead of our tank wondering if we would get through when we heard a shell fall directly on the road about two tanks ahead, and at the same time heard Lieutenant Williamson[5], of my section, call out. We rushed there and found him and his corporal down. As we were going into action, we could not stop the tanks on that heavily shelled bit of road, so we carried the two back and put them inside my tank. It was not possible in the pitch dark, any light being sudden death, to assist them much but, still on the move, we did what we could. A little later, on that same unhealthy roadway, Corporal Tait and I being still together ahead of our tank, a German inflammatory shell fell and burst close to us and flaming stuff fell on us both. We mutually and automatically slapped each other about until we were quite sure that our clothes were not alight, both abusing the Hun volubly. That was the first and last time I was ever in reach of one of those flaming shells, although I had seen them before and saw several that night. Shortly after midnight we arrived at Valley Cottages and thankfully parked our tanks along the hedgerows and immediately got Lieutenant Williamson and his corporal down into a gunner officer's dugout under one of the ruins.

If Williamson had one wound he had forty, in both arms and both legs. No bones were broken and they were not deep, but he was fairly flayed and full of splinters from the corduroy road. We slopped iodine all over him, regardless of his undying hatred, and sent him back at dawn on a stretcher. He finally recovered after many months at home. The corporal had one bad wound in his back which had pierced the lung and we heard later that he died in hospital.

The tanks were then turned over to the guard of reserve crews and we, the fighting crews, hurried back to our mess and camp at Voormezele to rest, eat, drink and sleep, preparatory to our troubles to come on the following night.

After the night of July 30–31 we returned to our tanks at Valley Cottages through incessant enemy shelling. Everyone agreed that it was the most spiteful and irritated front they had ever seen.

I found on arrival that my tank had lost most of the water in its radiator and the weary job began of finding water and then re-filling. In the intense dark with shells falling all over the place it was trying work. All tanks had to re-fill with petrol (gasoline) also, and the petrol-dump was not a normal one. The petrol tins (of two gallon capacity) were scattered in threes and fours in shell holes all over an area of about ten acres to minimize enemy shelling as much as possible. This meant much more floundering around in the dark, and dodging of shells, imaginary or otherwise.

It was 2.30am before my tank was completely refilled and ready for action. I collected my crew in the tank, and Captain Dudgeon, my Section

Commander, and I stayed with the men, all trying to sleep; but so many enemy shells were falling about and many of them so very near, that at any moment we expected the finish.

My section's orders were to attack with the second wave of tanks one hour after Zero, viz. 4.40am. We were to go along Observatory Ridge, down through the gap between Sanctuary and Armagh Woods, across the German front line trenches, then along Green Jacket Ride past Stirling Castle and across the Menin Road close to Clapham Junction; and farther, if possible, to Poldhoek. But no one reached the Menin Road; the infantry being held up close to Stirling Castle on our sector of the front. All the night our guns had fired only in a normal manner and they did not answer the very heavy enemy shelling. They were vainly trying to deceive the enemy who, as I have said earlier in this account, knew all our plans for attack at dawn. Just before Zero we all, foolishly, got outside of our tanks and when, on the second of Zero, all our guns burst into a great chorus of sound, we saw the same beautiful display of red and green and yellow rockets shoot up from the enemy lines.

We watched the first wave of tanks lumber forth to battle and all of us were delighted, thinking we had a surprised and demoralized enemy to deal with. Soon we were to be woefully undeceived, for the enemy shelling increased perceptibly and shells were crashing all among us. One burst alongside the tank next to mine on my left, literally taking Lieutenant Ley's head from his shoulders, killing one of his crew and wounding several others, amongst whom was my corporal with a splinter in his cheek. As soon as I could, I collected all of my crew and ordered them to get inside my tank and stay there, assuring them that a direct hit would finish them no matter where they were, but that the tank would preserve them from flying fragments. And not one of them suffered any more damage.

I then noticed a shell burst, it seemed to me, directly on another tank of my section to my immediate right, but, almost at once appeared Lieutenant Brockwell[6], its commander. He came to me and said, imperturbably, 'Did you see that shell – fell between the horns of my tank?' I asked him if there was any damage done. He said 'No, the men are all inside and all right but my pigeons are killed.' I asked him how that came about, and he explained that it was so hot in the tank that he had taken the two pigeons out, in their basket (we all carried two into action), and carefully placed them between the horns of his tank for air and for their health; and there they were killed. I asked him what he had done with them and, with a grin and with one movement, he produced a dead pigeon in each hand from the pockets of his trenchcoat. I inquired what he was going to do with them and he answered 'Eat them tonight when we get back.' And he was lucky enough to do so – with my help.

While all of this was going on and soon after the attack had started, Major Bryce[7], of No.6 Company, arrived with one of his sergeants to see No.5 Company start into action, and stood by my tank most of the time with me. Not being on duty he really had no business to be there at all, but you could not keep Major Bryce out of trouble if there was any of it about. He told me he had brought two men along as runners but he had left them in a dugout about twenty yards ahead of us. Shortly though, a No.6 Company man came running to the major to tell him that both of his runners had had the left foot blown off at the ankle as they were sitting at the entrance of the dugout.

With a despairing utterance of 'I gave them orders to stay inside', the major hurried away. The next horror to appear very soon was my Section Commander, Captain Dudgeon, who had been looking after his section interests; he was hanging onto his right arm and the blood was flying two feet or more from an artery around his thumb. A bit of shell had gone sideways through the back of his hand breaking every bone on its way. This meant a tourniquet of the tightest and I hastily fetched a 'Tommy bar' (small iron rod about the size of a pencil) from the tank and applied a tourniquet above the wrist till the bleeding stopped, but it was highly painful for Captain Dudgeon. Major Bryce and his sergeant had returned in time to help me in this and just after we had persuaded Captain Dudgeon to go into my tank a shell burst just behind us, and the sergeant, who was between Major Bryce and me, fell down calling for help. This was a very bad affair for pieces of shell had passed through both his thighs breaking the femur in each case. We did what we could for the poor chap, whose number was up, until the stretcher bearers came and then I would have given worlds for a wash but there was no water to spare or time either because time was flying towards 4.30am when my section would start into the actual action.

One of the tanks of my company farther along our hedge had been put out of action completely by a direct hit and a good many of the crews were casualties. On examining Corporal Tait's cheek, in the tank, it was much swelled and discoloured but he fairly begged to be allowed to go into action.

The time to start was very near and Major Tucker, of my company, (he had had three brothers killed in the war) ordered us to get ready. To my amazement, Captain Dudgeon staggered up and said he would show us over our front lines. On the roundabout way we had to go, via the gap between

Sanctuary and Armagh Woods, the front lines were half a mile away, and he could not have walked 200 yards as he had lost a lot of blood and the tourniquet, still on, had turned his hand and wrist quite black. Then Major Bryce chipped in and said: 'Nonsense, Dudgeon, you can't go. I'll take them over.' This from the major of another company who really had no business in the fighting that day at all. But I assured the two majors and Captain Dudgeon that I needed no help, because a section of tanks had gone through that gap an hour ago and all I had to do was to take our section over their tracks. All I wanted to do was to get away from that spot as quickly as possible – action seemed preferable to being a target. They finally agreed and the section, my own section from then on as it happened, tanks Bandit, Brigand, Buccaneer and Barbarian swung away from that loathely spot and rumbled off cheerfully towards Observatory Ridge and the gap.

Major Bryce very soon afterwards became Colonel of B Battalion, commanding the regiment to the end of the war and gaining the DSO and three Bars, all of which he thoroughly earned.

My good luck failed me while we were lurching down the slope of Observatory Ridge, Bandit leading a long line of tanks, for my engine failed through that radiator-leakage trouble. Inside it was like a steam engine with pipes almost bursting, and all we could do was to swing out of line and let the others go by. We tried to remedy the trouble but as the seat of it was really want of water it was hopeless to think of going into action. It would be very good fortune if we could bring the tank back because the Ridge was being incessantly shelled with heavy stuff and a stationary tank was a mark at once. So we hastily covered Bandit up with our camouflage net and, removing the Lewis guns, clock and compass, left the tank there, under charge of two of the crew in a near-by trench, to cool off, while we hurried back for more water and to report for further orders.

Major Tucker, on my report, agreed that it was useless to think of going on with Bandit into action that day, adjured me to get the tank back as soon as possible and, in the meantime, while the engine was cooling off, to take a basket of six pigeons, and two men to act as runners, and go up to the front lines and watch the progress of our tanks in action, sending back pigeon messages at once. This we proceeded to do and we returned minus the pigeons about noon, after witnessing the most intense shelling of the war, in our estimation, and the destruction of most of our tanks. Only two of them, out of ten that started from Valley Cottages, came back and sundry tank officers and fragments of crews dribbled back on foot with hair-raising experience to relate. Our Brigadier, Brigadier General Courage, to whom the pigeons flew, must have had an unhappy time on that morning.

In my absence pigeon-running, the remainder of my crew plus members of our Salvage Corps, patched up Bandit so that at 2.30pm, it very slowly and heatedly crawled back to Valley Cottages and we parked nearly in the same spot. I found that, in the dark the night before, we had unknowingly parked Bandit right on the top of four British graves along the hedge. The crosses were still there but knocked askew and no real harm was done.

We buried poor Ley and one of his crew and then, about 3.30pm, what was left of No.5 Company returned to the camp near Voormezele, feeling that the day had gone very badly for us and for our infantry, who had only captured the first line of objectives instead of the third. It was nearly six weeks later before we captured Poldhoek on the line of the third objectives.

The next morning, 1 August, as Section Commander of No.1 Section, I turned my tank 'Bandit', with my own crew, over to Lieutenant Dalby[8], and together we returned to Valley Cottages to bring back Bandit and Barbarian, the only tanks left in No.1 Section. Eventually, we salvaged Buccaneer, but Brigand remained a rusty, contorted, burned-out relic near Stirling Castle.

We found Bandit had suffered a direct hit from a shell during the night. The right 6-pounder gun was displaced and scored with great grooves, and a big hole had appeared in the plating of the right sponson. Inside it looked hopeless but, out of habit, we tried to turn the engine over and found it would and, as the tracks and secondary gearing seemed to be workable, we patched up some broken piping and wiring, and at about half a mile an hour we spent the whole well-shelled day in getting Bandit back along that corduroy road, past Spoil Bank and again across the canal to safety. In the end Bandit returned by rail to the main tank workshops at Erin, behind St. Pol, and was successfully re-arranged. About a week later I was sent in charge of a party to Tank Workshop Headquarters for new tanks and, four days later, returned with sixteen brand new, Mark IV, fighting, big tanks; all thoroughly equipped and ready for action.

Although we did our best and worked very hard and went through all the arduous preparation for action in a big fight, the weather was now against us and the incessant heavy rains made the ground impassable for a tank. We could take them where the ground was not raked and combed and spaded up by shellfire but, on the ground east and south-east of Ypres, shell-torn for three years, it was impossible.

Since July 31st, the enemy had been driven back several miles and the front on our sector was at Black Watch Corner and Glencorse Wood, well across the Menin Road, so we de-trained at a very hastily and flimsily constructed ramp just on the southern edge of Ypres itself. For ten days or more we tried to bridge over various marshes on our route to our front lines, and my letter dated October 15th explains our troubles. Once, we took the tanks close to Valley Cottages again, but heavier downpours of rain than ever made the job a farce, and we were brought away from there and entrained again and sent back to Wailly, near Arras, to prepare for the first Battle of Cambrai.

This account sounds uninteresting, simple and tame, but it was memorable for the extremes of discomfort, the incessant work most of which was black, wet night-work, in unspeakable conditions of mud.

To Miss F. (near Voormezele)

In Belgium, 8 August, 1917

We are still going strong and keep cheerful. I have been most lucky. On the 31st of July, in the last big fight, we were in the thick of it, all day and all the night before. They shelled us all that night with heavy stuff and caused us a number of casualties. At dawn of the following day the same direful uproar of guns all along our lines, the same red flares and SOS signals from the Boche, the same bursting shells all about us.

Out of five officers in my section three were casualties; two being wounded and the other, poor old Ley of Devonshire, had his head blown off. This all happened close to me, of course, and the place was a shambles. All in the half light of a misty dawn after a sleepless and busy night under heavy shell-fire. No joke, I can tell you. I was bandaging, iodining, and putting on tourniquets until it was time for us to start into action ourselves.

Breakfast on a thick, stodgy sandwich and water, with hands red with other people's blood and no water to wash in. That is what you might call a bad start, and I was glad to get away from it and go anywhere into anything.

Then I had bad luck with radiator trouble and a hot engine, and had to stop before really getting into the fight. I returned to Company Headquarters and the colonel sent me off with pigeons and two men for runners into the battle area to send back news. I was glad when this was over for, apart from shells in great numbers, there was a lot of machine-gun fire about.

Later in the day I returned to my old Pumpkin, hoping it had cooled off, and found a shell had directly hit the old dear. But it so happened that the engine could run and the necessary adjuncts and I had the pleasure of bringing the old warrior back to safety.

So you see I had a day of it. Then after that was all over there is always the walk back of about three miles, every one of which is shelled and shrapnelled, but which we consider to be nothing and perfect safety.

Until you pass the wide zone of our batteries you are liable to get a shell in the back of your neck at any time, more or less. They are firing themselves blue in the face and the Boche is trying to knock them out, and there they are at it hammer and tongs. But our lot all that day did excellently and most of the officers came back and most of the crews, but not all, worse luck. These casualties in my section have made me a captain so please kow-tow to me. Military Cross and a captaincy in two months from a Second Loot.

Whatever happens now I do feel that I have done something for the cause besides enlisting and carrying-on. Our command is more or less resting now, but some of us have an aftermath of work to do, which I have not quite done. Yesterday I was up there again all among the wild-eyed crumps for most of the day, doing a job which had to be done.

In about a week I expect home-leave for about ten days and I absolutely need the change. My nerve is just as good as ever, it is not that, but I am physically tired and stale. After leave I shall come back like a two-year-old and go at it again.

Letters to Ida (near Voormezele)

From Belgium, 28 August 1917

Back (from home leave) at the same old place and fairly in harness once more. I am acting second-in-command of the company now, owing to the real thing being on leave. This means more interesting work and much marching at the head of the men. Infantry drill is coming easier to me than I had expected after three years of cavalry drill and I am not making many bad breaks. By the time I get my own company, I shall know how to handle them, and all the niceties of the formal parade ground. We are very busy getting ready for another 'push'. And it looks to me as if it will not be long before we are slammed in again. Some of our lot 'went over' a few days ago in pouring, pelting rain and, of course, could not do much except catch the very devil, poor chaps. Brigadiers should study barometers in our business and not gaily trust to luck, and they would if they went over themselves. To send us over on a low and steadily falling 'glass' was not clever, even for some Staffs. All yesterday and last night it blew a full gale and poured with rain in buckets. The wind is still very high. Last night our mess tent, a big one, blew flat and many smaller tents, and the big guns (ours) sullenly growled and barked at the disgusting enemy all through. The state of the country is quite pathetic. Mud is king! Birnie and I lunched with Edward[9] and he did us very well and is fit and well himself and seemed very glad to have us. After the usual dismal return journey we arrived on the following day after leaving you. I found my canvas cot and bath affair in camp when I arrived, so that problem is solved.

I am enclosing your latchkey which, most surprisingly, I found in my pocket. It is amazing the surprises life stores up for one.

(near Neuve Eglise)

In France, 3 September, 1917
News just came in. We are going back to the line and going into action again. Leaving tomorrow, most probably. Given decent weather we shall do very well and make the Boche very unhappy. So there it is! The more we hammer the reptile, the sooner the war will end – in our favour. No time just now.

(near Ypres)

In Belgium, 7 September, 1917
Since I wrote last we have been travelling and changing camps and indulging in hideous and piteous discomforts, the weather being quite outrageous. Rain, and winds that bite and tear you and, of course, the ever present mud of Ages. Much of it is night work amid shell holes and wire and the debris of former fights, and a musty smell that even I can appreciate.

Just now, I and my friend, Captain Porter[10] are in a topping dugout and, when we are not sleeping, we are going in search of food somewhere, and the rain and wind are vanquished. These blessed times are to last two or three days, mayhap, and then the Deluge I expect. Farther than two days it is not possible, profitably, to speculate, but all I know is that if we go into Action (capital required this time) I shall win ten francs. We are in exactly that same loathely part of the front that we had just left, and its behaviour has not changed very much. All around, in the rain and woeful mud and raving winds, the guns are going off, day and night, and the Disgusting Ones are hurtling about all kinds of disgusting metal. Their aeroplanes were busy last night, so I was told, but caused our lot no harm. You, in London, must have had an exciting time in the daily raid and I am overjoyed they left you and the wee hoosie alone. I hope we bomb some few of them in their own foul abodes and then they will stop, amidst a terrific squealing.

Please send me two spare batteries for my Oriflux electric lamp. You know the kind you sent before. Also a complete new set of straps for my waterproof, canvas valise, the thing I always bring on leave. I put it against the smoke-stack on the boat going back from last leave and dried the straps to the consistency of wood.

Send me also some more of those long bootlaces for my big boots. The mess has used up all that fine supply you sent before and this is the big boot season commencing. Also please send two more of those canvas bags and sacks we got at the Army and Navy. My man packs my bestest ties and collars with my dirty boots, sort-of sandwiched between. This dugout is very dark and I can hardly see to write. I know I want something else but cannot remember. Yes! A pair of those gloves we got at Gorringe's in Buckingham Gate. Leather, with a band and snap, no buttons, and some woolly, white fur inside, and be sure that they are big enough.

This country is a dreadful sight, but everyone is very gay. Our last Push was a grand success in terms of dead Boches. The best, perhaps, we ever had. They started to attack just as we began our great attack, and our appalling barrage caught them in the open and their front lines and reserve trenches were packed with all the four tribes of Germany. All of this mess we gathered in, dead, smashed up, or very scared prisoners.

(**Note by FVA**: We tried to go into action through the Hooge gap on 9 September 1917, but the rains had made marshes of the shelled ground and, as most of us stuck fast, our attack was called off.)

(Wailly, near Arras)

In France, 10 September 1917
On the 5th, I got orders to take the advanced party of my battalion to the new place we have gone to, and prepare a camp for said battalion. The first day was spent in a lorry, with six more coming behind, and we arrived at the rough expanse of field to be our camp after dark and under a positively passionate rainfall. Thunder was crashing and lightning very busy. The least said about the discomforts of that night the better. A duck would have

quacked with joy all night. The following days and much of each night have been spent in riotous labour and it wound up in an all-night session last night when the [rest of the] battalion arrived.

Till after dawn, in a thick mist, I was doing the collie dog act in bringing in our fat monstrous sheep from their grumbling wanderings here and there and off the right direction. It was full light before I retrieved the last one but the whole of them are safe and sound. It seems to me a thankless job, this of advanced party, because, there is a major over you and a colonel and a brigadier, besides adjutants and other gilded beings! All of these dear people appear in motor cars, sleek and happy, and they come for the sole purpose of finding fault; some fault by them must be found or their existences are not fully justified, so all of them have their say and frequently, without knowing it, they contradict each other. If you take the matter seriously you would never have a camp ready because the time is short and your number of men to work with is limited. The great thing is to show no annoyance (which is futile at any time and anywhere) or anxiety but to put them each in a good temper. A cup of tea or a whisky and soda are the best answers to turn away wrath, I find. They leave and the job goes on much as before. When the battalion arrived it tucked itself away quite happily and then all was well. The beings with the halo and the existence which must be justified, at least verbally, believe in letting contented and sleeping dogs lie quite still.

At any rate we are now away from that fearsome place up north (Ypres) and this place is peaceful. No Boche 'planes buzzing over your tent at night and emitting soul-rending crashes around, no 'Whistling Percy' and his war whoops. Just Peace! Seven miles away there is a war on, they say, but we begin to doubt it.

In France, 19 September 1917

We have a new major who is determined that we shall have no rest and he keeps us bucketing at nothing all day. This can be done owing to the grand weather and the new broom is holding up his reputation. Parades all day of a ceremonial sort that fairly sicken me and make me wish the war would end at once. None of our own special work. We might be infantry of a mongrel breed. But I have had one trip into the big town (Arras) about four miles away, which has been almost in our front line for over two years. The Dirty Ones are nearly six miles from it now, gnashing their yellow teeth, and the fine old town is more or less rid of them. Every street is scarred and marked and some streets badly smashed up, but the town can be easily re-built after the war. Except the Cathedral, that is knocked down almost to its foundations. The Hôtel de Ville is gone. A few fragments show what a lovely old building it was before the Swine broke loose from their tribal midden-heaps. It seems so natural and proper that swine should deface and defile beautiful things. But, without a doubt, the French nation, in its dignity and love of beauty, will rebuild this lovely old city. The square of houses around the obliterated Hôtel de Ville is a dream still, of ancient wonders in architecture, of pride and pleasure. Even swine cannot destroy everything. What the French have suffered is immeasurable!

All is well with us in every way.

To P[11]. in Honolulu (Wailly, near Arras)

In France, 25 September 1917
Many thanks for your very kind letters written from so far away. I always think a letter coming a long way is worth more than one from just round the corner. You seem to be somewhat knee-deep in clover. It is only a vision to me, a bibulous dream. In some past life I believe I was on an island myself, quite surrounded with peace and clean and beautiful things. As it is, in the present, we wallow daily, in body and thought, in unclean atmospheres, and I can see no quick end to it all. America coming in so strongly and sanely is going to hasten matters but even then it is not possible to say when this horror will end. All we do clearly know is that it will end some day in the complete defeat of the Disgusting Ones.

We have recently left the actual snarling, fighting front and are back about eight miles behind, licking our wounds and preparing for more murder in the near future. The sector we left is where our troops have just won and consolidated impregnable woods on the last high plateau of all (Passchendaele Ridge), an important victory, and it was the grimmest sector on the whole western front. How human beings ever come out intact from such localities is the marvel. But men live there for weeks at a time and fairly dodge big shell-bursts continually, and the shelling never stops there day or night. No-one feels certain of his life for five minutes consecutively. All the same, our fellows are quite cheerful and absolutely confident. The British Army is in full stride now. Every man in it now looks like a veteran, feels like one, and work goes quite smoothly. Experts at their special work is the impression you get. Near us is a US Railway regiment and I have had several talks with some of the men. They all come from New England and seem to be enjoying themselves immensely. Working with them on the railroad as section hands, etc., is a multitude of Hillmen from the Himalayan foothills. Fierce, dark fellows hung with charms round their necks and big conch shells in their ears; and faces tattooed variously. Their native 'boss', or chief, carries a two-handed kukri knife, or sword, heavily tasselled with long red horsehair. Nearby are thousands of Manchurian Chinamen doing the same work, and also African natives from central Africa, working in the sun in nothing but cloths. This whole world is upside down and will never be the same again. It will never be the same again but it will be a better world which is something rather fine for this generation to bequeath to posterity.

I try not to miss the interest out through the life becoming a normal one, but a newcomer would find it marvellous. The effort on our side and on the enemy's side is too big to grasp. It is going on, rain or shine, night and day along the front and behind the front to the sea, and across the sea and all the seas, indefinitely. Our efforts increase progressively and their efforts have about reached their highest pitch. And all because a clique of men, just ordinary men, were greedy mentally and materially.

We may go into action again this autumn but I do not know yet. I am a captain now and have more responsibilities in action and so proportionately less chances of winning through. So far luck has been with me continually and I believe it will stick to me to the end of the trouble. After the war I have not the faintest idea what I shall do.

Remember me, please, most warmly to all your dear ones and let us hope to meet some day next year.

Letters to Ida (just outside Ypres South, on way to Passchendaele Ridge)

In Belgium, 15 October 1917

I have not written much of late because there has been nothing much to talk about except rain and mud, and shells, and cold and damp. We found a dugout, which we named the 'Root Heap' because it exactly resembles one in size and height and shape.

This abode saved our lives, I think. In it we dug a fireplace on the side and conducted the smoke to the surface outside by a channel in the stiff clay. A nearby coal dump tendered to our wants most unconsciously and, coming in wet and disgruntled at any hour of day or night, we found a snug fire waiting to dry by.

It has been too wet for us to go into action and we have been busy preparing a roadway over a small stream near the scene of future operations. This stream has been shelled so that the course of it has been diverted and re-diverted until the poor thing gave it up and sat down and formed a marsh in disgust.

All about on slightly higher ground are batteries of big guns, almost in the open, that blare and boom at most disconcerting intervals. Nearby are two main roads, made of planks laid on the all-embracing mud, leading to the extreme front and covered by a motley procession of lorries, limbers and ambulances, weary, muddy men and horses, coming and going continuously. As far as one can see, in all directions, are guns and men and horses, all busy as ants. Some guns always going off, with sharp roars and shattering growls, for these are all Heavies. Long strings of men in single file going towards the front in the distance like slow-moving ants. On the skyline, horses and riders or limbers, like toy soldiers, and all the time the guns at work.

Our work was heavy, carrying material over awful ground, shell holes full to the brim and framed in mud. The Boche was always shelling all about, big stuff worthy of our Heavies. Colossal duels between monsters perhaps ten miles apart. Titanic, blind encounters causing disturbances like those of nature.

All very well to read about but most unpleasant to those on other duty near-by. Several times these roaring masses from afar just comfortably missed our small party, hurling up and over us prodigious masses of dripping mud and water impregnated with dead horses and mules.

One shell, especially, landed about twenty yards from me and almost in the gun-pit of a Britannic Titan, with a most appalling rush and roar from the sky (you have no idea of the volume of sound). I saw men throwing themselves flat in all directions, then a dense wall of smoke, flame and mud spreading out like a fan towards and over me and, from the wall, smaller and harder particles going high into the air, tins, mud in chunks, all sailing up in a circle. I bowed my tin hat to the storm and half a paraffin tin came hustling out of the sky crumpled up like a concertina, just over me by about four feet. For twenty seconds or so, other things came from the sky and splashed and thumped into water and mud and shell-holes around. When the cloud dispersed there was one man in the battery lying very still and one man being dragged away by friends. Later on this man walked off supported by two friends. Other aerial cyclones fell near us at work and spoiled our appearances but only this man was hit, on the very top of his tin hat by a piece which came from on high and a long way. He was only stunned and went to work again in less than ten minutes. But we were very, very fortunate.

Many sights were to be seen. A lorry smashed up and hurled half off the crazy road by a shell. At once the ants clustered around, removed the obstacle and mended the road. Our guns roaring and barking all the time. A shell fell on the same road close to an eight-horse limber coming back empty. The two leading drivers were knocked off and most likely killed, and the horses hurt. Anyway the lot bolted down the road until the ants swarmed and stopped them. The dead are picked up and the road again is mended and the road traffic to Berlin is again in full swing; and so it goes on, day and night, and every day and every night, through rain and shine and heat and cold. But I would rather work anywhere else than in the paths and neighborhood of the Ultimate Heavies when they are throwing things at each other into the void. 'Whistling Percy' is a frequent squealing visitor around the Root Heap but last night all our Heavies simultaneously, for half an hour, pooped off, rapid, on counter-battery work on our right flank where the Boche is nearest and, strange to say, Whistling Percy is quite silent today. Probably his whistle is broken. Boche 'planes negligently drop bombs every night, usually in open fields, and then buzz off home again followed by our frenzied and foolish archies.

I have seen Dickie Bowlby's grave several times lately and have written to Bessie [his mother]. It is safe and sound somehow, but the cemetery is pitted with shell holes and every cross splintered or broken by shrapnel. We are camped quite close here. He is in one of the proudest spots on this globe, at any rate. Perhaps most historic place on the front.

Owing to the weather and state of the ground I believe we are going back to whence we came in a day or two, not sorry on the whole but reluctant to leave the heart of history. Personally I never have an ache or pain and never miss an hour's work anywhere. The youngsters are the ones that crumple up, it seems to me.

(Wailly, near Arras)

In France, Saturday 20 October 1917
We are back again at that same peaceful spot from which we departed about two weeks ago, and not sorry either, considering that awful country up there and the mud and rain and mess. As it was impossible for even infantry to fight

under those conditions, our special form of fighting was out of the question, and here we are. In a few weeks we go to other winter-quarters on the coast and I hope to get some sea fishing in the little French fishing smacks.

We had a quite miserable time leaving, having arranged our big selves for a fight.

It means much night work and if the weather is bad, night work is not nice. Apart from hostile demonstrations, the wet and mud and pitch darkness and pitfalls and wire are enough to undo all the patience you may have collected during life. The train journey is always the same. Very slow with frequent long stops. And one seems always to detrain at night or at early, shivering, unshaven, unwashed, hungry dawn.

We slept most of yesterday and this morning begin to feel very much alive. Just before we left from up there, a fine young greyhound walked into our mess and attached himself to me, and I brought him along to this place. A very handsome and well-bred pup of about eight months. He is going to catch hares for us this winter and in the mean time he sleeps at the foot of my bed and affords us all much long-legged amusement.

I expect our troubles are over till next spring and then, if the Boche is still outside his own foul country, we will go and bat him once more.

(Wailly)

In France, 27 October 1917
We are still in the same quite peaceful place but up to our middles in mud, more or less. The rain it raineth night and day and it cannot be stopped. Tents are not nice quarters in cold, wet and wind. The recent gales have tried our tents sorely and the question of tent drainage is most serious.

In my case, as usual, I have made myself very snug by gouging down two and a half feet inside the tent and digging, out of the clay, a fireplace with a flue running on a slant under the wall of the tent outside for about three feet. A sheet of corrugated iron curled up makes a good chimney, and there you are. It burns wood and coal equally well and coal appears miraculously and I ask no questions.

Extra care is needed to keep the outside drainage perfect or we would find the hole two-and-a-half feet deep in water, but we have even done that and our quarters form a sort of club as far as I can see.

An old KEH brother officer[12] came from home to us on a sort of a Cook's tour of the front and, when he returned, I got leave, two days, to see him off from the coast. This meant a hot bath and some good meals and sheets. Oysters, yea verily, and lobsters and game birds and fizz. I brought back with me fifteen books and thirty pounds of chestnuts to roast in my tent, but the trip there and back was made in blinding rain and wind, and very fast; by car, of course, in the hands of a wild Irishman of a driver who horrified and scandalized the Military Police and never stopped to argue.

We are 'standing by' to go into action again but I doubt if the weather will give us the slightest chance. The dear French have shaken up the Disgusting Ones delightfully. I was at the coast when the news came and the French were radiant with joy and pride[13].

Everywhere everyone's face was smiling and excited and cheerful remarks about 'les animaux and les grosses Cochons' *were happily passed around. And it is true. The Boche to me is no longer human but purely and disgusting animal.*

(Wailly, near Arras)

From France, Tuesday, 13 November 1917

Am writing from a different place and can say no more. If possible am more busy than ever. It is a case of very little sleep and much night-work of the hardest kind. With foggy nights lately, the dark has been inky, thick and solid, which means many tumbles in outrageous mud, into holes and tree stumps and trenches and riff-raff of all kinds. When you need sleep you do not care when you fall after a bit. But you would give large pearls of value for a light. My dear, do you know I am the last surviving officer out of five, of my old original section? I am the only one left. One having been killed shockingly and the other three seriously wounded. In every case I was between two and twenty feet from each of them. Last night one of the officers of my section, a grand chap, was talking to me and, the next instant, with no warning, he was down and mad with pain. The worst thing I ever saw or could have conceived. Someday I may tell you. We got skilled help and worked on him and put him on the stretcher and carried the poor chap, such a great friend of mine, to the nearest ambulance station and sent him off to operation tables and good nurses, etc. And then you have to trudge back in the black dark to the very place where it occurred and try to forget where. One of my best corporals was lately so hurt too that he died three days later. Two inches of his femoral artery was shot away and we kept him alive till the doctor came fifteen minutes later by pressing the artery on the bone with our thumbs, taking it in turn. It is dreadful to have a man's life literally under your own thumb. The doctor gave us full credit and did his best later. Anyone who thinks war is fun had better come along with me for a bit. Between spells of horrors you do get some fun or you could not carry on, but it is a weary business. I have no doubt that, on this front, the Boche finds it more weary than we do. That is some consolation but it is not one that sparkles.

Chapter 8

The First Battle of Cambrai,
19–22 November 1917

This battle was the first one of the war in which GHQ gave to tanks the opportunity they had craved for months. In all previous battles, tanks played a very minor part in the general plan of attack and the element of surprise for them was entirely wanting. In all previous battles, tanks had been asked to fight over ground mangled by shellfire for years where they were lucky if they could move at one mile an hour. They were sent into action following the infantry after the Zero bombardment had started and the enemy wire had been cut by shellfire in the old orthodox way. The result was, on the whole, a disappointment to the Tank Corps and probably to GHQ.

We wanted to be sent in to a big attack over ground not much shelled and without any preliminary bombardment at all, and we guaranteed that we would demolish the enemy wire better than our guns would. Sent in at dawn, the element of surprise would be perfect and result in saving the lives of many of our infantry.

These conditions were given to us in the First Battle of Cambrai and continued in all tank fighting in later battles.

The Cambrai sector for our attack was a part of the Hindenburg Line and supposed by the Germans to be invincible. There had been little fighting on it previously and the ground was in good condition for us to travel fast and safely over.

The German defence consisted of two very wide and deep trenches, the front and support trenches and a forest of wire. The wire was designed to keep our infantry back as it would take so long to cut with gunfire that they would have ample time to bring up reserves.

The trenches were nine feet wide and eight feet deep and were designed as an impassable barrier for our tanks. Thus they could hold that line with relatively few men and use the balance elsewhere.

We dug trenches of the same width and depth behind our lines and found that our tanks could not cross them. The tank would nearly get over, then the stern would drop to the bottom of the trench and the tank was left standing on its tail. But the Tank Corps evolved a remedy. Great cylindrical bundles of fascines[1] were made, ten feet in length and four feet in diameter, weighing three tons each. These were hoisted to the nose of the tank by the tank's own power and were carried in this wise to the trench. At the edge, the fascine was dropped in, reducing the trench to nine feet wide and four feet deep, quite easy for a tank to cross. Every fighting tank in our Army was on that ten-mile sector, 300 big tanks, and each had a three-ton fascine balanced on its nose. These fascines were very difficult to handle and entailed much risk and it was a wonderful relief to finally get rid of ours in the Hindenburg line.

A great rehearsal was held near Arras about a week before the battle, at which several hundred of our Staff were present, and three tanks out of the four of my section officiated successfully. At last we moved to the battle area and detrained at Fins in the first week of November, moving by night to a big wood which was packed solid with tanks. Zero day was to be 20 November, the day that the tank was to come into its own. There was to be no bombardment and tanks would lead the way at dawn and break down the wire, and our infantry were to follow right behind the tanks.

In the night of 19–20 November, as silently as possible, we took up our positions close behind our front line trench; it was 2.30am before I got my four tanks on the pegs I had placed for them a few nights before. My own orders, then, were to return to the wrecked village just behind, Villers-Plouich, to the dugout of the brigadier of the infantry going over with us. Here I was assigned a young infantry subaltern who led me to where his men were lying out in the fields. Men were lying in the open along the hedges in the dark and cold, in a drizzle. I stumbled over the feet of one and woke him. I said, 'What do you think you are doing out here?' and he said, 'Waiting to get shot at dawn.'

I guided them all to my tanks and the men lay down again behind the tanks, waiting. It was 4.30am before this was done and as Zero was at 6.10am and I and my section had to start at two minutes before Zero, there was not much time left to sleep. It was foggy and damp and raw.

The attack started absolutely silently at Zero, no gunfire, no machine guns at work, and it was not until we were well across no man's land that the enemy waked up and began to shoot off rockets of all colours and also other things more offensive. As it happened, the fascine on the tank I was in, Bandit II, suffered a severe jolt in crossing our front line trench which loosened it in a downward direction and, after going through a shell hole or two in no man's land, it jolted still further down until it entirely obstructed our view to the front. That tank was virtually a blind one. But we knew our direction was right so we locked the differential which kept the tank going in an absolutely straight direction and went on till we reached the great Hindenburg line front trench. Here, with a sigh of relief, we got rid of our fascine and endeavored to cross the trench. Unfortunately, we had happened upon an extra wide part with crumbly ground and we stuck for about half an hour, finally getting over with our own power. Another of my tanks, Barbarian, also stuck for a time and had to be towed out by Brigand, and all this was done without any casualties, although we were back and forth outside the tanks, and it shows how demoralized the enemy was by this horrible surprise effect. Our orders were to rally just behind the Hindenburg support trench on Highland Ridge and to get orders from our major. This we did, and the orders were to go as fast as possible down the valley, leaving Ribécourt on our left, to Marcoing, and to take up our objectives in that town. There were fourteen tanks of my company in action that day, all having rallied together, and there developed a point-to-point race across country as hard as we could go. On the way we saw two German machine guns in action and we diverted our headlong course, giving them the benefit of our 6-pounder guns. By the time we arrived the German machine gunners had bolted down a sunken road behind them and we jumped out and threw the machine guns, intact, telescopic sights even in place, on to the roof of Bandit II and, at once, wallowed off at top speed again for Marcoing which was nearly five miles away.

As we ploughed and hurtled our way through and across obstacles I noticed with pleasure that there was only one tank ahead of us, and that was young Lieutenant Gordon-Clark[2]. His was a female tank and they carry less weight than a male so I despaired about catching him. Nearing Marcoing there was a bridge to cross over a small stream but the enemy, roused by this time to a fine pitch of fury, was shelling it so diligently that Clark shied away from it, aiming for another crossing lower down, and I followed Clark's good reasoning. Having crossed the stream safely there was a straight road of half a mile into Marcoing, the last lap, and within a few hundred yards of the town I noticed a machine gun at work about eighteen inches from the ground through a hole in the brick wall of a small outhouse. This gun was foolish enough to fire at us instead of lying low and waiting for our infantry on that straight road. Clark failed to see it and went on so it was up to us to put it out of action. Other tanks were roaring along behind us so the job had to be done in the quickest way if we were to preserve our pride of second place in the race. Therefore we simply ran the tank into the brick side of the outhouse and collapsed the whole affair onto the top of the gun and crew, then backed out in a great rush and hurried back to the road, getting into Marcoing just behind Clark.

Bandit II's objective was the railroad bridge near the station and canal and we had to travel down the main street, with all the cross streets intervening, where one had numerous excellent targets all the time. To reach the bridge by the shortest way, for we expected the enemy to blow it up and speed was essential, we turned off the road at a level crossing, crashing through the gates and onto the railroad track where we bumped and clashed our way along on the sleepers. As the railroad here crossed a small valley, Bandit II was soon up on a high embankment of cinders and, before we reached the bridge, we saw about fifty Germans come running out of a wood towards the bridge and towards us with bayonets fixed in a most warlike manner. But we brought every available gun to bear on them and the 6-pounder, I think, filled them with especial horror, for what was left of them turned and bolted back into the wood. Soon we were at the bridge and we held it intact till our infantry came an hour and a half later, about 12.30pm. Here we had a steady fight with nests of snipers in the railway station and in a hotel just opposite the station, but the 6-pounder guns drove them away finally and when our infantry came they had hardly a single casualty. Before the infantry came to where we were, they took over most of the other part of the town while nests of snipers were still busy firing at us, and my corporal (Tait) jumped out of the tank without any orders and almost at once he was shot through the upper arm. To this day he has a crippled arm through nerves being out and he has no one but himself to blame. Shortly after this, I saw Major Henshall[3] and Captain Birnie, walking down a road which turned and led direct to these snipers. At first I thought they knew of the danger around the turn but, when I saw they were about to make the turn, I jumped out of the tank, followed by one of my men, and called to them to go back as there were snipers ahead. They stopped and walked back, but a sniper took a shot at us and the bullet landed at my feet and threw a piece of cinder into the back of my right hand and also bits of cinders through the puttees and under the skin of the leg of my faithful man. We scuttled back into the tank and put the 6-pounder to work at that sniper and the fire from that quarter stopped very soon.

The infantry soon arrived and our work was done and the cavalry was galloping back and forth through the town and beyond. Our fourteen tanks were all intact and we had had very few casualties and the Regimental Sergeant Major of the 1st Norfolks told me that his regiment had only four casualties all that day. The enemy was gone and, as he was shelling the town with small guns in a very feeble way, we parked the tanks on the edge of Marcoing itself. By evening it was raining and cold and we soon retired to some very deep dugouts in the chalk where there were a number of German wounded. These could not be sent back because no ambulances could get there yet, on account of the roads being all torn up. We gave these men cigarettes and food and tried to talk with them.

Owing to some super-German ideas of ventilation, the draught in these dugouts was excessive and it was freezing cold and damp, so I left about 10pm to find a warmer place. A burning house near-by promised warmth and we found that only a part of it was burning, the rest being very comfortable with a kitchen and stoves and food, so I returned and very soon No.5 Company of B Battalion was in these new quarters. Further search of the house revealed about 200 bottles of good red wine, about a dozen bottles of liqueurs, two cases of champagne and twelve live chickens in a coop. The night, alongside fires dragged from the burning part, developed into a festive one and war, it was voted, was the only trade to follow. The next morning we found that this was a German Brigade Artillery Headquarters and we collected a multitude of their maps and aeroplane photographs and turned them in to Colonel Bryce.

Apart from these we found a complete dinner set, plates, cutlery and glassware and linen for sixteen officers. All of which went the same way. Later in the night, we found a piano in a house on the side of the town. Eight of us officers with a two-wheeled gig on springs under the same inoffensive but regular shelling, ran the piano on that slender structure to our own headquarters to add to the gaiety of the times.

On one of my walks in the town, I entered a nice house whose doors were wide open and I found a good and well-bound library. Examining the books I found that a German officer of the name of Meyer had drawn a line through the French owner's name in every single book and had written his name underneath. I spent a long time in drawing a line through 'Meyer' and in re-writing the Frenchman's name.

The town was full of food. Quantities of bread and fresh meat and potatoes, principally, and there were stores of clothing and blankets in plenty. As our new supplies of petrol (gasoline) and oil, etc. had not arrived we could not do much, but a few tanks did go and help our infantry to take Noyelles on the 21st, and Cantaing on the 22nd, without suffering much hurt. On the evening of the 22nd, Captain Birnie and I were ordered to take the petrol and oil from the remainder of our company tanks and to fill up three tanks each of our respective sections, preparatory to going on to attack Bourlon Wood on the 23rd.

Chapter 9

The First Battle of Cambrai,
23 November 1917

Just before Captain Birnie, with three tanks of his section, and I, with three of my section, left Marcoing at 6pm, November 22nd, we were given our orders by Colonel Bryce: to join in the great attack on Bourlon Wood, which was the key position of the whole Cambrai attack.

If our troops could capture and hold Bourlon Wood and village, both of which were on the high and commanding position of Bourlon Hill, the enemy's line would be forced back to Douai and Valenciennes and rolled back northwards to Arras. In detail our orders were to circle round the wood along the southern slope of the hill to Bourlon village, which was in the north-east corner and where we should meet other of our tanks from H Battalion coming from the opposite direction. This attack was to be at dawn and the importance of the undertaking was impressed upon us warmly.

We left under a wet and cold drizzle and travelled steadily until about 2am, having been delayed by several very deep and steep-sided sunken roads which had to be crossed in the dark. Our stopping point was a long sunken road running between Cantaing and Anneux, parallel with the front lines, with six tanks of No.4 Company of B Battalion and later, one reserve tank of our company, making thirteen in all. The 23rd was a Friday and the omens looked badly to me. As a matter of fact, this reserve tank with its officer and crew was completely destroyed and none of its personnel ever seen again.

In this sunken road, besides, was the best part of a Highland Battalion, Camerons who had scooped little holes in the bank for shelter. They told us they had been fourteen days in front trenches, three of these days being days of hard fighting, and, in their mud-plastered, unshaven condition, it was difficult to distinguish officers from men. This was the battalion that was to follow us and, as it turned out, they had a very hard time and lost heavily in trying to do so. The enemy had not bothered us with shelling while travelling but he seemed to mistrust that sunken road and repeatedly shelled it with 5.9s without, however, doing any damage.

Before dawn our orders were changed: we were to go through Bourlon Wood direct for the village; later, they were changed again and we were not to start until 9am and then to attack and hold the village of Fontaine-Notre-Dame on the right flank of the Bourlon attack.

These changes, added to thirteen tanks and the day being Friday made me feel superstitiously uncomfortable.

At 9am we started, tanks in single file, with Bandit II leading the line and Lieutenant Dalby as tank commander and myself and our crew of seven men inside[1]. We were assisted (and also much hampered) by a smoke barrage put up by our guns and, it being broad daylight, the enemy shelled us heavily but with no success.

There were two main German trenches to cross and the village was still about a third of a mile behind them. By this time, the surprise effect of the tanks had worn off in this battle and the German infantry and machine gunners had been served out with their famous K or armour-piercing ammunition. Being the leading tank, Bandit II came in for much concentrated machine gun and rifle fire and two of the crew were put out of business before we crossed these trenches. In both cases the bullets entered a slit-window and one man [Coleman][2] was hit over the eye and the other in the groin. They lay on the floor, one on each side and were very much in the way.

Both of them were 6-pounder gunners and most useful men. We were in action and could do little for them. Coleman had a groove cut in the temple bone and lay quite unconscious. From time to time, I could spare a moment to pour from our drinking-water tank a cupful with a splash onto his head. This gradually recovered him. The other man was in much pain but not seriously wounded.

We crossed the trenches and, nearing Fontaine, the tanks scattered to various objectives. Our entry and that of the two other tanks of my section was at the church and our fighting point, the south-western precincts of the village. Unluckily Bandit II knocked down a telegraph pole; the heavy wires entangling the muzzle of the 6-pounder gun on the right side held the gun firmly and, before the tank was stopped, the clip rings on the mounting were so bent that it was impossible to traverse the gun any more, and there it was sticking out at right angles to the tank. In the narrow streets of the village this gun was always bumping into something and caused us a deal of trouble.

This was the result of carelessness and was avoidable. The two best 6-pounder gunners were knocked out. One of the substitutes was a reserve man, keen enough, but devoid of intelligence – not untrained but wooden. A tank fighting crew must be composed entirely of picked men or the weak link will snap when the strain comes.

The village was very strongly held by the enemy and every house seemed to be full of snipers and bombers, but we drove them ahead of us, chiefly with the 6-pounder guns, until we got the tank into a very advantageous point in a small street on the south-western edge of the village, where it overlooked open ground between it and La Folie Wood to the south. Across this open ground the enemy was bolting from the village to the wood and he offered us many good targets. Time was passing and there were no signs of our infantry. About 3.30pm I saw one of my tanks, Brigand, on the edge of the village apparently in trouble and we went to it and manoeuvred our tank so that we were head to head and could talk, with no fear of damage from machine guns. Lieutenant Law[3], commanding Brigand, told me that his radiator had been shot through and that all his water was slowly but surely leaking away and that, so far, he had had no casualties. I instructed him to try to return home at once and told him further that, as the oil pump in our engine was working very badly and getting worse, we would follow him and, if his engine failed for want of water, we would pick him up with his crew. It was then nearly 4pm and there were no signs of our own infantry anywhere. Brigand at once started to leave the village homeward-bound and Bandit II followed about 100 yards behind.

So far all was well, but Brigand disappeared behind some scattered houses and I have never seen them again to this day (1920) because, as soon as we were well in the open and going very slowly for want of a proper working oil pump, a German pip-squeak battery began to range on us. The first shot short, the next nearer, and the third over us and we were 'straddled'. Direct hits must follow and they did. We still kept crawling on. The first hit blew in the heavy steel door of the right sponson, injuring and shocking the two gunners on that side. The next struck us, for we felt the concussion, but no damage was done inside and we kept crawling on, hoping to get out of direct sight of that battery. Later we found out that this shot had broken our left track and we were done for because we were simply running off that track. The third direct hit (and they all three came very quickly) hit us squarely in the centre and to the stern of the tank, bursting open the radiator which filled us with steam and set us alight. I gave the order to 'clear tank' and in a remarkably short space of time we had the wounded out and ourselves. Jumping out last, I was immediately shot in the elbow by rifle or machine-gun fire and, in searching for cover for us all, I was hit three more times, but these later ones were luckily grazes which did little else but ruin my clothes. The crew at once disappeared like moles under the tank which was still being shelled. It was a very poor place to choose and cover had to be found. Lieutenant Dalby was also searching for cover and he was shot down about five yards from the tank. He fell on his face and I thought he was dead, but I called out to him to ask if he was badly hurt and he lifted his head a trifle off the ground and gave me a deliberate wink; unbelievable, unless actually seen. Machine guns were still steadily playing on us and Dalby was again hit slightly, lying where he was, so he crawled to the tank side. We then decided to disturb the crew underneath the tank (by kicking the soles of their boots which were sticking out into the open) and take chances and to run across the open and back to the village, as there was no cover where we were except a burning tank which was still being shelled. This we did and, I must say, I never saw badly wounded men run so well before. We all reached the village untouched, although the air seemed to be full of buzzing bees, and I got them down into a cellar where I hoped to be able to bandage and tend to our hurts, for we were five wounded out of nine, and to quietly wait for infantry to appear. Even then I never dreamed but that our men would come and that we would return with them. As it happened, the enemy must have seen us disappear into the house and, as our tanks had by that time either been knocked out or had gone home, they appeared in force at the entrance to our cellar, before we had finished bandaging each other, and I surrendered the whole party. Apart from wounds, we were completely exhausted, having travelled all the previous night and been in action all day with no food except a sketchy breakfast at dawn. It was useless to show fight because I was the only one of us armed (having my revolver) and one bomb thrown would have finished us all. The men, besides, had fought splendidly and deserved consideration and I am glad to say that all of them recovered from their wounds and returned safely to England in the spring of 1919. We were marched into Cambrai, arriving there just at dark, as prisoners-of-war, and the rest appears in my diary kept while a prisoner in Germany.

I would like to add, that none of our troops entered Fontaine again until October 1918, about ten months later, when the Canadian Army took Fontaine and Cambrai.

To Mrs Dalby, mother of A.A. Dalby by N.J. Gordon-Clark

A diary was found on a dead German recently in which he describes the attack by us on the day when your son was taken. He says that the courage shown by the tank crews that were stuck in the village was extraordinary and that no men could have behaved in a finer way. I think that a tribute like that from an enemy is worth a lot.

Yours sincerely,
N.J. Gordon-Clark.

Chapter 10

Prisoner of War

Telegram to Ida (from War Office)

War Office, London – 5.55pm [No date]
Mrs Corbett, 12 Gayfere St., London, England.
Regret to inform you Capt. F. Vans Agnew, Tank Corps, reported missing November twenty-third. This does not necessarily mean either killed or wounded. Further news sent immediately on receipt.
Secretary War Office.

To Ida (from Captain H.V. Diamond)

11 December 1917

Dear Mrs Corbett,
You will have been notified by now from the War Office that your brother Captain F. Vans Agnew is reported as missing in the action which took place on November 23rd.

I am afraid I can add no news to this, though my delay in writing has been in the hope that I might be able to.

On the morning of the 23rd, he took his section, which had already done splendidly on the 20th, into action, [and] the tank on which he was fighting through the enemy's lines into the village of Fontaine. This is at present the last known of either tank or crew, and though I may point out that owing to some cause of breakdown the tank may have been surrounded and the crew captured, it is impossible to give you any definite surmise.

Every enquiry possible has been made to ascertain whether he has passed through the dressing stations, but with no result.

If, as we all hope, he has been made prisoner, you will, when this is known to the authorities, be notified by the Prisoners of War Department.

Should any kind of news reach his old company you may rest assured that I will at once communicate with you and I will esteem it a great favour if you would write me, if news reaches you.

I need hardly say how sincere our sympathy is for you in your anxiety, for he was held in the highest respect, admiration and friendship, by all his brother officers, and the loss (even if temporary as we hope) to us is a personal one.

Believe me, Mrs Corbett
Yours very sincerely
(Signed) H.V. Diamond[1], Capt. (2nd in Command) No.5 Coy. B Bn Tank Corps.

To Ida [from Major Henshall, Frank's commanding officer]

B.E.F. 15 December 1917

Dear Mrs Corbett,
I regret that I have not had the opportunity of writing to you before now to let you know any news of your brother.

Unfortunately I am unable to give you very satisfactory information but no doubt you will like to know all that I can tell you.

On the morning of the 23rd your brother was in command of a section in my Company, which attacked Fontaine.

The tanks started at ten o'clock in the morning with orders to capture the village which would then have been consolidated by the Infantry.

All went well and all the tanks entered the village, but there they met with tremendous opposition which afterwards turned out to be so great that the Infantry were unable to enter. They repeatedly attacked but by nightfall they had only been able to reach the outskirts. The tanks fought splendidly but unfortunately out of the thirteen which started, five of them failed to return from the village which was never really in our hands, and one of them was the tank BANDIT in which your brother went into action, accompanied by the tank commander, Lieutenant A.A. Dalby.

The five tanks which are missing were all seen in the village and a conversation was exchanged between your brother's tank and another (Law's tank). At that time all was going well.

What happened after that I am unable to say. Whatever your brother then did I am confident it was the right thing, as I have every faith in your brother and Dalby.

We all have every hope that they were taken prisoners, as they would be quite unable to defend themselves against so many Germans, who were holding the village in strength, and being unassisted by our Infantry who could not advance owing to inactive gun fire.

I can assure you that everything possible was done to obtain some definite news of them; I personally did not leave the battlefield until late that night, until I was satisfied that nothing further could be done.

Your brother is missed by us all, we were a happy family, and 'old Vans' was one of the cheeriest. [Illegible passage]

I am sorry that you have been given so much pain by the message which the press state to have been delivered by General Elles[2]. It is, as I hope you had imagined, a gross untruth. I am enclosing a copy of the only special orders which the General issued, previous to the battle which I hope will clear up the statement in your mind.

You have my personal sympathy during the anxious time that it must be to you until we hear some definite news; anything which reaches me in the future, I will send on at once.

Yours sincerely,
(Signed) [Illegible] Henshall. Major.
Commanding No. 5 Coy Tank Corps.

Enclosed: SPECIAL ORDER. No.6
Tomorrow the Tank Corps will have the chance for which it has been waiting for many months – to operate on good going in the van of the battle.

All that hard work and ingenuity can achieve has been done in the way of preparation.

It remains for unit commanders and for tank crews to complete the work by judgment and pluck in the battle itself.

In the light of past experience, I leave the good name of the Corps with great confidence in their hands.

I propose leading the attack of the centre division.

Hugh Elles. Major Gen. Commanding Tank Corps.
19 November 1917.
Distribution to Tank Commanders

To Ida (from the War Office)

M. S. 3. Cas/518.A. WAR OFFICE, Whitehall, SW1. 4 January 1918
The Military Secretary presents his compliments to Mrs Corbett, and begs to inform her that the enclosed communication from Captain Frank Vans Agnew, Tank Corps, who was reported missing on the 23rd November, 1917, has been brought to his notice by the Postal Censor.

The Military Secretary is desired by the Secretary of State for War to congratulate Mrs Corbett on the safety of her brother, and begs to say that steps will now be taken to have his name published as a prisoner of war in the official casualty lists.

Enclosure: Postal card to Mrs Vans Agnew Corbett
'Fill up this card immediately'
I am a prisoner of war in Germany.
Name: Vans Agnew
Christian name: Frank
Rank: Captain
Regiment: Tank Corps
Slightly wounded

Date: 26 November 1917

Chapter 11

Münster Lager

Note by FVA

This diary was not kept daily between the dates, 23 November 1917, when I was captured, and 31 January 1918, when I was finally discharged from the German hospitals, but I have given a short account.

From January 31st the diary was kept daily. On 1 September 1918, the German censor at Fürstenberg took it and kept it until the 18th, heavily and indignantly censoring it with indelible blue pencil. I at once, on September 19th and 20th, re-wrote almost everything he had obliterated and, by cutting a slit in the lining of my tunic under my left armpit in which I placed the diary book, I evaded the search of the German censors on our departure from Germany on 9 December 1918, and brought it safely home.

I have added a complete list of every parcel received by me in Germany, giving the date it was sent from England and the date of its arrival in my hands. This list includes parcels (chiefly of bread) received from Berne, Switzerland, and from Copenhagen, Denmark.

All sentences typewritten in capitals comprise the subject matter censored by the German censor at Fürstenberg. I was able to remember everything, almost word for word, and re-wrote them in the same diary at once.

Account opens

The German NCO in charge of the men who captured us was, luckily for us, a very decent and humane person. He took us back into a street whose houses and brick walls afforded protection for all. Here we were halted and, at once, I could see that it was going to be a toss-up whether we were to be shot or not. Tanks were not popular at all in that village. No German officer was there and the men had a free hand.

A noisy argument began, into which the NCO joined in our behalf, and I heard him use the word '*Kultur*' a number of times most earnestly. Possibly German *Kultur* saved the day. Who knows! One giant of a young, fair-haired German came running up with a light machine gun on his shoulder. This he planted before us, with an unholy grin. As it happened, a German officer turned up, a fine looking, dark haired man, well iron-crossed. At once the conclave broke up and silence ensued. The officer ordered us to be sent back at once and I personally breathed more freely. None of us had said a word. We had all shown a complete indifference to the proceedings, being tired out, five being wounded, and no one cared much about anything.

Then began a weary trek back into Cambrai – a mile and a half away. Our own British barrage had to be gone through and it was evident that the Germans treated our guns with more respect than we had for theirs. The same German NCO took us to Cambrai. He went from dugout to dugout, most cautiously, with often long waits between. Finally, just after dark, he took us to a large building well into the town which had an open courtyard of considerable size in the centre. Here we halted and stood silently for perhaps half an hour.

Suddenly from the main building came a tall, dark, black-haired, slim, hatchet-faced, lantern-jawed Staff officer, with long strides. At once he began to harangue us in French and he worked himself up until he frothed at the mouth. He told us that England started the war and that every British prisoner should be shot on sight and much more to that effect. Being most insulting in word and manner. Then he asked who was the officer in charge and I raised my hand. He rushed at me, seized me, by my sore arm as it happened, swung me round, and ordered me to follow him. He dashed off in a great hurry while I strolled behind. Then he would look round and run to me, shaking his fist in my face and shout '*Schnell – schnell*'. But I was irritated by him and did not hasten. This continued until we had crossed the wide courtyard and entered the main building. Here we mounted stairs for two flights and went along a passage to where a sentry stood by a door.

We entered a smallish room where two grey-haired senior officers sat behind a table, side by side, with an interpreter standing half-left to one side. My enemy stood behind me. I liked the look of both of the senior officers. They showed the type of the old professional soldier and looked like gentlemen. Through the interpreter, I was asked various questions – how many men I had, how many wounded, where we were captured, and I signed papers referring to rations for us and so on. Then I was asked to what corps I belonged and I told the interpreter to please tell the generals that that was a question which an officer did not answer. He told this to the generals and, to my astonishment and pleasure, they both grinned and nodded their heads, as if to say that I was quite right. After conferring together, they said

I might go. I wanted to get even with my enemy behind and I hastily asked the interpreter if I might say something to the generals. He asked them and they said I might. So I told the interpreter to please tell them that I and my men did not mind being taken as prisoners-of-war or being wounded, or any of the hardships of war, but that we did mind being insulted by a German officer while prisoners-of-war. When they heard that, both of the old boys began to get purple with rage, and the oldest-looking of them rapped out something, which the interpreter told me meant 'Who was the officer?' I jerked round and pointed to my enemy behind me. Neither of the old chaps said a word, but the senior of them glared at my enemy and shot the forefinger of his right hand upwards in a vertical line in front of him, and I heard my enemy's heels come together with a loud click. And that is how I left them.

I was then marched down by the sentry and turned over to the same corporal and guard. At once we were marched out of Cambrai to the village of Rieux, a good eight miles away, and it was quite midnight when we got there. Luckily, it was fine weather and not cold. Lieutenant Dalby had lost a lot of blood, having been shot through the briefs, and was light-headed. Coleman had a wound which grooved the bone (he now wears a silver plate there), and we had to support him all the way, taking it in turns. I thought he would die. The guard was considerate and allowed us ample time to rest. My left elbow had bled much and my sleeve was full of caked blood, but it was not so painful then as it was later when it turned septic. My other wounds were nothing at all: two which just missed my left hip joint, lying side by side, and one over the back of my right hand. So I was feeling quite strong in spite of all. None of us had eaten a bite since dawn when we had had breakfast in the trenches at Anneux.

At Rieux we were taken into a guardroom full of German NCOs and men, all snoring in wooden bunks bedded with straw below and blankets above. Here came to us a doctor of sorts who dressed our wounds in a kindly manner and we were given food. This consisted of black bread in chunks and acorn coffee. I was hungry and ate well, but some of our wounded ate nothing and lay down on the floor to sleep and rest at once. There was no other place for them to lie. I was the last to lie down. No sooner was I down when a German with rifle and bayonet entered and demanded of us the senior in rank. I answered and he told me to follow him. Out we went into the dark and I was feeling very uncomfortable not knowing what was the cause for this. He marched me through streets and, in a short time, to a house, which we entered. There was a sentry at a door inside; he stood aside and saluted, and I went in. I saw a mess table prepared for a meal and five German officers sitting at it. At the head of the table was a major, and there was a captain and three subalterns, or the equivalent German rank. They all smiled in a quiet and friendly way. To my astonishment, the major spoke to me in perfect English, with no German accent, and introduced me to all present. They all stood up and bowed and clicked heels. The major then told me that he had asked for me, without any intention of getting knowledge from me in any way; that he had heard there was a wounded British officer in the village, and that he wished merely to offer him the hospitality of their mess. And he wound up by saying, 'What would you like to eat and drink?' That question being easily settled I asked if I might have a wash, as I was in a disgraceful state. After that I had a small bottle of claret (French) and some cold meats and bread and butter, much regretting having eaten that black bread and acorn coffee.

The major then told me he had been educated at Harrow and that he had many friends in England. The captain was, to all intents and purposes, an American. He spoke pure American and he told me he had a brother, who was an American citizen, in Buffalo, New York. I fancy he was American-born himself and of German parentage, and was probably caught in Germany when war broke out, on a business or pleasure trip. The three young subalterns spoke no English at all but they beamed upon me happily. The major said that his lot had only recently come from the Russian front, where they had had a very easy time of it, and he added that when his men, who were in front of Marcoing on November 10th, saw our tanks coming lumbering down the Coing valley slope to the town, they 'ran like rabbits', to use his own words. It was interesting to talk with him.

He pooh-poohed the American Army. He said that it was not their war and that when they had had a few men killed they would go back to America again. He also said that the German submarines would prevent them from crossing the seas. I politely disagreed with him and he asked for my reasons. I told him that the convoy system would ensure the passage of troops in spite of submarines, and then I said to him, 'You know how the Canadians have fought'. He assured me, 'Wonderfully well', and then I mentioned the Australians, New Zealanders, South Africans, Newfoundlanders etc. He agreed that all were fine soldiers and had fought well. Then I said, 'What is the difference between all these men and Americans', and he was silent, thinking deeply. I told him that the Anglo Saxon is the same the world over and that seeing their dead makes them all see red.

He then asked me about my quarters in the village. I explained the situation. At once, he told the captain to go and see that all of my wounded, including myself, were given a bunk with blankets and straw. After polite farewells, I left with the captain. As soon as the captain entered the guardroom his manner changed and he barked like a dog at his men. They all sprang half asleep from their bunks and saluted, stiffly at attention. He found several men who had no business to be in there at all. These were ordered out and in a short time all of my wounded were in their bunks and one was allotted to me.

He then told me that, early in the morning, we were to go in a cart to hospital at Caudry, about nine miles away and that he would, personally, see us off. This he did. The cart was a two-wheeled farm cart, with a big carthorse in the shafts. I was bare headed all this time and it was cold. In action, in the tank, I was too hot and I had long discarded my head-piece. French peasants, old men, boys and women, greeted us with sympathy and tried to bring us food, but were always ordered away. About noon we arrived at Caudry and were put to bed in a ward, if wounded. No hospital clothes were given to us and we lay in our dirty uniforms. The doctor asked me if I had had an anti-tetanus injection. Although not true, I told him 'Yes', for I mistrusted their injections; never once would I accept their morphine injections in other hospitals when my arm was thoroughly septic and extremely painful. As it happened, I was right, for at Heidelberg and at Fürstenberg, in prison camps later on, I met two of our officers, both airmen, whose wounds were only in the arms and both of them, after injections, became half-paralyzed in the legs. Neither of them could walk properly when I knew them. We spent the night and next day there.

The next night we went by tram to Le Cateau where the hospital was in a big factory building. We were in a very long and large room, officers and men all mixed up, about seventy beds. The dressing room was at one end, merely curtained off; there were German wounded in there, too, a few. All the agonized yells and howls and exclamations from some of the wounded, whose wounds were being dressed, were clearly audible to everyone else in the ward. There was one doctor and one nurse for all of us. By the time I arrived at Le Cateau my arm was septic and much swelled under the bandages, feeling as if it was on fire and burning merrily. When the doctor took off the bandages, there was a rush of discharge from the elbow, and I heard him say, under his breath, '*Mein Gott!*'

Several incidents I remember well. One day someone, British also, was making a fearful noise with yells and shouts while his wound was being dressed and we found out that he was an officer. I, being able to walk, was deputed to go and see him and to tell him to keep his mouth shut in future as he was a bad example to our men. I found a weedy, pimply, youth in bed and I gave it to him straight, telling him never to do it again and to bite a wad of sheet or blanket when dressing time came. He never made a whimper on other occasions. The few German wounded we had in there made more noise than enough at all their dressings, but it is totally unnecessary to make a sound under any provocation provided you have something to bite on.

A gunner officer, in a bed opposite mine, had five bullet wounds through his chest. He would sit up in bed, and strictly against orders, would smoke cigarettes on every possible occasion. I firmly expected to see the smoke come curling out from the holes in his chest. He said, quite cheerfully, that he would probably die in any case and he might as well enjoy himself. Whether he did or not I do not know.

In the bed next to mine, when I arrived, was an under-officer of Indian Cavalry. A Rajput, I think, and I have forgotten his name. He told me that he had had three horses killed under him the day he was captured. His wound was not serious, a bullet through the calf. The food was execrable and scanty, black bread and skilly soup. This Indian could not eat beef owing to his religion. Therefore, for fear there might be beef in the soup, he never touched it once, and this meant bread and water for him only.

Our only hospital orderlies were some miserable Belgian prisoners. Weakly, vicious-looking men, they prowled about day and night, never attending to the wants of the many horribly wounded men. The men might ask for water in vain as far as these rats were concerned. Their sole object was to steal anything they could find of value from the desperately wounded. My arm was very bad and I never slept. So I could watch the rats at work. They tied my arm to the ceiling in an upright position, heaven knows why, and tried all kinds of queer supports, strings and wire cages. The doctor and nurse, a hard featured, elderly woman, were kindly and both of them did their best but they were hopelessly overworked. Result being that our wounds were dressed about once in three days on an average. Of course everyone was going septic unless the wound was a simple one and drained itself naturally.

After my Indian officer friend left, they put a small, thin, British officer, next to me. He had been shot through the head in a later fight than ours, probably when the German counter-attack took place in the first Cambrai show. He should have been dead as a stone but he was not. He was, nevertheless, doomed, and the doctor and nurse never came near him. All that evening and that night, he lay in his breeches, tunic, belt and boots, under a blanket even to his head, and talked incessantly. He was evidently in the Machine Gun Corps and he was expecting a big attack. His batman bore the name of 'Pike'. He would call 'Pike; Pike; Pike', gradually louder, until Pike appeared. It was like listening to a man talking at one end of a telephone. A long conversation would follow with Pike. Then he would send Pike for his sergeant. The sergeant would arrive and he would discuss unendingly with him how to post his guns in the most advantageous position. Suddenly, in a tense whisper, he would say, 'Here they come, here they come', and tell the sergeant perfectly coolly to 'Warn the men – warn the men.' Then there would be a break and dead silence and, in about five minutes, he would start calling for 'Pike' and go over the whole thing again in almost the same words. He lived till, I think, noon of the next day. It was hard to tell, on account of the blanket, but he became silent after that and he was removed. A great relief to me, as the situation was a very trying one for all of us in hearing, and we were so desperately sorry for him, even though he suffered absolutely no pain.

A very young Tommy, not over eighteen I should think, was lying in bed, shell shocked, without a wound of the smallest description anywhere. This boy did nothing but call loudly for his mother and complain of his lot in life. His monotonous calls kept many badly wounded from their sleep. Tempers were frayed and fevers were high. The men retaliated with roars of rage at him and obscene remarks. This went on for several days and nights, until the lad just died in his bed. Unharmed and skin intact, he died of sheer fright, and the gruesome part was that many men were delighted and said, 'Good riddance to the blighter, now we can sleep'.

I spent twelve days in this hospital and I was the last one left of our tank crew. Lieutenant Dalby healed up well and the men were patched up sufficiently to be sent elsewhere. We parted with intense regrets on both sides. When I finally left with several other officers whom I scarcely knew, we wrote a letter to our doctor thanking him for his work and kindness, all signing it. He was much pleased and touched, and said he would frame it and keep it as a prized possession. I shall never forget my drive in a lorry to the railway station at Le Cateau over cobblestones on metal tyres. My arm was in a wire cage, thoroughly septic, intensely painful. I had to sit because standing was impossible, and every jolt was like a white flame in the arm. But once we reached the train, my immediate troubles were over.

By hospital-train we went, two days and three nights, to Münster Lager (good train, Red Cross, warm and comfortable and fair food). Best food since capture. Arrived at Münster at about 12pm. Were all (200 or so with 10 officers) unloaded onto farm wagons with poor horses, and drove one half-hour to the Lager. Very cold and jolty. Dreadful for the wounded, for us all. At the Lager all were put into one big shed and made to lie on the floor on straw, all piled up close together in a heap. Four men died on the floor that night. Sleep impossible. Next morning we were sent to other sheds and given beds, etc.

The censor at Fürstenberg on 1 September 1918, tore out several pages here about our treatment at Münster, the Heidelberg censor having passed my whole diary without censoring a word, before this officious official got his claws on it. I re-wrote this account at once on September 18th as follows.

Münster Lager
We arrived at Münster on 8 December, I think, and I described our arrival and first night. The next day we (ten officers and four sergeant majors and 200-odd men) were put into several big ward-huts, with beds of straw mattresses on boards, with blue and white checked sheets and pillows; the German sack-sheet affair that you put the blankets into. At any rate, we got our clothes off and went to bed. For food we got imitation coffee in morning and a chunk of bread to last all day. At noon a bowl of thin skilly soup, potatoes and carrots (meat rarely); in the evening a bowl of thin skilly soup. The men got less for they rarely got the potatoes and carrots. We gave almost all of these away to them. After a day or so we, the ten officers and four sergeant majors, were removed to a smaller ward-hut by ourselves. Each of the huts was warmed by a stove which was quite insufficient, even if going all the time and, as they were often out for want of coal, it was hopeless. All had two thin cotton blankets.

Here we got occasionally some pink jam, made from beets or turnips, a very small bit for all day. The orderlies were nearly all Russians and they did very well, especially in dressing wounds. They were so big and helpful and gentle over it, while the German orderlies were rough and clumsy, not on purpose but just naturally being built that way. The doctor was a good kind sort but not a good doctor professionally. In the Army he would be called a 'dud'. We had Colonel Elliott Cooper[1] with us, badly wounded in the hip joint. He suffered the pains of the damned but never whimpered once. His language was very bad but a joy to hear, and, when at his worst, he hurled things about. He got a VC for his work before he was captured. The poor chap died in Hanover Hospital a month later. If he had gone to Hanover [direct] from Le Cateau he would be alive today, in my opinion.

I know my arm got steadily worse at this place and grew black and the nails came off and, if I had stayed there a week more, I should have had to have it off. The doctor kept talking about operating. Luckily for me and us all, we suddenly were sent to Lazaret No.2, Hanover, on December 20th. The same awful journey to the station in farm carts over the frozen mud, ruts and stones, and a wait in the cold at the station out on the street, where every loafer scanned us, for over two hours. Some of the stretcher cases were numb through and through. All the men and the four sergeant majors were left behind. Poor chaps! I was sorry for them, God knows how they got well there of bad wounds.

Frank Vans Agnew, left, in Roosevelt's Rough Riders in 1892 and, right, in 1917. *All photographs are from the Vans Family Archive unless specified.*

In the centre of the picture, Ida Corbett, 'my fighting suffragette-sister' tackles Herbert Asquith, the Prime Minister, in the campaign for votes for women. *Mary Evans Picture Library*

The 'pink slip' that sent Frank into action with Walrond (above, *unknown source*), Carey and Foster. 'Walrond was killed later, as was Carey, and Foster was so badly wounded he went home and never came back.'

'Some of my troop', King Edward's Horse, 1914. Is that Walrond at the extreme right?

C Troop, 2nd King Edward's Horse.
Above: at Woodbridge, 1914, Frank one from the left in the front row, Lieutenant Grosvenor in the centre.

Below: Privates Scallon, *WW1Photos.com*, Meiklejon, *Kissimmee Gazette*, and Sherris. *WW1Photos.com*

Ernest Wilmot Scallon
King Edward's Horse.

Guy Sherris
King Edward's Horse.

Above: Colonel Cradock, who commanded 2nd King Edward's Horse throughout the war. He 'looks at me quite sideways', Frank wrote after two of his fellow officers also applied for the Tank Corps.

Left: Brigadier General John Seely who commanded the Canadian Cavalry Brigade.

Below: Frank, in the centre, now a 'Second Loot' with his Mounted Gun Section, 21 June 1916.

Tanks from B Battalion perform for the King. 'My tank, a male or 6-pounder Hotchkiss-gun tank, carrying two big guns and four Lewis machine guns, and the tank commanded by Lieutenant Doyle, a female, were selected to perform. Other tanks of other companies performed perfectly and B Battalion nearly blew up with pride.' *Bovington Tank Museum*

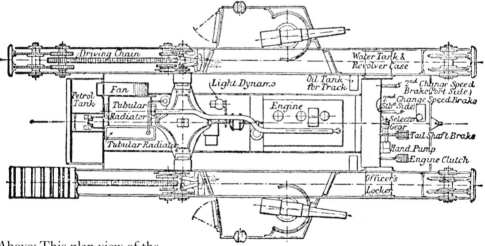

Above: This plan view of the interior of a Mk IV tank shows the middle of the tank occupied by the huge, hot, noisy and fumy, 16-litre petrol engine around which the crew had to operate. *Florida Center for Instructional Technology*

Right: Interior, showing (l to r) the breech of the 6-pounder Hotchkiss gun, the driver's front slit and the engine. *Hans de Regt*

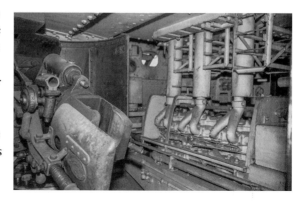

Above: Each tank carried two pigeons, the only way to communicate with one's commander; here a pigeon is released through the special hatch in the tank's right sponson. *Bovington Tank Museum*

Left: A camouflaged British tank on the side of the road near Neuve Eglise, July 1917. 'We moved up nearer to the front, by night, to a field and parked the tanks along the hedges round about. This required careful camouflage work with the nets to avoid being seen by enemy aircraft'. *Australian War Memorial*

German prisoners at Messines, on the afternoon of 7 June 1917, carrying their own wounded to a field dressing station, while the British Mark IV tanks advance towards the distant Messines Ridge where an enemy shell is seen bursting. 'The Green Line was gained and the Australians proceeded to dig in and to consolidate. Meanwhile we patrolled in front of them for a full hour to check any desire of the enemy to counter-attack the position.' *Australian War Memorial*

Friends and colleagues from B Battalion
Above: Arthur Dalby, commander of
Bandit II, wounded and captured with
Frank and the rest of the crew.
Left: Frank's great friend William
Birnie, killed at Fontaine.

Below: Private Frederick Coleman.
Courtesy of his family

Below: left, Captain Hugh Warren Victor
Benjamin Broomhead Diamond, second
in command of No. 5 Company, an actor
in civilian life.
Right: Captain George Edward Porter
MC and Bar, Devonshire Regiment and
Tank Corps. (Photo 1919 in 20th Bn,
Tank Corps.) *Courtesy of the National
Army Museum*

Bardit II is hauled away from Fontaine–notre–Dâme by its captors. *Bundesarchiv*

German engineers loading captured tanks at Fontaine, February 1918. *Bundesarchiv*

A German soldier poses proudly beside Bandit II; the damage to the tank is plainly visible. *Philippe Gorczynski*

Bandit II on its way to the German tank workshops after recovery to be repaired or, more likely, used as spare parts in the repair of other captured tanks; like Frank and the rest of the crew, a prisoner! *Unknown*

Frank, on the right, in Hanover Hospital, looking all his 49 years. The man in the bed is Lieutenant T.W. Morse, of Toronto, serving in the RFC, missing 20 Nov. 1917. The third man is unidentified.

The funeral of Lieutenant Colonel Neville Bowes Elliott-Cooper VC, DSO, MC, died 11 Feb. 1918, Hanover, of blood poisoning. 'His language was very bad but a joy to hear, and, when at his worst, he hurled things about. He got a VC for his work before he was captured. The poor chap died a month later. If he had gone to Hanover [direct] from Le Cateau he would be alive today, in my opinion.'

Karlsruhe Camp, March 1918

Above: 'Men I was in hospital with at various places. The Flying Officer on the outside, opposite to me, is to live with me in internment. He is a Canadian, Golding by name.'

Below: International group. Frank, centre. 1. Italian major 2. French captain 3. Serbian colonel 4. Belgian captain 5. Various British officers 6. Italian captain 7. Flying Officer Golding.

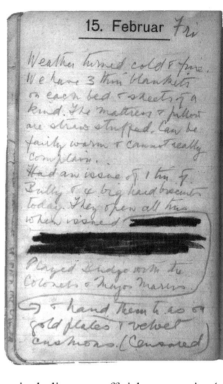

Karlsruhe Camp

Above: 'There is a library here with quite a good lot of books of fiction, travel, study, etc. You sign for a book as usual… one officer translates all of interest in German newspapers, including our official communiqués, and writes it all down in books in Reading Room.'

Above right: The censored diary entry from 15 February 1918.

Prisoners standing about; no doubt they did a lot of it!

My Hut & Quarters!

Heidelberg Camp
Above left: the main
building; right: 'My
quarters.'
Left: 'A botanical
enthusiast'
Right: 'Baths. Hot and
cold sprays!'
Are they of Frank, these
two? And if not, why did
he have several copies of
each?

The British Amateur Dramatic Society presents their Grand Christmas Pantomime, Sindbad the Sailor, Heidelberg 1918. 'Score, dialogue, costumes, music and orchestra of over 20 instruments.'

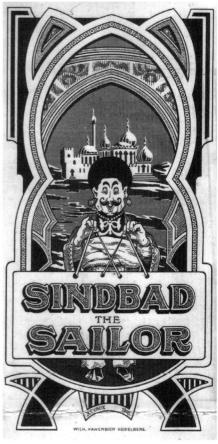

Fürstenberg Parade.

This remarkable photograph shows a prisoner's-eye view of the camp's perimeter wire; a German, perhaps the driver of the car, can be seen in the centre, behind the picket fence and, behind him and to his left a German soldier in the classic Pickelhaube helmet. 'Monday, 11 November 1918: Armistice signed. At 1pm a car arrived with several revolutionaries, all soldiers, not officers. Car had a red flag (40 H.P. Benz), belonged to Duke of Mecklenberg-Strelitz.' It has not been possible to confirm the make and model of the car in the photo.

Dinner and dance given for officers working on the repatriation of British ex-prisoners-of-war, Copenhagen, Christmas 1918.

Chapter 12

Hanover

At Hanover we found ourselves back in civilization in a regular hospital with proper nurses, orderlies and doctors. Professor Schlanger, the famous surgeon, was chief and here we got invariably the best of attention and kind treatment. The food was much better and more of it, but even then I was always hungry for more, but we put on weight here and were at least warm and clean. There were five of us in a small ward and we found Lieutenant Evans[1], RFC, there, who had been thirteen months in that bed, paralyzed in both legs. He is in England now. The nurses were very kind and considerate but I shall never forget the sights in the dressing room. At Christmas we had extra food and heard speeches most warlike and much singing of fine quality.

My arm began to mend on January 4th, when they put a tube in it and also poulticed it daily, and from that day it steadily but slowly improved. It had to be dressed every day and this was a very painful business. About January 20th when they took the arm out of splints and the doctor proceeded to try to bend the joints about, the pain was excessive and, if you did not squeak, he thought he was not hurting. At any rate, after it was all over I sat down on a chair and contentedly fainted.

To Ida (received 25 February 1918)

Reserve Lazaret 1, Hanover, Germany, 3 January 1918
You will be glad to hear that I am on the mend, at last. My temperatures have gone, the left arm is losing all its inflammation and I am not in any danger of losing the arm. The elbow joint may yet be stiff. That remains to be seen. The pleasure of being able to sleep again is coming back, for I have scarcely slept for five weeks, as I bar morphia. It was thoroughly septic after the fourth day of being wounded. The other three places where I was wounded have already healed up, as they were only grazes, luckily.

This is an excellent hospital, under one of the internationally famous German surgeons, and our treatment is most kind and considerate. Some day I will tell you of the other places we were at before we came here so providentially. But one must harp on the food question. It is quite necessary. You can find out in town just how much you can send, in number of parcels, weight etc. from British Red Cross or any of firms like Fortnum and Mason, Harrods, Army and Navy Stores, Selfridges, etc.

About bread: if sent from England, it will get mouldy unless in tins with oiled paper, etc., for I have seen it arrive here quite spoiled. There is another way to send it, and that is through a firm in Denmark, which...

(Whole page out by German censor)

P.S. I find I am allowed to write one more sheet. We are allowed to write two letters and four post cards a month only, which will be enough to send you any news and desires of mine. The German papers say there is to be a Commission of Enquiry[2] into the conduct, on our part, of the late battle (Cambrai). I am glad to hear it and wish I were there to give evidence. My being here is all a gross mistake on someone's part, for I obeyed orders to the letter and had not a ghost of a chance as it turned out. I attach not a bit of blame to myself in any way. I hope the family is not too disgusted, but please tell them what I say.

I can receive all the letters I like but remember to write nothing the censor will not approve of, or they are destroyed.

To Mr and Mrs P. A. Vans Agnew

Reserve Lazaret, Hanover, Germany, 9 January 1918

Ida has no doubt told you of what befell me on November 23rd last. Since then I have been having a bad time and no mistake. At present I am doing very well, but my left elbow is still most painful. I was wounded in four places by machine-gun bullets, but the other places were grazes and have quite healed. My capture was not my fault in any way, as I only obeyed orders.

We were told to go into enemy ground behind their lines and take a certain strong place and to hold it till our own infantry came and relieved us. So we went and I was leading the line and took the place and proceeded to hold on. It was a never-ending fight, it seemed, and after six hours of it, all my machine guns were knocked out and one of my big guns, and we were five wounded inside out of eight.

Then came enemy aeroplanes in numbers to spot us for their own artillery, and later came the shells. My affair had three direct hits from shells and was almost destroyed and we ought by rights to have all been killed. What was left of us then had to get out into the open and, while the men lay under cover for a few minutes, I looked for a place for us all to run to for safer cover, and it was then that I was hit three more times by machine-gun bullets.

We got to cover somehow and waited in hiding for our infantry. But they never came all day and we were, of course, captured. Our treatment, as prisoners, has always been kind but conditions have been very bad, owing to so many wounded, theirs and ours.

It was time something happened. Twenty-eight months at the front and three times wounded is about enough, or else I should have gone on and on, red hot, till I was buried for good and all in some shell hole. I never did miss a single fight and never would have, and I had tremendous luck, so I am sometimes relieved to be here. On November 20th we had a most successful day and gained all our far objectives. I captured, myself, two machine guns; and brought them back to our headquarters on top of the tank and then I, with Captain Porter and his tank, guarded and saved the most important bridgehead in the town. We captured and held it till our infantry came, an hour and a half later. So I was practically told by my colonel that I would get a Bar to my MC, but being captured three days later may cancel it. (It did.) Out of sight, out of mind!

We are only allowed to write two letters and four postcards a month and can only write in pencil. The pin-holes in the paper are because, with only one hand, the paper slips about and I pin it down to cardboard so as to be able to write. I can receive any amount of letters, no limit being given, so please write, all of you, to the above address.

I have done my level best all through and like Stevenson 'my damndest', and here I am as reward. At once I began to learn German. I find it most engrossing and a great way to forget troubles and kill time. There are swarms of Russian prisoners everywhere and I have had great practice talking to them. It all comes back fast.

To Ida (received 24 February 1918)

Kriegsgefangenen Sendung, Reserve Lazaret 1, Hanover, Germany, 19 January 1918
My arm came out of splints today and the wound is about healed, but the elbow joint and the wrist joint and fingers are very stiff and it will be some

time before they become supple, if ever. Officers of ours have been giving me hints about food for parcels and I am putting them down in order of importance. 1. Self raising Flour (5lb a month) 2. Fray Bentos tinned Bully Beef 3. Tinned Codfish Balls (American) 4. Desiccated Potatoes 5. Raw Haricot Beans 6. H. & P.'s Ration Biscuits 7. Dried Apricots. 8. Dripping 9. Bovril (in bottles) 10. Robinson's Patent Barley 11. Bologna Sausage 12. Potted meats 13. Egg powder 14. Curry powder Baking Powder. They tell me Plasmon Oats[3] is better than Quaker Oats.

I expect to hear from you in about a month from now and to get into touch once more, but it has been a long time since November 23rd. You would not call me 'fat as a pig' now for, no joke, I have had a bad time with my wounds and look back with relief. But we are most kindly treated here and the doctors are of the best. I am doing famously with learning German and getting on fast. You might send me novels to read at any time. Any good ones will do.

Chapter 13

Karlsruhe

I left Hanover hospital on 31 January, going to the Officers' Camp at Karlsruhe, arriving there on 1 February having passed through Cassel, Frankfurt (spent night there in a cold hut, with no blankets) and Heidelberg in trains (sometimes express) that were generally unheated and very cold. Traveled under escort of two smart Landwehr soldiers armed with rifles and bayonets, etc., in slippers, long blue Tommy's coat and cap-comforter[1]. Had lent my boots to Davey[2] to come to Karlsruhe in, a week before I left, expecting to get them back in time for my trip, by the escort, and lent my fine tin hat to Lieutenant Reader[3] who travelled with me. He was very lame and anaemic and dotty and not fit to travel at all. So I was a weird sight and did not care a rap.

Thursday, 31 January 1918
Travelled to Gutenheim by slow and ice cold train and changed. Waited one and a half hours IN THE PUBLIC WAITING ROOM WHERE WE WATCHED THE GERMAN PUBLIC EATING BLACK BREAD AND OTHER MISERABLE FOOD GLOOMILY. WENT ON to Frankfort IN ANOTHER ICE COLD TRAIN AND SLEPT IN A CELLAR. No blankets. Started at 7.28am and arrived at Karlsruhe BY EXPRESS train.

Monday, 4 February 1918
Saw the camp doctor and he examined my arm, told me my elbow would be always stiff and put me down for exchange to England or Holland or Switzerland. Invited to tea and bridge to quarters of two colonels (Troughton[4] and Baldwin[5]) and Major Morris[6] of D. Battalion Tanks. Had a fine tea and made ten marks at bridge, playing a mark a hundred.

Tuesday, 5 February 1918
Went to dentist in camp to get a front tooth put in. Must go again on Thursday. At this camp are French and Italian officers equal numbers, averaging perhaps a hundred of each; a few Belgians and one Servian

Colonel; among the British are many airmen, some few Naval officers and a few Transport and Merchant Skippers. These last hard-looking old specimens, ALL CAPTURED BY THE GERMAN RAIDER 'WOLF'[7]. There are two roll calls a day – one at 10am one at 4pm. Lights out at 9pm.

Wednesday, 6 February 1918
Having wonderfully fine weather. For weeks past, cold, frosty and dry. Our part of a big hut has seven beds, all occupied, and some have more. Each day two of us act as cooks and orderlies. No breakfast is given at all by Germany so it has to be cooked by us. None of us get parcels but others, who do, help by general issues and we usually have porridge and make toast. Coffee can be bought at German canteen, with a little sugar; apples also, ONE MARK FOR FOUR, FIVE MARKS FOR ONE CUP SUGAR.

Thursday, 7 February 1918
These we cook into jam or bread pudding; great help. (Follows an account of the German food issue, which the German Censor had obliterated with blue indelible pencil. They are ashamed to own the truth.) WAR BREAD AND SKILLY SOUP, POTATOES AND CARROTS.

Friday, 8 February 1918
Yesterday was invited to tea by several English officers in receipt of parcels and had best meal since was captured. Plenty of white bread toast, butter, jam, tinned lobster and good tea with milk and sugar in spite of (here I had joked about German submarines allowing all this good food to come to us from home and it was indignantly obliterated in blue indelible pencil by the fat-headed censor.) Today I saw camp doctor and was again passed for internment in Switzerland or Holland.

Saturday, 9 February 1918
Was told today that it would mean Holland. Had an issue of clothes today free from the British Red Cross: cardigan, 1 pr pajamas, 1 suit under-clothing, 1 shirt, pr socks, 2 handkerchiefs and 2 white collars, all most excellent.

Sunday, 10 February 1918
Expect an issue of food tomorrow. Sent by our Red Cross. About eighty Italian officers left this camp yesterday, which nearly cleared them out. There are about one hundred French officers here and same number of British. Our

Flying Corps officers outnumber the rest. Church service was held today, twice, so I am told. Last night was the regular weekly concert by British and French talent. They are hugely enjoyed and help to kill monotony.

Monday, 11 February 1918
Today we had the British food issue; four big hard biscuits, one tin of bully beef, 1½lb tin of cheese, ½lb tin of dripping, and ¼lb of cocoa. The biscuits and bully are to come three times a week and the rest weekly. This is all, of course, for men not getting any parcels. A most excellent issue. Was invited to supper this evening. Hot tinned meat with plenty of fried potatoes, toast and butter, cocoa, rice pudding and tinned fruits with a tin of cream.

Tuesday, 12 February 1918
There is a library here with quite a good lot of books of fiction, travel, study, etc. You sign for a book as usual. Two French billiard tables are in the concert hut and are well patronized; also a piano there, and several officers play violins; officers who play or act well are kept here permanently to get up concerts, etc. There is a small permanent staff of British officers to look after issues of food, library, church and so on, and one officer translates all of interest in German newspapers, including our official communiqués, and writes it all down in books in Reading Room.

Wednesday, 13 February 1918
This is a great help with the news of the world and the war. Of course, it is German news and must be taken with salt. Flags were flying on the streets yesterday in honor of the Russian peace. Much good will it do them! Had an issue of one tin of bully beef and four biscuits today. Had a false alarm of an air raid today; sirens and whistles are most loudly blown in the town to drive people to cover. Most of us stood out in the open to watch for our or French planes.

Thursday, 14 February 1918
This camp is in a small park in the middle of the City itself. It is so placed purposely, so as to keep French planes from bombing the town; it does not cause such a result. Am keeping up my German every day, making good headway. New officers keep coming every day or two.

Friday, 15 February 1918
Weather turned cold and fine. We have three thin blankets on each bed and sheets of a kind. The mattress and pillow are straw-stuffed. Can be fairly warm and cannot really complain. Had an issue of one tin of bully and four big hard biscuits today. They open all this when issued, and HAND THEM TO US ON GOLD PLATES AND VELVET CUSHIONS. Played bridge with the colonels and Major Morris.

Saturday, 16 February 1918
On the 14th I received a letter from Geneva saying they had forwarded my telegram to Ida on February 8th – so that is very satisfactory. Borrowed Morley's *Recollections* in two volumes from a friend and find them grand reading. The library here charges six marks for upkeep and the buying of new books, etc. and there is a deal of good reading in it, and I have always the German language to fall back on. After dark I take an hour's good sharp walk for exercise and because lights are out at 9pm.

Sunday, 17 February 1918
Have written two letters and three post cards already and am sending last of my allowance to Ida today to ask for immediate postage of *The Times*, as soon as she hears of my being interned. Another false alarm of an Allied air raid today. Sirens and whistles blew and nothing happened. Looks like 'wind up'. Fine cold, clear weather.

Wednesday, 20 February 1918
My last postcard to Ida was returned to me today, officially, as I had exceeded the limit of two letters and four post cards per month. Irritating, but true!

Thursday, 21 February 1918
Weather broke – rain and SW winds. My beloved pair of boots arrived from Hanover today, just in time for the weather. Now, with my tin hat, I have a complete uniform, such as it is. Moved to a three-bed room in a different hut, with Captain Dickinson[8] of Indian Cavalry and RFC (pilot) and Captain Johnston[9], RFC (observer). Both wounded, crippled, about like me, and booked for internment in Holland or Switzerland.

Friday, 22 February 1918

Still squally weather and rainy. Boots great joy. Our room snug. Good stove to ourselves, and spring mattresses instead [of] straw ones on boards. Nice and quiet, too. Other hut for eight had very noisy neighbors every night till midnight. Have a delightful little French orderly who tends us tirelessly. Two Russian orderlies here too, who will wash clothes for us, and two British orderlies who bring us oatmeal and bread to sell at reasonable prices. We are in clover.

Tuesday, 26 February 1918

Was photoed today; once with officers of my old hut and once in an international photo. I was given the place of honor in centre, seated. Captain Dickinson got three parcels today. Terrific excitement to us. Hurried off to draw them and found they were all <u>books</u>. Tottered back, dumbfounded.

Thursday, 28 February 1918

Rain all day. Last day of month. Can write more letters and post cards tomorrow. All officers here had to sign a declaration that we were under martial law as to destruction of German crops or any agricultural arrangements. Not much use to us here! No letters. Captain Tragett[10], who wrote from Münster Lager on December 9th and sent address of Soltau, 3605, exactly as I did, received a letter today from his home. He had been officially declared 'killed' for a month before his people knew he was alive.

To Ida (received 4 May 1918)

Officers Prisoners' Camp, Karlsruhe, Germany, 1 March 1918
So far I have had no letters from you or anyone else, and no parcels and here it is the first of March. A long time from 23 November 1917. But in a week I expect bread parcels from Berne because chaps who wrote a week ahead of me got some today. You must not think we are starving, though, by any means, for at this camp we manage grandly. The Red Cross issue of food and clothes to officers per week is good and, added to the official issue, keeps us better fed than ever I was in the hospitals. It is monotonous; bread, porridge, bully beef and rice and biscuits are the main supplies; but there is enough, and that is everything. I have also got my beloved boots back, which I had lent to another chap. We have no definite news of our last and final Medical Board for internment but it is most heavily rumoured to be

coming here very soon. As soon, please, as you hear from me that I am in Holland, or Switzerland, send me your daily Times *and any other papers or magazines you care to.*

My left arm is of course better and less painful, but the elbow joint is still very stiff and rigid and I begin to doubt if it will ever move again. Nevertheless I am very glad and very lucky to be alive at all. The enclosed photos were taken here a few days ago. The small group comprises the men I was in hospital with at various places, and the large one is an international group. They insisted on my sitting in the place of honour. On my right is an Italian Major, on his right a French Captain. On my left a Servian Colonel, on his left a Belgian Captain. Another Italian Captain, with a beard stands behind and a tall Servian is in the extreme rear. The rest are all British and friends. In the small group the Flying Officer on the outside opposite to me, is to live with me in internment. He is a Canadian, Golding[11] by name, a bank manager in Toronto. He crashed behind the German lines, and, literally, broke his back. Now he can get about, slowly and cautiously, and is improving by degrees. Very nice fellow in all ways. If you have not sent any of my kit yet, please hold it until I get to Holland or Switzerland or, failing that, to some permanent camp. Kit floating about looking for an owner might sink somewhere. Did you ever get the Scribner *for last August I wrote to you about? If so please send me one when I am interned – with the* Times, *etc. About pipe tobacco, please send me ¼lb a week of 'John Cotton' and get it and the cigarettes sent out 'in bond'. It is far cheaper and any tobacconist worth the name can arrange it for you. I am systematically working at German and French now, and with my Russian, which I have brushed up wonderfully since my capture, I shall soon be fair at these languages; perhaps best at Russian.*

Friday, 1 March 1918
Still wet and cloudy; heavy rains at night, but warm. Good many French officers left this morning. In evening was told a parcel had come for me yesterday which had not been posted up. Went in bounds and found a packet of cigs, from Ida, sent January 25th to Soltau 3605 (Münster Lager) and forwarded directly here, missing Hanover. Great excitement ensued. Wrote Ida a letter enclosing photos of self in two groups and one of donkey and parcel cart.

Sunday, 3 March 1918

Rainy, muggy day; warm and very close. Spent day on French grammar and cooking. Cooked oatcakes fried in dripping. Great success. After dark, walked about three miles. Round the circle in the grounds is 150 yards, paced, and twelve times go, roughly, to a mile. Am quite fit, except for the arm. We manage to buy from various orderlies, oatmeal, rice and biscuits, enough to keep us going. Got ¼lb of tea today.

Monday, 4 March 1918

Rained all night steadily, drizzling. Same today. Received a parcel of two loaves of good white bread from Copenhagen which arrived yesterday. This is the best bread sent to prisoners of war. Went before the doctor again for internment, as per order this morning. But he waved me away and said, 'No need, you are going.' Accent on 'You'. And I saw my name marked by blue pencil. 'Int'. Looks a certainty! No letters from home.

Tuesday, 5 March 1918

Cleared up, bright and fine and colder. No letters or parcels still. My letters will come in a batch, no doubt, from long back and recent ones, together. Today arrived about sixty officers captured by the German sea-raider *Sea Wolf* – British, Japanese, all sorts and ranks. Three Australian Army captains in room next us; they were captured seven months ago and have been cruising ever since. Travelled 20,000 miles since were captured on coast of New Guinea, mine-laying. Fifteen RFC officers left yesterday.

Wednesday, 6 March 1918

No letters, or parcels. Today more 'Sea Wolves' arrived. Every allied nationality is now represented here. They are all skippers and mates and engineers of captured and sunken ships. One is a Japanese Lieutenant Commander of Navy, captured on a liner. Many of the skippers are old men from sailing ships and cargo boats of all kinds. Some were held on the German ship as long as a year. They all say the officers captured were well treated, the men not so well, and speak well of the skill shown by German captain in evading capture and laying mines in tight places. It certainly was a most creditable piece of work.

Thursday, 7 March 1918

No letters today but received four parcels, two food parcels and one of cigs from Ida, all in good order. And one parcel of two loaves from Red Cross, Copenhagen; these were mouldy, green, and a mouse had lived in one. Saved some bits and ends for puddings. My first food parcels from home. Coffee, tea, milk, sugar, br and wh, tins of ham and bacon, lamb and peas, etc., baked beans, spaghetti, dripping, little chocolate, mustard, pepper, salt – no butter, jam, oatmeal, rice and vegetables. But most heartily welcome – great jubilation.

Chapter 14

Heidelberg

Monday, 11 March 1918

We were warned at 6am that we would go about noon today to Heidelberg and go we did after much photographing and goodbying. There were forty-eight of us for exchange or internment and most of the Wolves. Quite a big party of about seventy. Arrived at Heidelberg at 2.15pm and were marched, after usual delays, to the officers' camp about a mile and one-half out of the town. This is a big German barracks with grounds enclosed by wire: two big buildings and outhouses and about a dozen huts of usual type. Johnston, Dickinson and I got a three-bed room in No.3 Barracks. Much delay in being searched and in signing usual forms, etc. Seems to be a fine camp.

Tuesday, 12 March 1918

Same continuous fine weather. Cold at night with sunny days. About 500 British officers here and good many French. Many of them, most in fact, have been here for months and get parcels, so the camp is full of food in plenty. Everyone very kind, gave all the newcomers a good dinner last night with good pipe tobacco, cigs and cigars. Today we got a grand food issue from the Common Box, to which receivers of parcels contributed readily for the less fortunate. All sorts of tins of succulent food and sugar and milk. Invitations poured in to tea and dinner and breakfast next day, and I have had several fine repasts.

Wednesday, 13 March 1918

Yesterday the commandant, a fine old officer, gave us a speech, interpreted, about camp rules and general behavior. There are two roll calls a day, 10.30am and 4.50pm, more or less, and a bugle horn affair, which they call a *'tube'*, warns ten minutes before. All go out into the open parade ground and it is soon over.

Here we have a cold spray bath at five pfennigs a time every day till 4pm. Also hot bath only twice a month, 15th and 30th, which are great hardships, especially after Karlsruhe.

Friday, 15 March 1918
Colder than ever today, but fine. Snow threatening. The huts without coal were not very pleasant and I regret Karlsruhe where there was plenty of coal. This was bath day (one hot spray bath every two weeks) and an event. At Karlsruhe, three hot sprays a week. Am personally more pleased with K camp. Received one parcel of bread, two loaves, from Copenhagen. It had just begun to mould in spots. This bread is made from rice largely, while the Berne bread is made from flour and rye. Our mess of three lives quite happily now. No letters.

To Ida (received 15 May 1918)

Offizier - Gfangenenlager Heidelberg, 15 March 1918
Your first letter reached me only yesterday, dated 17 January, and not the long letter you mention. I was so glad to hear from you and to feel that you and the family do not feel aggrieved at my capture. I fairly loathe being captured but in my circumstances it was inevitable if the snails had to leave their shells perforce. I am afraid Birnie and Mercer[1] were killed for I saw disastrous signs, which pointed at them, after my capture, and I have heard no word about them from this side. Please write to Miss Mercer and tell her that I have had no word about him (her brother, who was in Birnie's section) but it is possible that I may yet. If alive they should have been heard from; if in hospital they must be very badly hurt not to have written for so long. I have drawn money on Holt from here as it was absolutely necessary to get things and food at times, and prices are terribly high here.

My arm is as rigid in elbow joint as ever, and quite refuses to move at my requests and apart from that, I am well and what may be called 'contented'. Can you get for me all the casualties and promotions of our Corps, from the London Headquarters since my capture and send on to me?

Sunday, 17 March 1918
Glorious weather. Blazing sun and no winds. Sit and walk in it all day. Have made arrangements to work at French with an old French officer who is working on English. Played two games of chess with Captain Groves[2],

RNAS, three years prisoner, and beat him both games. Was invited to dinner by Lieutenant Paravicini[3], son of the famous cricketer. Very nice boy, indeed. Gave me most pleasant evening. Archie guns near here fired six rounds near an aeroplane up very high, in afternoon, but the plane went on and dropped no bombs here.

Monday, 18 March 1918
Was invited to the pantomime tonight by members of British Amateur Dramatic Society (BADS), to see *Sinbad, the Sailor*. From 7pm to 10.15pm. Good orchestra, mostly French, but conducted by Lieutenant Bullock who composed much of the music and songs.

Tuesday, 19 March 1918
A really good performance with good costumes and well staged. Scenery carefully prepared and painted. The chorus girl imitations most lifelike, likewise the girl programme-sellers. No letters today. This was my day to get a French lesson from Commander Richard[4], of a French Colonial Regiment. One day I talk English to him and the next he talks French to me and we criticize each other. He has served in French Tonkin, New Guinea, New Caledonia, Madagascar, etc. and was captured, wounded, in 1914 at Liège.

Wednesday, 20 March 1918
Weather stayed warm, but more cloudy. Very good on the whole. Received the equivalent to five pounds from Holt and Co. through the Camp Office, and got 127.60 marks at rate of 25.52 marks to the one pound sterling. Exchange was recently as low as 22 marks. Played chess with Lieutenant Fry[5], supposed to be best chess player here and beat him after long hard game, which he opened with Four Knights opening; I queened a pawn finally. Today I received a service cap from Keenan and Phillips with Tank Corps badge intact, luckily. This evening took Major Richard (Fr) to see the Pantomime again; he was much pleased. It was the final night and the performers turned themselves quite loose.

Friday, 22 March 1918
Cloudy, inclined to rain but not cold. Received today two parcels of bread (four loaves) from Copenhagen, in splendid condition and a small clothes parcel from Ida. This contained some socks and a wool helmet from Minor and Marian in Florida. Most acceptable they will be. Also two handkerchiefs,

four collars and two ties, all khaki; also a Boot Bag. I cannot place the responsibility for the last named.

Heard today that the Great German Offensive began yesterday, in big type. Germans here are much excited.

Saturday, 23 March 1918
Seems strange to be in the sun on dry grass and read, while a big push is really on. German papers claim 16,000 prisoners and 200 guns and all our front lines on 80 kilometre front. If our attacks were held up at enemy front lines on the first day, we considered the attack a failure, for the element of surprise has been lost and measures can be taken, more or less, safely, to throttle the attack.

Sunday, 24 March 1918
White frost at night, but a beautiful sunny day to follow. German newspapers claim now 25,000 prisoners and 400 guns and (only) 300 machine guns which latter seems nonsense. More field guns than MGs! They claim capture of Ribécourt and Flesquières, etc., which we got on the Cambrai front first glorious day. Looks as if they have only flattened the salient we formed towards Cambrai and not much else. To say nothing of their own losses or casualties. Read Justin McCarthy's *Short History of Our Own Times*, from 1880 to Queen V's death.

Monday, 25 March 1918
Fine, but windy and colder. This is a p.c. writing day and I wrote one to Ida. Every five days you can write. In each month on the 5th and 10th a p.c., on the 15th a letter, on the 20th and 25th, a p.c. and another letter on the 30th. Got no letters or parcels today. Billiard tournament began today; there are some very fine players here. Our official communiqué today is quite reassuring. An article by Philip Gibbs, translated from German papers, shows that there is no reason to feel alarmed and that the enemy lost heavily. This evening about fifty British officers arrived from Karlsruhe. Found friends.

Tuesday, 26 March 1918
Received four parcels; one from Berne (two loaves bread, fresh) one food from Ida, one containing a wool scarf (donor unknown), one from Mrs Micky (two pks cards and two bridge score pads), most thoughtful and necessary, the latter. This evening about fifty more officers came from Karlsruhe,

British, Jap, French and Italian and two Portuguese. They have emptied that camp to make room for new officers from the offensive.

Wednesday, 27 March 1918
War news is not unduly alarming. The enemy claims a great deal but no one here believes half of it. They claim Albert and to have forced the old Somme defences, but we must have some reason for any such advance of theirs. Billiard tournament finished at 9pm. Lieutenant Fry, won it easily, giving the next best a big handicap. Wonderfully fine player!

Thursday, 28 March 1918
Received five letters today. All from home and not from Ida. Dates run from January 16th to February 9th, all arriving same day. Medical Swiss Commission is believed to be coming next week and the camp is full of cripples (like me) for it. No parcels yesterday or today. We are well enough off for food though and are able to help out the less fortunate.

Friday, 29 March 1918
Rainy and unpleasant, but not really cold. Have begun French with a new French officer, who knows very little English. From 5 to 6pm, we walk about and converse in spasms of appalling French and English and then we correct each other and laugh much. From 4 to 5pm, I go to another French officer who is going to teach me Spanish. This morning (Friday) a be-spectacled typical old German bookman, with his small son in a sailor suit, who speaks English, came on his weekly trip with a great variety of books of all kinds and languages. Novels also. Books of art and full of artistic drawings. Also grammars and dictionaries in every kind of language. I bought an English–Spanish grammar.

Saturday, 30 March 1918
Cloudy and rainy, but not bad. Very busy on Spanish in morning, preparing exercises for my teacher. Have met two French officers in the camp who knew Razzie (Captain Gower[6]) very well in various camps. They were delighted to hear he was in Holland. Keep my French up also from 4 to 5pm, most instructive, and amusing, too. In evening went to cinema in camp. This is the second film I have seen here; the first were all German and very stodgy, but these were American and quite lively. All the descriptive talks are in German and the long and ugly words are treated with derisive hoots from audience.

Sunday, 31 March 1918
Rainy and low clouds, but not cold. Easter Sunday. Worked hard at Spanish and find it very easy after Russian and German, or even French. The study of languages eats up time and keeps one fit in every way. At 7.30pm went to a French orchestral concert in camp. Orchestra of over twenty violins, cellos, a piano and a horn or two. English officer plays the piano and two English officers are violinists. Really good orchestra. A few songs were sung, very poorly, and a Jap doctor (naval) played his national instrument, a kind of clarionet, sounded like a bunch of excited guinea pigs, but we encored him three times and laughed far too much.

Monday, 1 April 1918
April Fool's Day in full swing. Still rainy, but not cold. Sports began at 2pm. Throwing cricket ball was won by Lieutenant Haight, a burly Canadian baseball pitcher. Of course! Long jumps and high jumps will be won by an Englishman, Locke, who is a really fine jumper. The French and Belgians try hard but they are not in his class at all. Going to cinema again tonight. Easter festivities are the rule. No parcels or letters given out today as it is a big German holiday. Yesterday (Easter Sunday) every officer was given a bottle of white wine (Hock) by the Kommandatur.

Wednesday, 3 April 1918
Clear, fine, cool day, with bursts of hot sunshine. Ground still too wet for sports. Received three parcels today. Two were very old food parcels from Ida, January 16th and 23rd. The January 16th one was all broken up and almost all missing; the other was crumpled and torn, but still [all] there I think. The third parcel was clothes from the tailor, a new tunic, very fine with Tank Corps badges and buttons, a new pair breeches and a lovely thin pair of dress puttees. Played my first game of billiards, French game, and by a superhuman break of nine beat my man at the post; my arm is a nuisance.

Thursday, 4 April 1918
Beautiful sunny day and warm. Received a parcel of three loaves from Berne. All fresh and good. We give away a good deal of bread and other things to chaps who get no parcels yet; I am looking after an old Skipper, who was captured by the 'Wolf'. He is seventy-four years old and a grand old chap. Another old boy over sixty, also a Skipper, taken by the 'Wolf', has been torpedoed three times. He is oozing with tropical malaria but keen to return

to sea and try to be torpedoed again. Received letter from Mrs M. Sports in heats were run today and finals to be decided tomorrow, weather permitting. The foreigners are not showing up well. Britishers will capture everything, it seems.

Friday, 5 April 1918
Managed to finish sports today. It was a clean sweep of 'firsts' for the British. A few 'seconds' and 'thirds' went to French officers. No one had trained a day, so conditions were even. A lot of them are hobbling round today, very stiff and disgusted. No letters or parcels. It is quite credibly reported that the Dutch and Swiss frontiers were both closed on March 20th and that they will be closed three weeks. That means we only get parcels and letters which are in this country now. War news still good – especially in Messpot.[7]!

Saturday, 6 April 1918
Went to a French piece today in the theatre, *Adventures of M. Tic*. Could follow the dialogue quite well. Excellently acted and staged. The French act so much better than we do, and go into it so faithfully and with so much vim and spirit.

Monday, 8 April 1918
Today played chess with a young Canadian, Harvey[8]. He is a sort of prodigy at it. Played me blindfolded, i.e. he turned his back to the board and we called the moves to him. He made a few errors which we kindly pointed out, but he never looked round, corrected them, and beat me in the end.

Tuesday, 9 April 1918
Last night was the Fancy Dress Ball from 7.30 to 10.30pm. All kinds of quite amazing costumes. Some hired in the town, majority made in the camp; many made of paper of all colors. About twenty ladies in ravishing garb and about one hundred on the floor, all told. Good deal of white wine was drunk and the end most hilarious but not in the least uproarious. The paper costumes collapsed at the end and a charming 'lady' turned into a muscular male in a few secs. Prizes were given and we, the spectators, voted for our choices.

Wednesday, 10 April 1918
Fine, warm and sunny. Received two loaves of bread from Copenhagen. Bread was good, but edges starting to green mould. No letters at all. This

afternoon played tennis from 3 to 4pm. Borrowed shoes and racket. Tennis is played on the group system. Twelve men to a group, and there are three full-sized courts of fine rock and gravel; each group has the three courts for one hour each day. Tomorrow we go on from 4 to 5pm, and so on. Very much out of practice and finding left arm much in the way, but it is good exercise and I can manage well enough.

Friday, 12 April 1918
Heard from Major Henshall, my Company Commander, yesterday. His letter was dated 8 February; tells me that Birnie, Evans[9], Mercer and Simpson[10] are killed, at any rate still missing. Christmas[11], wounded at home. Myself and Dalby prisoners and wounded. Seven officers from seven tanks. Only one tank returned to camp (Doyle and Law of my section, the only officers to return). Clean sweep almost, that day. Received two loaves from Copenhagen. Went to an English play in evening, 'Arms and the Man'. Quite good, considering it was in a prisoners' camp. Scenery superfine. Our acting does not touch the French, though.

Saturday, 13 April 1918
In morning the Germans were out in force, drilling just outside our camp. A mixed lot of uniforms but all good and in good order. They have a lot of machine guns always, which is part of their battalion drill, it seems. There is much shouting of orders and noise. No letters, no parcels. There is a Commission coming on Monday to examine French and Italian aspirants for Switzerland. Much commotion in the French and Dago quarters.

Sunday, 14 April 1918
Played tennis from 11 to 12am. Can hold my own, I find. About 11.30am, a German aeroplane that was flying around had to make a hasty landing and landed just outside our fence. Nearly tipped over and smashed his propeller. POOR FELLOW, SO SORRY! News came today of enemy drive at Plug Street Wood and advance therefrom. None too good but not fatal at all. He laughs best, etc. Very familiar country to me and should be hard to capture without heavy losses.

Monday, 15 April 1918
War news shows that the big attack has struck our real defences by Neuve Eglise, and the hills and valleys, well planned and arranged as far back as 1915. Lovely country of machine-gun defences. Beautiful fields of fire.

To Ida (received 21 May 1918)

15 April 1918

My slacks have not yet come, and will you please send me some towels. Medium sized rough ones, please, for the daily cold spray, and some more shaving soap. As soon as you get my wire from a neutral country, please, send me a pair of tennis shoes (no.7), some thinner socks, and a tennis racket. Please get one of weight 14oz and with a thin handle. Not these ones with big and thick handgrips. We are still awaiting the final Medical Board and know nothing of it, of course. I have heard from my Major, a few days ago, that of nine officers who went into action, four were killed or have never been heard of since, another is wounded and at home, Dalby and myself are out here as prisoners, both wounded. So, you see that it was a very strenuous fight. Our company is not displeased with us. Only two officers got back. War news is serious but not in the least disquieting to us. We have faith in the final finish!

Tuesday, 16 April 1918

War news today is distinctly good. We are evidently causing very heavy casualties to the enemy, and knowing the country around Neuve Eglise so well, I can quite believe it. My refugee friends there must be in a bad plight again. Hot bath today.

Wednesday, 17 April 1918

Played tennis from 8 to 9am. Yesterday the time of the camp was advanced one hour. No warning was given of course. Went for a walk outside today with a party of British officers and two Italian officers. You sign your parole before starting and it lasts just for the walk. A German officer comes along and two soldiers, unarmed. We went about four miles through some villages and along the Neckar Valley. Very fertile ground, many fruit trees, gardens and grain crops. Reported we leave for Aachen (Aix-la-Chapelle) on 27th to meet the Commission.

Thursday, 18 April 1918

Played tennis from 7 to 8am. Most energetic. Then the usual cold spray and breakfast at 9. Have agreed to give a lecture or talk on the Kirghese Steppes on Sunday at 2.15pm, and Dickinson is going to draw a fine map for the occasion, enlarged from an atlas in camp. These lectures occur every Sunday afternoon, as a rule, and embrace most of the world and all sorts of subjects, and are very well attended.

Friday, 19 April 1918

Helped Dickinson with the map of the Steppes most of day. Too cold to enjoy anything much. In evening went to the French operetta called *Vertu, Vertu!* The best private theatrical I ever saw. All local: dialogue, music, orchestra, scenery, costumes, etc. A curtain raiser first, part English and part French, was most funny and well acted. Written by two French officers who have also learned English in captivity. The mistakes of a French interpreter, who pretends to know English in a French hotel, with English guests. *Vertu, Vertu*, was amazing. All the music composed and orchestrated in camp; the play written in camp also. Well acted, well sung and well played all round.

Sunday, 21 April 1918

This afternoon gave my talk on the Kirghese Steppes, etc. to a good house (about 150) and they seemed to enjoy it. Dickinson's map was a great feature and I am keeping it.

Monday, 22 April 1918

This morning at roll call, my name was called to prepare to leave tomorrow morning at 9.45am to meet the Medical Board. Great excitement. Intense! Those for England, amputation cases, etc., were to come in a few days. Our cases are for internment or back to camp again. Packed up and generally got ready. After dark there was much celebrating done and lots of noise made.

Tuesday, 23 April 1918

Left Heidelberg Camp at 9.45am after much handshaking and cheering from the fellows left behind. Rainy, bad day. There were twenty-five of us; those of us able to marched to the station and we left at about noon. Travelled up the Rhine all the way to Köln (Cologne) via Mayence. Most enjoyable scenery. The river and river traffic, hills, castles (operatic), vineyards up the steep southern slopes, and general view of the rich Rhine Valley. Arrived at Köln at about 10pm and were conducted to a Red Cross place in the station with beds (and lice).

Wednesday, 24 April 1918

Started at 5am, arrived at Aachen about 8.50am. Were marched to a big sort of hospital place not far away and assigned a bed, etc. Very good treatment all round. Spent the day expecting to see the Commission at any time. Several hundred Tommies here also, all on the same business. Most of them are the Old Army, prisoners of 1914, and they have great tales to tell. A meatless day.

Thursday, 25 April 1918
Rainy weather every day and all day. It will give the great Offensive some mud to deal with, something we always had in ours. Waited, all day again in vain. Food, coffee (?) at 7am, brown bread (quite good), honey (?); at midday, brown bread, oatmeal gruel, noodles, potatoes plus cabbage and sausage. Quite good and sufficient. At 3.30pm, coffee and bread and honey; at 7pm, more gruel, bread, potatoes and sausage. On the whole good food. Better than the hospital at Hanover.

Friday, 26 April 1918
At 10am we officers began to go before the Commission. Went in alphabetical order and I was No.30. There were five doctors, two Dutch, one Swiss and two German. Very perfunctory examination. Twisted my arm about, asked my age and seemed contented to send me to Holland, but another German doctor came, twisted me some more, and then, I think, turned me down. So I expect to return to camp.

Saturday, 27 April 1918
Better weather, luckily, for at 9am I was on the list called out to return to the camp at Heidelberg. Ten out of twenty-five were rejected and go back at once. We finally left about noon, changed at Köln, stopped at Wiesbaden from 10pm to 6am in a Red Cross place. Slept on floor on a quilt, and slept well.

Sunday, 28 April 1918
Went on as far as Darmstadt till about 9.30am. Stopped there till about noon in another Red Cross barn and had a meal of stockfish soup, noodles and meat stew and a glass of beer. We had some food from English parcels with us and got on quite well. The trip along the Rhine is delightful scenery and especially at this time of year. Arrived at Heidelberg about 2pm. Marched back to the dear old Lager. Great amusement among our friends there. This is my birthday, too, my fiftieth, and be hanged to it. Thunderstorm at night and heavy rain.

Monday, 29 April 1918

Lost our nice three-bed room in the hut and am in another hut, Captain Dickinson, Niall[12] and self, with seven Belgian officers. Am in a bunk up in the air above a lower one. A gymnastic feat to climb up for a one-armed sort of cripple. Went to see the camp doctor to demand some treatment for the arm, and he said he would 'propose' it and took our names. If they won't send us where we can get treatment, they must in all fairness do it themselves. I have had no treatment since end of March and arm is really no better.

Tuesday, 30 April 1918

Have moved into another hut, the hospital hut, with Niall and Johnston. Here there are five, all told, and comfortable beds. Saw the town doctor this morning. He passed us for the Commission at Aachen and is quite annoyed at so many coming back. It reflects on his professional opinion. He gave us another careful going over, and was more annoyed than ever. As he talks good English, this was easy to discover. He told us he would send us to the next Commission and seemed most willing to help us. So we may get away yet.

To Ida

1 May 1918

Your first long letter written on January 16th reached me on April 16th and that is the first and only letter from you since March 26th. I do not know on what system the postal affairs are handled in this country, but that is the result. That long letter of yours gave me a lot of much needed news and I thoroughly enjoyed it. Now, I have bad news for you. On April 23rd I left this camp to go before the Commission (Medical Board). It was a board without rhyme or reason and the examination was really a farce. Two of our worst cases were rejected and two with practically nothing the matter with them were passed for Holland and are in Holland by this time. The examination of all twenty-five of us did not occupy thirty minutes by the watch. My elbow is as stiff as ever and my shoulder, wrist and fingers still semi-stiff. They asked me my age also which apparently made no difference at all. So I am back at Heidelberg, arriving here on my fiftieth birthday and making the very best of a bad job. Since our return in fact yesterday, the doctor from the town, who passed us for the Commission, sent for us all and gave us another careful examination. He talks English well and did not tell us much but I gathered that he was quite annoyed at the action of the Commission in rejecting so many cases he had recommended. It certainly does reflect on his own professional opinions, and I gathered that he would send us before the next Commission, whenever that may be.

You mentioned in a letter that I was on some list in England for internment or repatriation. What does that mean, and what actual steps do they take, or is it a mere form? If there had been any justice about the findings of this Commission, I would not feel dissatisfied but as it stands, now, I feel entitled to a grievance.

(Note added by FVA: There were five doctors, four of them were neutrals and one was German. The latter was a bald-headed, grizzled old square-head, who said the final word. The four neutrals passed me. The German asked me what Corps I belonged to. I replied 'Tank Corps.' He whirled away from me and, with his back to me, said, 'Back to the Camp.' One friend, blind in the right eye, was passed for Holland; another, blind in the left eye, was refused! Another friend with a comic thumb was passed – nothing else wrong with him!)

Wednesday, 1 May 1918
Cannot get down to working on foreign languages yet, but have dug up a new French officer to practise our respective tongues. Went to a French musical comedy and parody in evening and enjoyed it hugely. They are wonderful at that kind of thing. War news is most encouraging. I am absolutely certain now that we shall win the war, hands down.

Thursday, 2 May 1918
Fine day with patches of sun now and then. Played tennis in evening from 5 to 6. Great for exercise and courts are really excellent. French orchestra (and four English, too) played 'Poet and Peasant' and Toreador (Carmen) this evening to a crowded house. It is amazing what a fine lot of musicians there are here. War news is grand. Our center at Arras has never moved at all in all this great attack and the enemy has done nothing of any strategic value, and has lost a great number of his men. Now, he will never break through!

Saturday, 4 May 1918
Nothing startling going on. Major Morris, A Battalion Tanks, and Captain Young[13], Rifle Brigade, tried to escape but were caught before getting

through the wire. They were sentenced to six days confinement. Very easy.
Got books and parcels, etc. I had a few words with the major through his
window till I was 'moved on'.

Tuesday, 7 May 1918
Hot, misty, steamy day. High winds at night, as a rule, now. This morning
eight officers (all friends) left for that idiotic Commission at Aachen, and
because they all should pass, being all wounded badly, I feel sure some will
be rejected. Played tennis in heat of day, and enjoyed it. My French teacher
is a Belgian officer[14]. He lives near Ypres in peace times and knows Neuve
Eglise well. His sister-in-law owns the brasserie (brewery) there. By this
time the brasserie looks like a parrot cage but I did not tell him so.

Thursday, 9 May, 1918
Cinema in evening. Poor films. Very heavy and lacking in humour except,
maybe, to a German.

To Ida

10 May 1918
*I have been to see a specialist down town here, yesterday, and he tells me I
shall get some electric massage two or three times a week. So that is all to
the good. I steadily keep repeating that my slacks have not come, in case
you should think otherwise, as I am so tired of wearing breeches and puttees
all the time. Summer is here. Hawthorn, lilacs, chestnuts, laburnum in full
bloom.*

Friday, 10 May 1918
In evening the BADS gave three short sketches. One by Conan Doyle, one
by W.W. Jacobs and the last a local spasm. Very good they were, all three.
Even the French were pleased. They had made a cardboard grandfather-
clock which ticked loudly.

Saturday, 11 May 1918
Rainy weather. Received a set of chess men and board from Mrs M. after a
very long delay in coming. Most thoughtful present. Also got a food parcel
from Lieutenant Clark[15] who had his left leg amputated at thigh and has
gone for England. He signed his parcels to me till he stops them at home.

Also got a letter from 'Boy'[16] most cheerful! Only hope he pulls through safely, as he is for the front. Bravo America!

Sunday, 12 May 1918
The tournament, open singles, begins tomorrow. I have entered and drawn Captain Gibou, French Artillery, as antagonist. He is twenty years younger and is good, and it looks blue for me. Weather permitting, this week will see some fun, as there are some very fine players here, especially one very big young French officer, Lieutenant Bayard[17]. He is almost first flight, to my mind, certainly out of top drawer.

Monday, 13 May 1918
Played Captain Gibou at 1.30pm. Very stiff to begin and he beat me 6-4, 3-6, 6-4, so he won all right. Very fine chap and a pleasure to play against. Long sets and good game and large and enthusiastic gallery.

Tuesday, 14 May 1918
These days, unless I am interfered with, I do an hour or over in morning on French with a French baron who talks English very well, also Russian, German, etc. Very fine chap, indeed. Then in evening, I teach English to a Belgian officer, who lisps badly, and incidentally pick up some excruciating French. This is a good chap, though, and tries hard.

Wednesday, 15 May 1918
Better day and tournament in full swing. Went at 9.30am down town to get arm treatment. Was put on several machines which tried the old fin quite severely, but beneficially, I hope. Walked down and back and enjoyed the many wisteria creepers just now in bloom. It is a gloomy looking nation, indeed! And a most beautiful old town and the river Neckar is most smiling scenery. Too bad!

To Mrs M.

15 May 1918
Ida writes to me that Micky has been wounded again (in the feet) and is now at home in hospital. I am very sorry to hear that and please tell him so. It might have been worse, of course, but all the same I am so sorry when anyone cannot be at the front itself. It is the only place, after all, when a

war is on. As for being stuck out here, words cannot and do not express my true feelings. Even Kirghese will not. I am getting treatment for my arm at present and I believe it will do a deal of good after a while, but it was a great disappointment being turned down by the Medical Commission. That was the final commission, it seems, and my chances are now very slim. Its workings were ludicrously unjust. One case, an officer who had lost a left eye was passed for Holland, the same day they rejected an officer who had lost his right eye and the poor chap, bewildered, returned with me. The chess men and board arrived a few days ago, thank you for them more than very much, and I have had several games on it already. There is one quite young Canadian who plays us all, blindfolded, and beats us, too.

G. (J. Pennington Gardiner) wrote me, quite seriously, that he had made arrangements 'to procure for me 300lb of maple sugar', to be sent out in 5lb packets. Isn't he delightful, and isn't that the real American spirit? I had sent him a message, half joking, to send me some maple sugar, with visions of a pound or two.

Your letters are a great treat and please continue, quite indefinitely.

All kinds of good wishes to Micky. Tell him to get well and go forth again, ad libitum[18].

Thursday, 16 May 1918
Tennis tournament pursues its sweltering course. Find it almost too hot in the huts for study and there are no shade trees in this camp. Food parcels come in regularly and a good thing, too, for we hear the frontier is closed again for some time and we may need reserves of food.

Friday, 17 May 1918
Hot and glorious. Am translating one of O. Henry's books, *The Voice of the City* into French, with the Baron, who much enjoys the American slang.

Saturday, 18 May 1918
Quite hot and sunny. Bayard is smashing his way to a victory, most certainly, and it is a treat to watch him at work. He uses all the strength he has on his strokes and he is a very large and perfectly made young chap. O. Henry continues to afford us much amusement. Play bridge in evenings a good deal.

Wednesday, 22 May 1918
Fine warm day. Went down with three other British officers and two French to the Stadthaus Hospital in Heidelberg for treatment on the arm; forty minutes walk to get there. Give you first 'radiant air' or 'hot air'. Your arm is in a kind of cardboard or canvas box with dry gas heat underneath, and you leave it there about one-half hour. Very good treatment. Then a massage for twenty minutes, then exercise on the machines. Then walk back. We are to go every Monday, Wednesday and Friday in future.

Friday, 24 May 1918
Left at 8.30am for more hospital treatment and we usually get back at about 1pm. See many German wounded down there and many crippled men; otherwise, the town looks normal enough.

Tuesday, 28 May 1918
Good, fine weather, and grand aerial observation. Rumors of a big German attack between Rheims and Soissons. Bigger the better, for the war will be sooner over and in our favor. This evening the French gave a dramatic performance, *'L'Idée de Mdlle Françoise'*, Delightful costumes, scenery, acting and spirit.

Wednesday, 29 May 1918
This evening ninety French and Belgian officers left for Switzerland from this camp; most of them were captured in 1914. Very pleased, but very quiet. Four years subdues them.

Thursday, 30 May 1918
Today some German staff officers came to inspect the camp. Not impressive people at all; rather the reverse. The place is all cleaned up and tidied beforehand. Just like our inspections, colonels or brigadiers at front and at home. All of them are farces and everyone knows it, I suppose. Two of the Belgian officers who left yesterday wore their swords still. They were from Liège. All Belgians captured there were allowed by the Germans to keep their swords. Rather nice thing to happen in this disgusting war!

Saturday, 1 June 1918
Rather amusing incident has occurred. Trouble between an English and French officer over cooking pots on the common stove. E.O. says F.O. moved

his pot and then pushed him, and E.O. got best of pushing match. F.O. went to F. Commandant and demanded a duel. F.C. agreed solemnly. E.O. was quite willing; has been sixteen years in Army and eight in Cavalry and likes sabres and pistols. It is up to F.O. and we are awaiting his next move. [FVA did not say what happened afterwards.]

Wednesday, 5 June 1918
Went to hospital down town in morning and much enjoy the walk and view of the people and gardens and flowers; roses, standard and climbing, do very well in this climate. It is a very orderly, clean and pleasant town, but the people do not look either well or happy. They look gloomy and most discontented. This long war must be disconcerting to people on strict rations. In evening, a Zeppelin sailed about over us and Heidelberg for two hours. Very fine! And a perfect mark for archie!

Monday, 10 June 1918
The German crops look quite perfect here. Potatoes and all vegetables. Any amount of fruits, apples, pears, cherries, currants, etc. Grain, too, is in perfect condition, wheat, rye, barley, etc. and all roots. So far the season for agriculture has been ideal.

Thursday, 13 June 1918
At 8.30am went for a walk with sixty other officers (all English and two French). All on parole, of course. Went up the mountainous molehill nearby and got a good view of the town and river Neckar. Could see Mannheim away off west. Woods are beautiful up the hill–slopes, and the same kinds of tree and undergrowth as in Virginia. It might have been a bit of the Blue Ridge.

To Ida

15 June 1918
Will you, please, send me enough good sole leather to sole and heel a pair of boots, as it is impossible to get here, and again I will mention my unfortunate 'slacks' and the pair of boots which went astray and have not turned up.

Yesterday a Swiss Commission came here for the French, and, to my astonishment, I and three other British officers were sent for to be examined by them. They put me down for 'Internment' as before; but this commission,

*being for the French, has no power to send us anywhere. All they can do is
to send us before another commission at Aachen where we may be refused
again as I am convinced that the commission there is all guesswork. Still it
is another chance and I shall leap at it if it comes.*

*The Prisoners of War Conference at the Hague is most interesting for us.
Even if they agree on the same terms as the German–French agreement we
shall be much better off. In this agreement, officers and men of over forty-
eight are interned after twelve months captivity. I have put in nearly seven
months already.*

*In the meantime we are having delightful weather and, in this camp, we
have a quite pleasant time; enough food, enough exercise, enough to read,
and plenty of fun, concerts, cinemas, chess, bridge, tennis, so do not think I
am languishing in sorrow.*

Monday, 17 June 1918
Young, very young, German officer in hospital told us the war would go
on for five years yet and then, he said, the French and all our Allies would
abandon England. About time, too, it seems to me! We smiled upon him,
mysteriously.

Wednesday, 19 June 1918
Went to hospital down town. To the young German officer patients there
who try to patronize us as to the war generally, we answer in German, 'It is a
good war and I am well satisfied.' That always shuts them up. And it is quite
true after all.

Friday, 21 June 1918
Big meeting of British officers to discuss whether finances for theatricals,
football, tennis, library, etc. should be under one committee or under the
present system of separate ones, dominated by the BADS. The BADS
was well organized and voted us down forty-four to forty-one. I am all for
centralization in everything and will try again.

Thursday, 27 June 1918
Fine day but cold and windy. Read and fought flies.

Postcard to Ida

Date – June 29, 1918 'This card given to prisoners to fill out.'
   I have received parcel, May 30, 1918, No.118
   1. Have you received your parcels regularly? Yes, thanks!
   2. Were contents in good condition? Excellent!
   3. Is your address as shown on the other side correct? If not, please enter your correct address below. Quite correct
   4. Do you receive your bread regularly? NO, and in summer it is usually mouldy.
   (Signature) F. Vans Agnew, Captain.

Saturday, 29 June 1918
Were officially informed that it is not possible to play football on the promised field outside because it spoils the grazing for a small flock of emaciated sheep. Censor sent for me today to decipher a letter of Ida's in her best hieroglyphics. He was much amused.

Monday, 1 July 1918
Fine, windy, cool, sunny day and went to the hospital. The German who massaged me told me he, also, was wounded at Cambrai on 30 November. MANY OF THE HOSPITAL ORDERLIES AND THE NURSES AT WORK HERE FOR A LONG TIME HAVE BEEN ORDERED TO GO TO THE FRONT FIELD HOSPITALS AND THEY ARE NOT AT ALL PLEASED.

Wednesday, 3 July 1918
Rumors of the new Spanish disease breaking out in Germany.

Thursday, 4 July 1918
Spanish influenza is in full swing. Captain Johnson succumbed and is in bed. Much good that will do him.

Friday, 5 July 1918
Johnson better today and Niall going down. Half the camp is more or less affected. Every room has one or more so–called sufferers. It seems to be a mild form of *grippe*.

Saturday, 6 July 1918

Most of the orderlies are imagining themselves very ill and it affects all their duties. Tennis courts are half filled. Roll calls half attended. All rather nonsense to me. Cannot understand it!

Sunday, 7 July 1918

German papers of course say England and France are devastated by the Spanish 'floo', and that, owing to scientific German methods, Germany is quite unharmed. They leave us out of their best methods, evidently. BUT THE DOCTOR IN THE HOSPITAL AT HEIDELBERG, A GOOD REASONABLE CHAP, DEEMED THIS AS RUBBISH. HUSH! VERBOTEN! FORGET IT!

Tuesday, 9 July 1918

About one hundred new French officers came today, all for the Swiss Commission. They brought two small dogs, which thrilled the camp to the bones. This was the Grand Duke of Baden-Baden etc's birthday and being a holiday for the natives, we got no parcels or letters; and flags flew and speeches (unintelligible to me, am glad to say) were made in the local vernacular.

To Ida

15 July 1918

Today came a kit parcel from you (a shirt, socks, collars, ties, and handkerchiefs), also a kit parcel from the tailor's containing a new and dearly beloved pair of slacks and a pair of pajamas. This last parcel they had addressed to Soltau and it had gone the long round of Soltau, Hanover, Karlsruhe and here. A cigarette parcel and a pipe arrived also. So this was a great morning for me and I can think of nothing but thanks! Letters may come yet today but the letter question is always very uncertain. Day before yesterday a parcel of six books came. I need no more clothes I am sure, but a pair of slippers would be fine and six tennis balls and another pair of the white canvas rope-soled tennis shoes. No one has been better looked after in the way of parcels and kit than I have and I am the envy of a good many. Thanks entirely to you!

Today the German papers announce that the Prisoners of War Conference at the Hague have finished their pow-wow and we ought to hear in a day or so what it all means. Being over forty-eight I should get away before winter sets in, it seems to me and that is most important from the point of view of coal. Another tennis tournament begins today and I have drawn a very nice partner. We shall not win but we shall enjoy ourselves very much.

War news is as good as can be and everyone here rejoices. I wish they would send the staff of the Manchester Guardian *into the front line trenches and never release them again. A burial party is what they need and no more! The wave of Spanish influenza has passed over and all the woebegones are now sitting up and taking nourishment – mostly liquid! It passed me by as usual and of course! We get warm and pleasant weather on the whole but rain is always quite near and ready to fall. Flies are a pest and mosquitoes are just starting to appear.*

Wednesday, 17 July 1918
Every night there are air raids by our people at Mannheim and Ludwigshafen near-by, and we hear and see the racket afar. Usually, at 12.30am to the tick. MANNHEIM IS WHERE THE POISON GAS IS MADE AND BOTH ARE FULL OF FACTORIES.

Friday, 19 July 1918
Major Morris (Tanks), Captain Young, Lieutenants Nathan[19], Goldstein[20] and Mann[21], all went to a new camp at Stralsund on the Baltic. They had all tried to escape recently at different times and go to a sort of Strafe Camp on an island. AS THEY ARE FIVE RATTLING GOOD MEN THEY WILL NOT MIND.

Saturday, 20 July 1918
The German attack on both sides of Rheims seems definitely now to be a total failure, and the German people here do not feel at all easy and are becoming very polite and friendly.

Sunday, 21 July 1918
Just had news of French and American counter-attack from Soissons to Marne and retreat of Germans over Marne again. Have been appointed President Tennis Committee.

Monday, 22 July 1918
Whole camp much bucked over war news. French claim 20,000 prisoners and 400 guns and are delighted with Americans.

Tuesday, 23 July 1918
Started a new Singles Handicap Tournament. Made arrangements, settled handicaps and drew for partners. A and B groups. B means 'dud'. Hope to begin play tomorrow.

First news of Prisoners of War Exchange Conference today. Fourteen months instead of eighteen seems to be correct. Rugby game in evening but, as it rained, had to stop before game finished. We did not mind the rain but the Germans did. The guard might get wet, I suppose.

Postcard to Ida

25 July 1918
All is well. Three days ago tennis racket came and is most satisfactory. A week ago I got a third single tennis shoe with a shirt, collars, ties, etc. Letters to all are very irregular and few, but parcels keep coming and bread as well. I may get special consideration on account of age in the exchanges, so please send me as soon as possible a certificate of age, fifty on April 28th last – because I may need to show proof. When I enlisted I gave my age at forty, when it was really forty-six, you remember, on account of the age limit in 1914, so that may make a complication. But you must cut the red tape in some way and I feel sure of your ability. I believe I may be exchanged to England on the age alone and apart from the lame arm. War news continues to be most favorable and we are all delighted.

Friday, 26 July 1918
Fine cool sunny day. Went to hospital in town. Saw German censor, Herr Wack. He told me a birth certificate is not needed. This man was twelve years in Singapore, Burmah, China, etc. and speaks good English, a very good sort. Played in tournament and was badly beaten by Brundritt[22], Tank Corps, 6-2, 6-2. He is very good and uses a twisting, cut ball in all strokes, low over net (just the kind I loathe) and places very accurately.

Saturday, 27 July 1918
Four English officers tried to escape last night. They mingled with a big batch of French officers going to Switzerland, hoping to escape in the confusion and dark. Rather a feeble effort!

Tuesday, 30 July 1918
Tennis tournament in full swing, many fine matches played. Rugby in evening from 4.15 to 6pm, acted as a touch judge. War news really most inspiring. Germans on the retreat from Marne, for second time, after three years fruitless fighting. Americans doing quite splendidly.

Wednesday, 31 July 1918
Last night the Germans had a night-training attack for their young troops with Very lights and bombs and rockets, etc. This excited us immensely and the windows of the big building were jammed with onlookers. When the Germans charged with fierce cries, they were drowned by a louder, humorous roar from us, which must have irritated them immensely. It was impossible to resist. Anniversary of the Ypres 3rd battle. Went over with the old tank and had a desperately hard day. Got my captaincy through casualties that day.

Thursday, 1 August 1918
At roll call in morning the German officers in charge remonstrated with us about the disturbance last night and said it would not do. They were quite decent about it, almost amused, and said they had not told the Commandant and would not, or he would 'strafe' the whole camp.

Saturday, 3 August 1918
German official [communiqué] of August 2nd says: 'Crown Prince's Army: Between Soissons and French Tardenois the enemy continued his fruitless attack yesterday. After warding off his attacks and evacuating yesterday's battlefield, we continued our movement during the night in this great rear guard action according to plan.' Verily these people have no humour, what!

Monday, 5 August 1918
Watched a German battalion at drill in steady rain. WATCHED, ALSO, GERMAN NCOS KNOCKING DOWN AND KICKING THEIR MEN. Another amusing bulletin of Crown Prince's Armies of August 4th.

'No engagements. We are on the Aisne (N and E of Soissons) and on the Vesle in contact with the enemy.' Delightfully vague and does not explain a hurried retirement of ten kilometers.

Must have lost a lot of guns in this rainy weather. Tonight learn that we have taken Fismes and recrossed the Aisne and Vesle.

Thursday, 8 August 1918
Four new British officers came today from hospital. All with jaw wounds; their mouths are full of wires and plates, poor chaps. One is from D Battalion of Tanks. He was just out from home four days and was picked up wounded in the retreat to Peronne. Saw no fun at all and feels very cheap.

To Ida

14 August 1918
Yesterday I had bad luck. I was warming up for a tennis match, our tennis group against the rest, when I slipped and fell on my bad arm. That has finished my tennis for some time and I am back to a sling again with the arm as sore as it was last March. Remarkably painful too, with any movement! It cannot be helped and there it is! The delay about the Prisoners Conference at The Hague is very trying, but I expect there is a very good reason for it and I hope our people are sticking out. Prisoners are much too apt to think that they are the most important people in the world and to forget that there is a war to be won yet. Two days ago I received a mosquito net from you and I hope you do not mind but I gave it to our Dramatic Society to be made into beautiful muslin dresses for the leading ladies in our coming comic opera which is being madly rehearsed. We have been removed from the barrack huts where flies and mosquitoes might have been a great nuisance, and I am now in a nice room, up high in the big stone and brick building, with Captain Dickinson and Walker[23], and we have few flies and no mosquitoes. We hear sounds of air raids in the distance sometimes at nights, and see German troops drilling feverishly almost every day, so we know that the war is still moving along. Am perfectly well in mind and body, barring the left wing, so do not worry at all.

Thursday, 15 August 1918
Fine weather, of course, when I cannot play tennis. Arm still in sling and taking life easy: breakfast in bed and the usual sham. A double air raid last

night and at 9am today. Big row last night and tremendous barrage put up, from Mannheim and Ludwigshafen by the sound. No letters ever come to anyone any more, almost.

Monday, 19 August 1918
Have joined a Spanish class, about thirty of us in three groups under three British officers who have lived in South America. Am an advanced pupil from my previous work. We spend from 2 to 3pm every day. Am keeping up French and my Russian, too. German, have dropped!

Wednesday, 21 August 1918
Beautiful, clear, sunny, hot day. Great day for aeroplane fighting and observation. Very useful as we are pushing Germans over the edge just now. Went to hospital and saw Professor Beische, the specialist. He told me to come on Friday for an X-ray on my arm, and wrote another chapter in my medical history sheet. Had some good tennis, five sets, and find my arm just allows me to serve. Enough is as good as a feast. Two parcels today.

Thursday, 22 August 1918
Full moon last night and clear and wonderful. Good air raid somewhere towards Mannheim. Sirens and tooters blared and local Germany disappeared into cellars, I suppose. Excellent war news. We seem to be out to win and keep on advancing.

Friday, 23 August 1918
Went to hospital in morning and had two X-ray photos taken of my elbow, both sides. Nice old lady in charge. Spoke English gloomily. War news probably is responsible.

Monday, 26 August 1918
Fine, but windy and uncertain! Two big air raids last night out Mannheim way. Tremendous barrage each time and could hear the boom of bombs bursting. Same local excitement here. Sirens and tooters and whistles.

Wednesday, 28 August 1918
War news keeps all of us, with the fine French officers, in irrepressible good humour. It certainly looks good for a complete victory next year. Did not go to hospital as I had a very good tennis set on. Berlin Exchange is going up.

I got 260 marks for 10 pounds today. Last time, two months ago, I got only 215.

Thursday, 29 August 1918
War news is exciting. We are back at Montauban and Delville Wood and Trônes and Bernafay Woods, fighting the old Somme battle over again and giving more than we get I expect. (SOMETHING CENSORED FOLLOWS, WHICH I CAN'T REMEMBER)

Friday, 30 August 1918
Fine, but cloudy and cool. NW wind. Went to hospital. Most of the young nurses and masseur-girls have gone to field hospitals near the front, we are told, and they are certainly not in sight. In the evening got the surprising news that every British officer in this camp is going to another tomorrow. Found out that three camps are mentioned. Fürstenberg (north of Berlin), Klaustal, and Schivemtz in Silesia. Arranged with Major Walker that Dickinson and I will go with him to Fürstenberg.

Saturday, 31 August 1918
Fine weather and cool. Great excitement today, of course, everyone (184 of us) packing, paying mutual debts, and trying to find things to pack into. Only fifteen of us going to Fürstenberg. Said to be the best camp in Germany. Sort of Donnington Hall[24]. We left at 8.45pm, marched to station and left at 10pm, third class carriages and crowded. Slow train and many long stops. Got to Frankfurt at about 6am.

Chapter 15

Fürstenberg

Sunday, 1 September 1918

Fine day, very much so. Everyone very sleepy and sore. We have to wait here so all went to a Red Cross place to get something to eat and a wash. Place is hung round with posters, 'Are we barbarians' is one, and they proved statistically and without humour, that they are not. Others depict the area for 'English' air raids. Another shows the value in mineral and agricultural 'loot' of Ukraine. Another shows the danger to German trade with Belgium if the Channel Tunnel is completed. Left at 1pm and travelled all day and night on towards Berlin.

Note by FVA

On our arrival at Fürstenberg, on September 2nd, the usual search of our baggage and selves took place, and my diary was taken from me to be inspected by the censor. It was not returned to me until September 18th. I wrote a general account at once of our doings during that time in the diary, which follows immediately, and on September 19th the diary continues in a normal manner.

Monday, 2 September 1918

Arrived there about 8am and travelled across from one station to another in a two-horse wagonette affair, fifteen of us. Place looks empty and forlorn and only saw two motor cars (staff cars probably). Went on, after breakfast in a station restaurant where we ate our own good food brought with us, until about 12am when we reached Fürstenberg. Here we carried our bags, etc. to the camp, quite close, after having been ferried across a fine little lake, where we are allowed to bathe daily, I believe. All this journey was in third class carriages and am glad it is over. The camp building is a kind of hospital sanatorium, just outside the village and is in sandy, rolling country, interspaced with many nice lakes and covered with forests of pine, beech, oak, etc. very well cared for. The grounds inside the wire fence are small, less than five acres. None too much for 160 officers. All British except one

Russian! Among these are about sixty of our Mercantile Marine officers, torpedoed from Rio Janeiro to Iceland and proud of it. These are the men who will never forgive Germany and time will show. Fine men they are, many gray-haired and very set in their ways. Most of the officers here were taken in the March 1918 show when German masses overran our thin line on the Somme. They are heartily enjoying the joke now when Germany is marching backwards 'according to plan'. Must have marched forwards merely for exercise and to keep warm, they suppose! Or according to another and a *bad* plan. The two tennis courts are outside the wire. Every officer and orderly has a parole card signed by him; these you hand over every time you leave camp for walks or tennis, etc. and, when you return they are handed back to you. An excellent plan.

As the camp was nearly full, we were scattered among the rooms, one here and one there. I was lucky to get in with two Capitanos, Ellis[1] and Lidiard[2], in a nice room on sunny side of house and Major Walker and Dickinson and self mess together. We brought enough food to last us till parcels will begin again regularly. Every day there is a walk from 9.30am to 11.30am, and again from 2pm to 4pm. On Saturday (in summer) there is a long walk from 9am to 4pm and we take lunch and picnic out. At 9am there is a roll call and another at 4pm. On Sundays, no walks or going out of camp at all, except to the church in Fürstenberg. This gives us much outside freedom which is not abused. The woods and forests are beautiful and the lakes are joined up by a canal system to Hamburg. So the walks are a great pleasure and the natives seem friendly or indifferent.

The 'skippers' have been toy yacht racing on the lake near-by and, every afternoon, they are out in rowboats testing or racing them. A cup is being fought for by the ten boats and twenty races are to be sailed. Reminds me of the Round Pond in Kensington Gardens. Sweeps are arranged and betting is brisk. There is a dramatic society and sing-songs and a very bad orchestra (I miss the French touch) and a debating society is proposed. A very good library of novels and a set of bound *Illustrated London News* of 1860 vintage and other ancient and interesting literature. Colonel Smith[3] is Senior British Officer and then there are three other Colonels, Bury[4], Sloggett[5] and Lord Farnham[6]. The tennis courts are quite good, asphalt and sand, but the system of allotting times to play not so good as at Heidelberg.

The war news up to September 19th (I am writing on the 20th) is wonderful but am not in the least surprised. I always felt we could win when we were ready and since being prisoner I see nothing super-human about these people. After years of living in America they seem to me slow and uninteresting. If they could defeat us we would well deserve it. It has been a grand war for us and Germany has done us a great kindness in precipitating it. This will leave the Anglo-Saxon on top for a century or so, maybe forever. And Germany must eat crow for a long time!

To Ida (Fürstenberg, Mecklenberg)

11 September 1918

Now I can give you some impressions of this camp. After a full week's travel we came north through Frankfurt, Cassel and Berlin, a long and tedious journey, but in parts quite interesting at this point in the world's history. The populace looks puzzled, curious and not hostile, some of it quite friendly...

The grounds are not large inside the inevitable wire fence but sufficient and a great many rabbits are kept by officers in rows of hutches. I spend all my spare time mowing grass with my fingers to feed them on and they never refuse. The camp is a very good one and I like it better than Heidelberg or Karlsruhe, both of which are good. German officers are kindly and polite and I see nothing to complain about. Will you please send me out a waterproof coat of sorts to use on walks. I had one in my kit. If it is not there send me a new one. It will do as a blanket also at night. A warm pair of slippers, too, please, for this is going to be a cold place later on, and gloves, my dear, as you love me! Gorringe's, Buckingham Road, don't you remember, fur lined, two pairs please, so as to always have a dry pair.

My left fin is gradually getting over the trouble I had, but is not back to its form of two months ago. All treatment for it has stopped, of course, since coming here, and it must look out for itself. Prisoners of War Exchange seems to have dropped out of sight and one has nearly given up the idea. Some day it may come to life and I may get away on account of age limit, but we read the official communiqués in the German papers and rejoice. What does anything matter when we are winning the war by leaps and bayonets! The study of foreign language is non-existent now, as we are all British but the previous time was not all wasted. There is a good library here which is really all I need. Bridge in the evening and chess.

I bought some very good maps of the front at Heidelberg and I follow each day's advance, French and British, and mark it in and date it on the map, and by this time it is a regular diary of progress. Wonderful effort, even on

a map! Tanks must have lost heavily, from enemy accounts, and I am very
anxious to get news of my own lot who must have suffered. It is truly tragic
to be vegetating here when such stirring times are going on in the world. And
I miss the papers and details of news and the general spirit of home-rejoicing
most confoundedly. It is ages since I had a letter from you or anyone else, or
any real news at all. I hope you are as fit as ever and snug in your wee abode
and garden. It will be the middle of next summer before I get back to see it,
I expect. I have had a few swims in a lake here and find I can manage with
one arm well enough, and dive too with one arm, about as well as before but
more circumspectly and with less abandon.

Thursday, 19 September 1918

Fine day, warm and sunny. Got this, my diary, back today from the censor.
The blue adornments in it previous to September 1st were his 'objective'
(the blue line). He imagines I have no memory, I suppose. At any rate, this
is a great aid.

Saturday, 21 September 1918

Got some new maps of the front this morning from our hosts (?) and was
busy on them all day, more or less. Very good maps and cheap, 1–150,000.
Show every name mentioned in all communiqués. Played tennis in evening.
Like these courts better than Heidelberg.

Thursday, 26 September 1918

Got a food parcel today. We are running very short of supplies. News from
Palestine and Macedonia will give the enemy something to ruminate on
during the winter. Give us two years more war and we will have another
Egypt out in Mesopotamia.

Friday, 27 September 1918

Yesterday evening two officers escaped. Colonel Bury and Edmonson[7], a
young Second Lieutenant, got away in twilight, not unperceived. Sentry
fired three rounds, somewhere. Usual excitement due to such occasions and
a roll call soon after. No parcels or letters for days. Our reserve of food will
soon be done! At Heidelberg I never missed any food parcels. Something
wrong up here, evidently.

Wednesday, 2 October 1918
Edmondson was captured after four days without any food. He lost it somehow. He was removed from here at once, somewhere. Colonel Bury seems to be still at large.

Thursday, 3 October 1918
Fine day. Went on walks and enjoyed life. Played tennis in afternoon. Just after dark when lights were on, they suddenly all went out. All of them in the building and all outside round the fence. Very soon rifles began to go off along the wire fence. Joyful and gleeful excitement. Windows and balconies full of faces, giving encouraging hunting calls and whoops to the escapers. Sentries charging about, and commandant and officers, into the woods and out again, along the road and back again.

Friday, 4 October 1918
Must have been over a dozen shots fired. They had to get electricians up from village before lights were restored, and then we had a roll call, about 10pm. Found Colonel Lord Farnham, Howell[8] and Ashburnham missing. Commandant quite annoyed. Announced that (as a strafe) only ten officers allowed on walk at a time, no football, no tennis, no cinemas. Everybody retired intensely pleased. To blazes with their strafe and a dozen like it!

Saturday, 5 October 1918
Yesterday at morning roll call, the German officer told us a few things. Intimated that we were taking or, at least, arranging for food to be taken outside for escapes during our walks when on parole, and so on. We promptly held a meeting. Decided, not unanimously am sorry to say, to turn in all our parole cards on the evening roll call parade. This was done, with few exceptions (mostly marine) and no one goes on walks at all. And nobody cares a rap.

Sunday, 6 October 1918
This morning news came of Germany's offer of peace negotiations and an armistice to the US. A sly but silly move! We shall say 'Get out of all your occupied territory. Go back to your beloved Fatherland, where you belong, and then talk about peace on our terms.'

Monday, 7 October 1918
Fine sunny warm day. Bulgaria is broken and squealing audibly. Turkey is surrendering most of her army here and there, and we are advancing everywhere. No wonder they want a peace now, if you please. Wish I had the making of it!

Wednesday, 8 October 1918
Fine day and warm. Fine advance. Parcels and letters are few and far between. We live from hand to mouth but manage all right. I can live on potatoes, war bread and good news easily.

Friday, 11 October 1918
Fine and sunny. Good fighting weather and we are making hay of the Hindenburg defences. Poor old Turkey. 76,000 prisoners! Almost the whole army accounted for. That comes of keeping bad company; always gets you into trouble, sooner or later. The Turk has not squealed yet, either, not audibly. Am quite sorry for Turkey.

Saturday, 12 October 1918
I subscribe to *Berliner Tageblatt* now and struggle with the weird language. The construction of sentences would explain a lot of their character as a nation. Excellent news – Caudry, where I spent two days in hospital, is captured, and Le Cateau, where I spent nearly two weeks, is on the verge of same blessing. On Monday some of us will go on walks again. Doubt if I shall.

Sunday, 13 October 1918
Fine day. Many games of golf, played with tennis balls and hockey or any sticks. Most amusing scenes. The trees are taking all the fine autumn tints and some woods blaze outright. We keep advancing 'according to plan' and the enemy keeps retiring, 'according to plan', and I suppose everybody is happy, doing what each wants and plans to do. Suits us to a T! The official German war communiqués are as amusing as ever.

Monday, 14 October 1918
Were told on morning parade by Captain Sandée (German from Alsace) that our parole cards would be restored, walks begun as before and tennis and football. Strafe is over. The Spanish 'floo' is beginning here. We had it all

before in Heidelberg. Several chaps down. It has taken a long time to travel north here and I do not anticipate pleasure seeing it twice.

Tuesday, 15 October 1918
Lidiard, my roommate, is down with 'floo'. High temperature and headache, etc. Same old thing. Seems to shy off me for some reason. Twenty or thirty other chaps are down and German papers are full of it. Grand war news. Wilson is being very firm. Good luck to him. Fight it out to a finish in the field is the best. Always wrong to stop a dog fight.

Wednesday, 16 October 1918
Got our new parole cards again today and played tennis from 2 to 4pm most happily. Heard 'whooping cranes' (big blue sand-hill crane) this morning for about an hour. They wanted to feed around our lake but were afraid. Must be migrating south. Reminded me of Florida and Siberia too. Ellis, my other roommate, is also sick now. Both in bed and very sorry for themselves, not for me!

Thursday, 17 October 1918
This morning was sent for by Captain Sandée who is married to a Russian lady and talks English very well. Fine man and much liked. He told me the Dutch Embassy had sent a request to find out about my health, arm, etc. They had rumors I had died over here and had not heard from me for long time. Explained matters as they stood and await results. Much 'floo' still in camp. Walked out in afternoon.

Friday, 18 October 1918
Ellis and Lidiard still down and in bed. Cleaned up our room today as our orderly is also sick. Got letters from Mrs M of August 19th and a packet of Gold Flake cigs. Food parcels are very scarce and our cupboard is bare to the bone. The old Turk squealed today, audibly!

Monday, 21 October 1918
Post up my gigantic war map of entire front. Scale 1–150,000 (in kilometres). Takes seven maps to cover the front which join together perfectly. A German map is very cheap. Have posted every gain in ground since July 20th and dated it so have a complete diary of our combined advance from the Marne to the Scheldt.

Tuesday, 22 October 1918
Foggy and raw. Getting parcels now and a few letters. Had several parcels personally and Major Walker and Dickinson, too. Our cupboard is now well stocked for a change but we must economize as times are uncertain. Am pleased to see that Wilson is being firm, for the change to 'good behavior' of this nation is so 'sudden like'!

Monday, 28 October 1918
Gloomy day. All these past days have been without local incident except that Colonel Lord Farnham and his two associates, who all escaped from here, have all been returned here. They report hard times: want of food and exposure to wet and cold and weather made them give in, finally. They got within forty miles of Holland border and did well to do that. Many amusing adventures they had.

Tuesday, 29 October 1918
Austria has squealed! Very loud squeal and not to be denied, a really whole-hearted squeal. Makes one almost sad to see a great nation like that. Everyone with his mouth wide open doing the same thing, quite regardless!

Saturday, 2 November 1918
The Armistice terms to the old Turk will make his Allah ashamed of him, and Mahomet to groan in his grave. That all comes of keeping bad company and may be a salutary warning to all the little Turks to come.

Sunday, 3 November 1918
Today the German medical chap was caught red-handed stealing parcels of ours. He re-addressed them to his wife somewhere. Captain Sandée caught him and arrested him promptly. His room was searched and much stuff found.

Monday, 4 November 1918
Dull clod of day. We translated the Armistice terms to Austria. All because of the same bad company they kept. Pitch will stick! Poor devils! And how infernally warlike the Italians have become all of a sudden. This settles Germany to the everlasting little Dot. Cashed a cheque for ten pounds today and got 296 marks for it. In Heidelberg I only got 215 last May!

Tuesday, 5 November 1918
Fine, still, warm day. Great war news, too. Up to Ghent driving on towards Mons. Across the Sambre-Oise Canal to well south of Guise. The Americans north of Stenay are pounding their southern line of retreat to Metz along their only railway. There should be big captures in a few days! Big as they are now, they will be bigger. Late evening paper brought news of the general retreat (they have not the face to say 'according to plan') from Valenciennes to the Meuse. Going as hard as they can split, a weary, dogged lot of men.

Thursday, 7 November 1918
It is a shame that such good fighting material as the German has been so misled and perverted by the leaders of their army and politicians. The men are worthy of a better fate. If they will thoroughly clean their house when they get home they will make a fine contented, friendly nation, welcome to all. But the cleaning will involve much bloodshed. Carlyle says 'There is no true reform without bloodshed'.

Friday, 8 November 1918
No news yet that the German armistice has been signed. The delegates have gone to Foch. No Berlin newspapers yesterday or today. All sorts of weird rumors! We have won the war fairly and squarely, nothing else matters. Big German retreat on, almost to Hirson and Sedan, which cuts their two main lines of retreat. Give us a week more and we scupper the lot. Too bad if they sign peace first!

Saturday, 9 November 1918
Fine day. Took long walk to village, five miles off and through grand woods of pine, fir, beech and oak. Quiet, peaceful villages, so neat and contented. Armistice terms not signed yet. We get wild rumors of what is going on, probably greatly exaggerated. Looks like a Republic to me, and a good thing, too. The people will gain in the long run; at any rate, their lives will be happier and much more secure.

Sunday, 10 November 1918
Put on all my best clothes and went to the German church (Lutheran) in Fürstenberg. About ten of us, with a guard, unarmed. On way we met an excited soldier on a bike who stopped and said armistice was signed and that he advised us to turn back and not go to the town. We pooh-poohed him and

went on virtuously. Good church, to hold 500, but only about fifty present, forty-five of them women. All very stolid. Hot like a French church. Met two sailors coming home and they smiled happily and greeted us.

Monday, 11 November 1918
<u>Armistice signed</u>. Gloomy day. Absolutely grey. At 9am, paper with Armistice terms came. Pretty stiff, but quite necessary. At 1pm a car arrived with several revolutionaries, all soldiers, not officers. Car had a red flag (40 H.P. Benz), belonged to Duke of Mecklenberg-Strelitz. They interviewed the German officers. All men and officers have taken off the Imperial cockade and the officers do not wear swords. Got news in papers that Kaiser and 'Little Willy' have abdicated. A good riddance for the German nation now a free Republic. Congratulate them!

Postcard to Ida

11 November 1918
All is well with us and there is no occasion to be anxious about us. Soon we expect to come home, as we hear that the Armistice was signed today and we are a part of the conditions. I hope we shall go back to Belgium and France but do not know. Have good food supplies and everything we need. These are most dramatic times we live in and we are most lucky to be alive and able to see them.

See you soon, dear. Yours always, Frank.

Tuesday, 12 November 1918
Heard today that the Kaiser and 'Little Willy' and Empress have gone to Holland and rumors that Holland will intern them. Most undignified exit, even to save one's life, before peace is signed and with his country still officially at war. Had good long walk. Country people greet us cheerily. Tomorrow we are to be allowed out as often as we like, I believe, but not in the town, for our own safety. Hope to leave middle of next week. Parcels and letters are coming all right. Both uncensored. So railway traffic must be resumed.

Thursday, 14 November 1918
Everything is very quiet down here and the town people want us to be allowed into the town. Hope we will spend money there, I suppose. The

armistice terms have been altered. Food allowed in, etc. Seems no harm in that if properly watched.

Friday, 15 November 1918
We are allowed to have English papers from now on and the camp has ordered ten *Times* a day from Berlin.

Sunday, 17 November 1918
Had Sunday walk with Captain Sandée. Very dull these days. No news to speak of and hard strain waiting. But there is no grumbling: the war is won with plenty to spare. Am packed and ready to go at five minutes notice. Few parcels and no letters these days.

Monday, 18 November 1918
Woke up to find all white outside – really white. And it snowed all day and going on all night by the looks of things. Stayed in all day. The soles of my boots are so bad that my feet would soon be soaked. Cannot get sole leather here and must wait to get soles at home. Lecture last night on 'Electricity' by a Lieutenant Boraston[9] of RE. Most amusing, and very efficient. I am down for a lecture on Siberia and one on Florida which I pray will never come off.

Tuesday, 19 November 1918
Went for hard walk, exploring. Put up three deer and tracked them in snow long way. Came home late through the deer's fault. Notice put up that we go via Copenhagen to Stettin by rail, then boat to Copenhagen, and then on home by Danish steamships. Sounds true and will save the long and icy cold train journey via Holland or Belgium.

Wednesday, 20 November 1918
Unpleasant day, but the English papers came, November 7th to 11th, *The Times, Morning Post, Telegraph, Daily Mail* and *News and Chronicle*. Quite a debauch of good news and am almost surfeited. Spent most of the day at them with a walk in afternoon. We hope to go next week. This is the anniversary of the Cambrai show.

Thursday, 21 November 1918
Very fine, clear, sunny and freezing in shade all day. Read English papers and am much enjoying reading General Von Bernhardt's *World Power or*

Downfall, written in 1911. It is as amusing as *Punch* now, or more so! There is a loathely skin disease running through this camp, here and there, and I only hope I do not get it. Probably the tinned food. Took good long walk in woods. Meet Russians now and then and always talk with them. They are very pleased men.

Sunday, 24 November 1918
Two new chaps arrived today, one RFC, other Infantry. They were just captured in the last fighting and were in Berlin during the Revolution. Their guards left them and joined in so they were on their own. Diverse people, friendly, looked after them until they were put in charge of more guards of the Workmen's and Soldiers' Council, and finally sent on here.

Monday, 25 November 1918
Long walk north to small village, seven miles away. Came back through Fürstenberg. All friendly. Went into shop and bought nine small glass, colored 'sausage' dogs, single figures (one double) on a slab for a letter weight, fine for Xmas presents and souvenirs. No news of our going yet. Cannot be long.

Tuesday, 26 November 1918
No news of our going. Exhortations from Red Cross come often by post and wire, asking us to be patient and not to 'straggle'. No fear! Got four letters today. Concert at night. Hoped to be the last.

Saturday, 30 November 1918
Disgusting weather. Am haunted by a tooth, too, with a pulse in it. Found a book on travels in Patagonia which helped. We get no definite news of leaving. Am afraid Colonel Smith takes everything 'lying down' and we shall be the last camp of all to leave. 'Lines of least resistance' are so easy. Got letters today but food is getting very sketchy.

Monday / Tuesday, 2 / 3 December 1918
Same grim weather and rain in eve. Cold. Cold. Damp! Yesterday had to go to a dentist or burst. Went to a lady dentist in town. She is a brick and knows her work, much better than the half-blind male thing (German) which worked on me in camp. This purblind worm was busy on the wrong tooth, so she said, and she was right. She finished my job, charged me ten marks,

very cheap. Paid her and gave her three cakes of toilet soap. She offered me back all the money and quite flustered on refusal. A good little body! Tried to buy rope for my box. Real rope was there – pre-war halter-shanks in harness shop. Asked me thirty-six marks for six thin halter shanks. Refused and bought paper rope at three marks for ten yards. No news, as usual.

Thursday, 5 December 1918
Still writing in this infernal book and the armistice signed nearly a month ago and no definite news. Needs patience. We are all out of food. No parcels for two weeks and all reserves gone except hope.

Friday, 6 December 1918
Colonels returned yesterday evening from Berlin. Seems to be a lack of transport by sea, but we should be home by Xmas. Shall go via Copenhagen. All out of food. Breakfast, dry bread, dripping and cheese with tea and no milk. May get relief parcels or our own, but seems doubtful.

Saturday, 7 December 1918
It is arranged for twelve officers to go to Copenhagen to help to get our men home, so I volunteered and was accepted. Leave on Monday (9th) and stay in Copenhagen till all men are gone. Dickinson went to a Man's Camp this morning. Major Walker goes to Copenhagen and I with him. Shall be there two, three or four weeks, perhaps. Heard in evening that all the rest leave for home on Monday via Lübeck, and perhaps true. Do not regret going to Copenhagen personally, as need some work badly, and glad to help the men.

Sunday, 8 December 1918
All arranged. We leave tomorrow 9.20am by train for Copenhagen. Going by boat from Warnemünde. Report of last night about the whole camp going – wrong. They go in next ten days in parties, including orderlies. Went down town this afternoon and saw a Sunday dancing hall. Rather dull. Very correct, and dull. Beer and dances mixed. Am packed and glad to go, for this is a disgusting country.

Letters to Ida

Phoenix Hotel, Copenhagen, Denmark, 11 December 1918

I telegraphed you on my arrival here and am hastily sending a letter by HMS Porto *taking troops back (PoWs) in a few minutes. I am busy now acting as Deputy Assistant Director of Transport on the British Repatriation Board. It is a mouthful, but means that I am in charge of all the motor lorries and petrol, sending supplies to about ten camps around here. I may be here six weeks or more and be pretty busy. It is only fair to let the married men and youngsters go home for Xmas, so please do not mind. Am very well and the Danes are immensely hospitable. Will write as often as I can.*

18 December 1918

Please address me c/o W. Vett Esq., Bergensgade, Copenhagen.

Just got your nice cablegram and am very contented. It seems a shame not to come back to spend Christmas with you but you know how it is, and you would do the same yourself. To see the boats going home laden with all your friends is quite a trial, I assure you. This cloud has its silver lining, of course. I have not more work to do than I can do well enough, although it is piling up. I am in a very comfortable billet. 'Palatial' is more the term. Mr Vett[10], my host, is the Wm. Whitely, Harrods, Selfridges, of Copenhagen, all rolled into one. He is a widower of about forty-five, with no children, and he and I live alone in his beautiful and delightful house. We are the best of friends and I have a latch key and the run of his best Havanas, liqueurs and a multitude of other objects of liquid art.

Every night, almost, he dines me out with great gusto, or we dine at his friends' palaces and they dance till all hours, most beautifully. Being a member of the Royal Danish Yacht Club, he takes me there a good deal, as he is a keen and practical yachtsman and abhors steam, just like me. I have seen more superlatively beautiful ladies in one week than I had for many years and am, in a senile manner, really enjoying it.

Everyone is falling over themselves to be kind to us and they really mean it. Of course, my host talks perfect English as do all his friends, and last and not least, he possesses a most entrancing wire-haired terrier of monumental pedigree.

I am doing my best to keep down expenses but prices are terrific here and I hope we shall be allowed some further allowance to our pay.

23 December 1918

A boat is just leaving, the Willochra, *so I am hastily sending you a line, and my hands are so cold I can hardly write. I just want to tell you all is well and to wish you and all others the finest brand of Christmas fun possible. Have been very busy in a blinding snowstorm all day and am just finished for the day. Expect a fine Xmas here myself as I have several kind invitations, so don't worry about me.*

26 December 1918

Another boat, the big Frederik VIII, *is leaving in about an hour for your side, and I will hand this to some chap leaving and trust him to post it. My word, this is a great town. I am having a wonderful time; my days till well after dark are very busy and then my host, Mr Vett, takes me about among his friends and relatives, restaurants and theatres. Christmas Eve is the great event here and I went to a great gathering of his family and the family Xmas tree; ten children, nice to look at and well-behaved, who all talk some English, and the rest grown-ups. They are all very well off and the many presents and the quality of them made my eyes bulge. To my own amazement the tree produced for me a gold wristwatch from my host, a thing beyond my own wildest dreams if I had to buy it for myself. You never saw such kindness. Last night I went to another family meeting (same family and children) at his sister's who is Baroness Wegel, Wegler (or something quite like that)[11], I am really apparently one of the family by this time.*

I am trying to get even slightly by taking all the children to the theatre some night soon. A few nights ago I was taken, after dinner at a strange house, to another house where there was a dance. There, I met Prince Waldemar[12], uncle of the King, and his two sons, one in Navy and one in Army. They were all most friendly and talked about the Germans worse than I ever have, I think. It was quite refreshing, and the army son, a very gay young man, attached himself to me to an alarming extent. Everyone was wearing orders and medals and crosses and sashes, even the ladies.

Then another night I went to a dinner and dance given to all the officers on the repatriation business, in a colossal house full of statues which looked very cold on account of lack of clothing. There I met the British Ambassador, Lord Kilmarnock[13], and before long I was in a game of bridge with him (or against him, rather) and beat him two straight rubbers. He is a very nice man, clever and earnest and not much to look at, most unassuming and I hope I shall see more of him.

So you see that I am not allowed to be forlorn while here. I find it all wonderfully interesting. Besides, since living with my host my expenses are much less, as he refuses to allow me to put my hand near my pocket when out with him having been trained in America. The men are comfortable and contented in the camps and boats are coming and going as fast as may be.

Note by FVA

Left Copenhagen on 30 January on a Danish 'butter-boat' steamer and arrived at Leith, Scotland, 31 January 1919.

Took a holiday till 1 March, when I went to the War Office where I was employed in Branch A.G.9 (Adjutant General 9) doing Tank Corps administrative work until the end of May.

A Medical Board then sent me to hospital where my arm was operated on twice. I was finally discharged from hospital on August 18th, and I remained on pay until I was repatriated on October 22nd to the United States, and honorably discharged from the Army by the British Consulate in New York.

Appendices

Food parcels

Frank's table carefully records the arrival of his food parcels, essential to life as a prisoner-of-war.

Arrival Date	Sent by	Date Sent	Contents	Days in transit
03/04/18	Keenan and Philips		Clothes, 1 tunic with badges, 1 pr breeches, 1 pr puttees	
03/04/18	Ida	22/01/18	Food parcel, damaged, 5 tins, sugar, oatmeal, etc.	71
03/04/18	Ida	16/01/18	Food parcel smashed up, 3 tins and 2 lumps of sugar	77
04/04/18	Berne	23/18/18 [sic]	3 loaves fresh bread	
08/04/18	Ida/ Lazenby		Food, 7 tins, raisins, dates, rice, tea, sugar, etc.	
10/04/18	Copenhagen	23/03/18	2 loaves bread – good order	18
12/04/18	Copenhagen	30/03/18	2 loaves bread – good order	13
20/04/18	Ida/ Lazenby		1 7lb bag flour	
24/04/18	Ida	07/03/18	100 cigarettes	48
24/04/18	Ida	07/03/18	Eggs (1 doz) 4 good	48
24/04/18	Ida	07/03/18	Food parcel	48
25/04/18	Ida	12/03/18	Clothes (pajamas, collars and ties)	44
25/04/18	Lazenby	12/03/18	Food parcel	44
26/04/18	Copenhagen	13/04/18	2 loaves bread - good	13
29/04/18	Lazenby	01/04/18	Food parcel - 6 tins	28

Arrival Date	Sent by	Date Sent	Contents	Days in transit
03/05/18	Copenhagen	01/04/18	Food parcel from YMCA, 2 tins	32
06/05/18	Copenhagen	20/04/18	1 big loaf - fair condition	16
07/05/18	Ida	20/04/18	5 good novels	17
10/05/18	Mrs M.	12/03/18	Chess board	59
10/05/18	Mrs M.	15/03/18	Set of chess men	56
10/05/18	Clark	15/03/18	Food parcel - 5 tins	56
13/05/18	Clark	29/03/18	Food parcel	45
13/05/18	Clark	11/02/18	Food parcel - 21 tins	91
13/05/18	Ida	27/03/18	Food parcel	47
15/05/18	Copenhagen	04/05/18	2 loaves bread – excellent	11
15/05/18	Clark	08/04/18	Food parcel - 5 tins	37
15/05/18	Ida	20/03/18	Food parcel - 6 tins	56
16/05/18	Ida	05/04/18	Food parcel - 9 tins	41
18/05/18	Ida	15/04/18	Food parcel - 3 tins	33
22/05/18	Ida	19/04/18	Food parcel - 5 tins	33
25/05/18	Ida		Clothes, 1 pr pajamas, collars and socks	
25/05/18	Ida	19/04/18	Cigarettes 100 – Gold Flake	36
28/05/18	Ida	29/04/18	Maple sugar principally	20
28/05/18	Ida	27/04/18	100 Gold flake cigarettes	31
28/05/18	Ida	27/04/18	Special food - 7 lbs flour, etc.	31
28/05/18	Ida	24/04/18	Food parcel - Lazenby – 9 ins.	34
31/05/18	Clark	17/04/18	Food parcel	44
01/06/18	Ida	13/05/18	Food parcel – special	19
03/06/18	Copenhagen	11/05/18	2 bread - all spoiled and green	23
03/06/18	Copenhagen	08/05/18	4 bread - all spoiled and green	26
04/06/18	Copenhagen	18/05/18	2 bread	17
05/06/18	Ida	15/05/18	Food parcel - special 6 tins	21

Arrival Date	Sent by	Date Sent	Contents	Days in transit
06/06/18	Ida	16/05/18	Food parcel – 7 tins	21
06/06/18	Clark	22/04/18	Food parcel – 7 tins	45
07/06/18	Ida	10/04/18	Food parcel	58
08/06/18	Copenhagen	25/05/18	2 loaves bread – good	14
10/06/18	Clark	15/05/18	Food parcel	26
10/06/18	Clark	14/05/18	Food parcel	27
15/06/18	Ida	01/06/18	100 cigarettes	14
15/06/18	Copenhagen	01/06/18	Bread – two loaves – good	14
18/06/18	Ida	10/05/18	8 hdkfs, 3 pr socks	39
18/06/18	Ida	10/05/18	Food parcel – special	39
18/06/18	Ida	11/05/18	Food parcel – 7 tins	38
18/06/18	Ida	07/05/18	Food parcel – 6 tins	41
18/06/18	Ida	04/05/18	Food parcel – 6 tins	45
20/06/18	Clark	20/02/18	Food parcel – 5 tins	120
20/06/18	Ida	18/04/18	Cigarettes 100	63
21/06/18	Ida	12/05/18	Food parcel 4 tins special	40
24/06/18	Copenhagen	08/06/18	2 bread – fairly good	16
24/06/18	Clark	18/05/18	Food parcel 6 tins	37
25/06/18	Ida	15/06/18	1 shirt, 2 pr socks, 1 suit underwear, 6 hdkfs, 1 pipe	10
25/06/18	Ida	17/05/18	Food parcel 6 tins	39
25/06/18	Ida	22/05/18	Food parcel 7 tins – special	34
29/06/18	Ida	30/05/18	Food parcel 6 tins	30
29/06/18	Ida	27/05/18	Food parcel 6 tins	33
01/07/18	Copenhagen	15/06/18	2 loaves bread – fair – 2 towels	16
02/07/18	Ida	31/06/18 [sic]	1 sack (7 lbs) flour, 2 tins	
04/07/18	Ida	05/06/18	Food parcel 9 tins	29
04/07/18	Ida	02/06/18	Food parcel 10 tins	32
05/07/18	Copenhagen	22/06/18	2 loaves bread – fair	13

Arrival Date	Sent by	Date Sent	Contents	Days in transit
05/07/18	Ida	05/06/18	1 tennis shoe, 1 boot, pa socks, 1 towel	30
11/07/18	Copenhagen	29/06/18	2 loaves bread – good	12
12/07/18	Ida	04/06/18	1 tennis shoe, 1 boot, 1 towel	38
12/07/18	Ida	04/06/18	Food parcel – special	38
13/07/18	Ida	04/06/18	6 books - good ones	39
15/07/18	Ida	04/06/18	2 collars, 1 towel	41
15/07/18	Ida	04/06/18	7 hdkfs, 1 vest, 1 tennis shoe,	41
15/07/18	Ida	04/06/18	100 cigs, Gold Flake	41
15/07/18	Ida	04/06/18	4 hdkfs, 2 ties, 2 pr socks, soap, pipe	41
15/07/18	Keenan Phillips	04/06/18	1 pr slacks, 1 shirt, 1 pr paj (Soltau)	41
16/07/18	Ida	18/06/18	Food parcel 7 tins	28
16/07/18	Ida	27/06/18	Food parcel 7 tins	19
17/07/18	Copenhagen	06/07/18	Two bread – good	11
17/07/18	Ida	18/06/18	Food parcel – special	29
20/07/18	Ida	18/06/18	Food parcel 7 lbs flour, etc.	32
22/07/18	Ida	01/06/18	1 tennis racket	51
22/07/18	Ida	01/06/18	lb John Cotton tobacco	51
24/07/18	Copenhagen	13/07/18	2 loaves bread – very good	51
27/07/18	Ida	22/06/18	Food parcel 6 tins	35
07/08/18	Ida	02/07/18	Food parcel 5 tins	36
08/08/18	Ida	25/07/18	Food parcel – special	14
12/08/18	Berne	22/06/18	French biscuits	51
15/08/18	Ida	22/06/18	Mosquito net – complete	40
15/08/18	Ida	22/07/18	Special food 4 tins	24
17/08/18	Ida	06/07/18	Food parcel	42
18/08/18	Ida	29/07/18	Food parcel (17 days)	20

Arrival Date	Sent by	Date Sent	Contents	Days in transit
20/08/18	Ida	15/07/18	Food parcel	36
20/08/18	Ida	11/07/18	Food parcel	40
21/08/18	Ida	19/07/18	5 books	33
21/08/18	Ida	19/07/18	Food parcel	33
22/08/18	Berne	19/07/18	Wooden box – Berne biscuits	34
23/08/18	Ida	19/07/18	Food parcel – special	35
23/08/18	Ida	24/07/18	Food parcel	30
26/08/18	Ida	15/07/18	Food parcel	42
30/08/18	Ida	15/07/18	Food parcel – special	46
14/09/18	Ida	27/04/18	Pipe and tobacco	140
16/09/18	Ida	27/04/18	Food parcel – special	142
19/09/18	Ida	27/04/18	Set of six tennis balls	145
23/09/18	Berne	23/08/18	Biscuits badly broken up	31
26/09/18	Ida	25/08/18	Food parcel	32
03/10/18	Ida	25/08/18	Food parcel – special	39
06/10/18	Ida	25/08/18	Food parcel – special	42
11/10/18	Ida	08/08/18	Food parcel – (good one) 15lbs	64
12/10/18	Ida	08/08/18	Pipe and tobacco	65
12/10/18	Berne	08/08/18	French biscuits (short)	65
18/10/18	Ida	08/08/18	Cigarettes - Gold Flake	71
19/10/18	Ida	28/08/18	Food parcel (Red X 15lbs)	52
21/10/18	Ida	22/08/18	Food parcel (Red X 15lbs)	60
21/10/18	Ida	22/08/18	Food parcel – special	60
22/10/18	Ida	22/08/18	Food parcel – special	61
29/10/18	Ida	05/09/18	Food parcel – 15lbs	54
05/11/18	Ida	02/08/18	Food parcel – 10lbs	95
05/11/18	Ida	30/09/18	Food parcel – special	36
06/11/18	Ida	26/09/18	Food parcel – 15lbs	41

Things that ought to be remembered

After the war we were presented with several well known and much read accounts of the war, dished up as novels, in which the neurotic, temperamental and sentimental authors had the hardihood to publish their experiences. They were no worse than those of thousands of other men, but their authors managed to convey to a large section of the public, both at home and in enemy countries, that their version portrayed the general feelings of the members of the British Army.

The mere fact that we were on the winning side and that we, in the past, created the British Empire and have held it against all comers for centuries, is sufficient refutation of these pernicious publications, but I feel that I must chronicle a few incidents which occurred in my sight and hearing during the course of my minute share in the war. I have no doubt that the 'thousands of other men' aforesaid could glean from their memories similar incidents to refute this small group of conscientious objectors to the morale of the British Army.

I was in the ranks during the first year of the war and I gained a commission in the same regiment after that period of time. While in the ranks in the spring of 1915, I volunteered for the bombing squads which were being newly formed, commonly known as Suicide Clubs. This I did largely to avoid thereby the 'fatigues' connected with the crude sanitary arrangements of the front lines, having found out that bombers were exempted from these and other less unpleasant fatigues.

In those days, bombers, in my experience at any rate, became positive habitués of no man's land. Most of the duties, wiring parties excepted, connected with that fascinating country devolved upon the bombers. Our bombing officer, Lieutenant Heath, was the perfect blend of irresponsibility and sheer courage, delightful to follow. I still have the pink trench 'telegram' addressed to 'The Grenade Corporal', Trench 135, whereby I was ordered to meet him at 9pm with my trusty squad of three – Walrond, Carey, Foster – at a named spot in the front line. Once there we were told that Brigadier General Seely desired us to capture a Hun, alive, that very night. This was a new game to us. Lieutenant Heath said finally, 'You will carry revolvers, a gas bomb in one pocket and a Mills in the other. If we see a German sufficiently isolated, give him the gas bomb, and if a crowd collects give 'em the Mills.' The bombers all had to be volunteers and naturally the more adventurous spirits in the battalion joined. It followed, in time, that those who survived the fray had much regard for each other.

My commission intervened and I was removed from no man's land to the Curragh for three months' training. To my horror, on return, the vacant post of Bombing Officer had just been filled. The CO was sorry and all that and gave me the job of OC Mounted Machine Gun Section, a dull game but better than nothing. Soon, however, all my bombing friends in the ranks, were asking for transfers to the MMGS, most irritating to the CO. Many of them transferred eventually. Then more trouble ensued. The MMGS became convinced that it was a dull game, through the leaven of the bombing element. We were removed from the front lines to a rest camp many miles behind, and, apparently, to some of my men, the dullness became insufferable. One of them, 'Snowy' Mitchell, a professional pugilist before the war, so named because he always looked, and was, so dirty, became a source of woe to me. A pearl in the front line, he was a pest behind the lines. An MP was a red-capped rag to him and Snowy was a professional 'pug'. The CO would shout at me, 'Why don't you keep your men in order, Sir.' I would like to see anyone keep Snowy in order.

The last seen of Snowy Mitchell, God rest him, was on the opening day of the Battle of the Somme. He was galloping over no man's land, armed only with the Spare Parts Box. He jumped into the German front line and I have no doubt was a professional 'pug' on twenty more until bayoneted.

Sharp was a transferred bomber, a big New Zealander, a man of means in his own country, a refuser of commissions. When he joined the MMGS I had to find out from him his destination when he would go on leave. 'Bailleul, Sir.' Rather taken aback I repeated my request. He said, 'Bailleul, Sir.' I said, 'Sharp, do you really mean to say that you want to spend your next leave in Bailleul?' He said 'Yes, Sir'. I went to the CO who was pleased. In fact he patted himself on the back, so to speak. Sharp went to Bailleul on his next leave. He told me guardedly that he spent it up in the front line with the Australians and much enjoyed himself. He survived the war but was a badly smashed up man at the end.

Wilson was a transferred bomber. He had a genius for scouting in no man's land and a complete ignorance of danger. We were at that same rest camp and he was feeling the dullness insufferable. One morning my sergeant, a grand little Canadian, came to me and announced that he was sorry to report that Wilson had disobeyed orders. 'What did he do, Sergeant?' I asked. 'Refused to get up, Sir', was the answer. 'Refused to get up?' I repeated, quite at a loss whether to blow up or to laugh. 'Yes, Sir, still in his blankets, Sir.' That seemed final, so I said, 'Does he give any reason?' 'Yes, Sir. Protest, Sir. Wants the battalion to go back to the front line, Sir.' 'Wants the battalion –

Oh, bring him to me, Sergeant, at once.' The sergeant brought him, and I excused the sergeant.

The upshot was that Wilson was offering himself up as a sacrifice to get the battalion back into the front lines. He knew that he could be shot for his action. He was extremely gloomy. I knew Wilson very well and he was an educated man, an Australian, so I said, 'Who gave you leave to speak for the MMGS in particular. Every man in the MMGS, including myself, is as good a man as you are and we all feel the same way. Now, give me your word of honour that you will drop this foolishness and obey orders in future, and I will not report this to the CO.' He did so, and became the real Wilson again.

Then there were two fine young fellows, not transferred bombers. One of them gained a DCM in the Battle of the Somme later. Hitherto, their conduct had been exemplary, but we were undergoing that deplorable rest behind the lines which, it seemed to me was destroying the morale of the British Army. One evening at roll call they were missing. They were absent for two days and nights and on their return were arrested at once. The next morning they were before the CO and I had, of course, to be present. Their sole defence was 'Drunk, Sir', 'Drunk, Sir', and I knew that neither of them were drinking men. They stuck impassively to that slogan and could not be shifted. I gave them the best of characters and the CO gave them fourteen days No.2 Field Punishment, not a severe sentence. He gave me a good blowing up, as an afterthought, 'Why don't you keep etc.'

Time passed and the order came to transfer the MMGS to the Machine Gun Corps. The men had to go but the CO would not allow me to go. The battalion was transferred to the Somme area which was being groomed for the battle, and to my sorrow I had to leave my MMGS behind. On the early morning of our departure I had just swung myself into the saddle when suddenly these men appeared, one at each stirrup leather. The spokesman spoke in a hoarse whisper. 'We want to tell you, Sir, what happened when we were away.' 'Go ahead,' I said, full of curiosity. 'We jumped a lorry, Sir, and went up to the front lines. Spent the night with the Australians.' I said 'Why in the world didn't you tell the Colonel?' 'He wouldn't have believed it, Sir. Thought it better to say we were drunk, Sir.'

In the month of May 1915, before I got my commission, we were force-marched to Festubert and into a recently captured German trench, which was the front line of the moment. The trench had not converted and we were facing a parados instead of a parapet. It was a thin protection. In the early afternoon of a Sunday we were heavily shelled. Next to me was an old friend who wore both the Boer War ribbons. He was doing sentry at a loophole, standing on the firestep. We were flattened to the sandbags in front at a lower altitude. A shell came through the thin parados and made a direct hit on him, I think, doing a good deal of damage in that bay. Then he spoke three times quite clearly and distinctly in an unhurried manner. He said, 'I'm hit – Fetch a doctor – Never mind!' and then he died. The marvel of his speech came to our understanding later in that night when we had to bury our dead in shell holes. It was with difficulty that we could lift him all in one piece.

I have dealt so far with incidents connected with the ranks but the spirit among officers was just as high, although necessarily more restrained owing to a greater sense of responsibility. In January 1917, having joined the Tank Corps, I was ambling along on an ice-cold train on my way towards St. Pol, behind which town lay the closed area where tank personnel received their training. Opposite the Thiepval sector the train came to a halt and a large Gordon Highlander officer blundered in, threw himself full length on the seat opposite me and went fast asleep at once. He was mud plastered, unshaven, completely worn out: Lieutenant Birnie.

On 23 November, after travelling all night, we found ourselves in a trench at Anneux and our tanks in a sunken road near-by, preparatory to going over very soon into the Bourlon Wood sector. It was cold at dawn and drizzling a fine rain. Someone had sent by post some cold grouse and we were breakfasting. As I remember Birnie was standing up, a positively noble figure of a man.

Entered on the scene his sergeant whose usual composure was replaced by most evident nervous embarrassment. He shifted from one leg to the other, tongue-tied. Birnie said, 'What is it, Sergeant?' in his friendly manner. The sergeant said, 'I've come to ask you a question, sir', and stopped as if shot. 'All right, Sergeant, go ahead.' 'Well, sir, the men want to know if you ever feels any different when you goes into action because you don't show it,' all said in one breath as if in a hurry to get rid of it. Birnie stood there looking down on the sergeant from his much greater height with a kindly but puzzled expression born of a great simplicity, and he said, 'But sergeant, you're only going to get killed.' The sergeant, speechless, tottered away in a maze. Birnie was killed that day. He and his tank crew were never heard of again. They disappeared. No doubt in a great blaze. The Gordons ought to remember this, the Tank Corps does.

[NOTE: It is not clear whether Frank intended to write more under this heading]

Afterword

fter a visit to relatives on Tresco in the Scilly Isles, probably for a well-earned rest, Frank returned to the USA on the SS *Lapland* in October 1919. Within a short time he was employed by the P.W. Shufeldt Company to map hitherto unexplored areas of British Honduras and Guatemala and to locate the chicle trees from which chewing gum was manufactured. Here in 1924 he drew the first known map of 'Uaxactun and Surrounding Area' and discovered previously unknown Mayan buildings.

In 1928 he married Olivia, Nelson Fell's younger daughter (her sister had married his brother Minor in 1914) and she joined him in British Honduras. It was she, no doubt, who photographed him holding an umbrella to keep the sun of Belize from shining on Charles Lindbergh as he worked on the repair of his plane, the Spirit of St. Louis. 'Looks as if it was only for me, but it was primarily for him, he was working in the open and under a hot sun,' Frank wrote. Typically, he could not bear to think that someone might judge him badly.

Brief interludes followed in Cornwall, where they grew daffodils for market, and Spain; later he managed a ranch in New Mexico and it was here that he heard in 1935 that his sister-in-law Marian had died, leaving her children orphaned (Minor had died in 1929). Frank and Olivia returned to England and took over the care of the four children, of whom my father, aged 11, was the third.

As the children grew up, Frank and Olivia again moved on, to France where they bought a villa near Cannes. There they lived peacefully, visited by the children during the school holidays until, on 17 June 1940, they took to the road to escape internment. A brief note written by Frank records five days' driving to catch a ship which left Bayonne on 22 June, and their arrival at Plymouth the next day. On 2 July they sent Minor and Marian's youngest child off to safety in the USA and on the 6th Frank joined the Home Guard in Truro.

Two years later he was, to his great irritation 'pushed out' of the Home Guard on grounds of age; he was 74. He promptly joined the Royal Observer Corps (there cannot have been much wrong with his eyesight at least) in which he continued to 'do his bit' until the Corps was stood down in May 1945.

He and Olivia returned to the south of France for a short while, then moved on to the West Indies and South Africa. In 1954 he gave his address to the Rough Riders' Association as c/o Barclays Bank, Jamaica. After a visit to England in about 1954, the only time I met him, Frank died in 1955 in Lausanne, Switzerland aged 87.

There are many gaps in these notes which it may now be impossible to fill. From some parts of his life, Frank and the family seem to have preserved every letter and photograph; from other times there remains nothing. I cannot discover which sister he referred to as 'Parrafine' in a letter to Olivia from Biarritz in 1897 in which he drew and criticized at length the 'loathesome [sic] little wretch of a dog' which his sister called 'darling sweetie yum-yum'.

If Frank travelled further than five paragraphs into the 'restless seas of the task' of writing the autobiography which he began in 1938, nothing remains. What he wrote is in a voice instantly recognizable from the letters and diaries of 1914-18: relentlessly positive, with a tendency to preachiness, devoid of any sign of human weakness on his part. 'It was my lot' he wrote, 'to have been plumped, with deliberation and with the best intentions, into the hurly-burly of the world without a profession or a trade, and my life became a joyous struggle to keep afloat with dignity and self-respect; the former failed frequently but never the latter.' Anyone who has read his war diaries will recognize the man at once. If he ever had doubts about what he was doing, he seems never to have voiced them and never, or hardly ever, to have lost his capacity to enjoy life or the courage to take on fresh challenges. In the family his reputation certainly has remained untarnished. Nevertheless he surely cannot have been an easy man to live with or to live up to. Sometimes he seems to have been unable to understand the everyday weaknesses of ordinary humans and though he rarely cast aspersions on the courage of the soldiers around him, he did not hold back from brutal criticism of any who gave in to fear or pain. He described boredom as 'the most foolish sin of all' but, perhaps, it was in fact because he was easily bored that he wandered so restlessly throughout his life.

Frank's attitude to the war and to life in general is now unfashionable and, I have to admit, unsympathetic. Reading his memoir it is often difficult to feel comfortable with his views and the way he expressed them; nevertheless I cannot assume the right, as I sit on my warm sofa at home, to criticize him for what he wrote in the stinking mud of Flanders. His opinions are honest and valid and no doubt shared by many people at the time, in the trenches and at home. He wrote because he saw that he was engaged in a chapter of history that should be understood and remembered; it has been my pleasure and privilege to be part of that process.

Frank Vans Agnew, biographical summary

Born: 27 April, 1868, in India
Educated: Kensington Grammar School

Career:

1884	Emigrated with his three brothers to New York, then Florida where he met E. Nelson Fell (ENF) and his family
	Farming in Minnesota and involved with a tow mill in Fulda, Georgia
1895	Graduated Ontario Veterinary College
1898	Enlisted in Roosevelt's Rough Riders as a farrier but saw no action
1900-1902	Worked for ENF at the Athabasca gold mine, Nelson, British Columbia as assayer
1903-07	Moved with ENF to Spassky in Kazakhstan where ENF ran the Spassky copper mine; FVA was assayer
10 Dec 1908– 6 May 1913	Postmaster, Kissimmee, Florida
1913	'Premier peach grower of section' according to the *Kissimmee Journal*

War record:

1914	Aged 46, claiming to be 40, enlisted in 2nd King Edward's Horse stationed at Woodbridge, Suffolk for training
May 1915	Posted to France/Belgium near Festubert
June 1915	Promoted Lance-Corporal
Sep/Oct 1915	Commissioned
Oct 1915	Trained at the Curragh, Ireland
Dec 23 1915	Returned to front near Neuve Eglise
Jan 1916	Machine Gun School
Aug 1916	Observed Battle of Somme from OP
Sept 1916	Saw début of tanks as observer

Dec 1916	Applied to join Tank Corps
	Ten days home leave
Jan 1917	Joined Tank Corps
June 7, 1917	Battle of Messines, tank commander, wounded
July 1917	Six days 'special leave' at Mirlemont, Paris Plage
	Visit of the King and tank demonstration
	Awarded MC for Battle of Messines
July 31, 1917	3rd Battle of Ypres, tank commander
Aug 1917	Home leave
Nov 1917	1st Battle of Cambrai: commanding 5 Section, on board
	Lieutenant Dalby's tank Bandit II; wounded and captured
Jan 1918	PoW at Hanover
Mar 1918	PoW at Karlsruhe and Heidelberg
May 1918	Examined but not passed for internment
Aug 1918	Moved to Fürstenberg
Dec 1918	Arrived in Copenhagen
Jan 30, 1919	Left Copenhagen for Leith

After the war:

1920–28	In Belize (British Honduras)
1928	Married Olivia Fell
1929–30	Scilly Isles
1930–33	Albion, Cornwall
1934	Spain
1935	Manager of a ranch in New Mexico
	He and Olivia now returned to England and took over the care of his brother's four children
1936–37	Romanhurst, Oxfordshire with the younger children
1938–1940	At the outbreak of World War Two he and Olivia were at the Villa Vans near Cannes, from which they escaped, driving for five days to catch the last British ship to leave Bayonne
1940–46	Joined first the Home Guard in Cornwall, then the Observer Corps
1947	France
1948	West Indies
1950	South Africa
1955	Lausanne, Switzerland, where he died.

Notes

Notes on the Text
1. Colonel A.C. Murray in a letter to P.A. Vans Agnew, 1 February 1918.
2. Royal Canadian Dragoons.

Chapter 1: To the Front, May–October 1915
1. Frank's 'suffragette sister' Ida, married to Frank Corbett whose brother and sister-in-law were for many years active campaigners for women's rights.
2. Lieutenant Colonel Montagu Cradock CB, CMG, (1859-1929) soldier and author, commanded 2nd KEH from its formation to 1918.
3. Frank's drawing of the airship no longer exists.
4. Mrs Meiklejon, wife of R.W. Meiklejon (see below).
5. Probably Frank's cousin Kate, married to Erasmus Gower; their son Erasmus was taken prisoner in September 1914.
6. Private John Dickson-Hill, 150, (1875-1915) born Dalmeny, West Lothian, enlisted White City, London, resident of Bedford, le Touret Memorial, Pas de Calais.
7. Private Robert Wright Meiklejon. Regt. No. 1239, known to Frank as Micky. Born 1879 in Scotland, he became a merchant seaman, was a rancher in Canada, but was in Kissimmee, Florida in 1913 when he and Frank organized the Sports at the 4th of July celebrations; he became a US citizen in 1942 and died in Florida in 1969. Micky married, in 1905, Helena Brooke Bodington (later known to Frank as Mrs Micky or Mrs M).
8. Private Guy Sherris, 1279, (1884-1915), formerly employee of Argentine Railways, le Touret Memorial.
9. Private Harry William Kingswell Hunt, (1883-1915), Regt. No. 1148, son of Mr and Mrs G.H. Hunt, of South Croydon; husband of Rhoda L. Hunt, le Touret Memorial.
10. Private Willy Herbert Alexander Auerbach, (1879-1915), Regt. No. 1145, le Touret Memorial.
11. Private Ernest Wilmot Scallon, Regt. No. 1172, son of the late Edward Brand Scallon and Frances Bradley Scallon. Educated Malvern College. Came from the Argentine to England and enlisted in 1914.
12. Private David Arthur Henry Alexander, (ca 1885-1915), Regt. No. 1400, from Vancouver.
13. Private Vivien Vere Willis, (1883-1964) No. 711, 2nd KEH and Tank Corps, solicitor.
14. Lance Corporal Lionel Brandon, No. 797, (1876-1935) 2nd KEH and Royal Army Service Corps.
15. Private James Joseph O'Hea, (1889-1976), Regt. No. 1128, later Lieutenant Colonel Liverpool Regiment.

16. Private Maurice Joseph de Verteuil, (ca 1893-1966) Regt. No. 1356, later Northumberland Fusiliers and Tank Corps.
17. Lieutenant the Hon. Gilbert Grosvenor, born 28 Aug 1881, died 15 Jun 1939, son of Richard Grosvenor, 1st Baron Stalbridge (though Frank refers to him several times as C.C. Grosvenor).
18. Sergeant Dan Morris, DCM, Regt. No. 1047 from Canada.
19. Second Lieutenant Francis Hillier Walrond, 2nd KEH and Ox and Bucks Light Infantry, killed in action 15 August 1916 aged 34.
20. General Sir Edwin Alfred Harvey Alderson.
21. Major later Colonel Arthur Cecil Murray, King Edward's Horse, Viscount Elibank, CMG, DSO, soldier and politician.
22. We have not been able to trace this reference.
23. Thought to be Theodore E. Foster, Regt No 731, arrived France 22 April 1915, commissioned Second Lieutenant 22 June 1917.
24. J. Pennington Gardiner, Boston, Mass. Like Frank, J. Pennington Gardiner served in Roosevelt's regiment of Roughriders in the Spanish-American war.
25. Captain Geoffrey Vaux Salvin Bowlby, killed 13 or 16 May 1916, Frank's cousin, brother of Dickie Bowlby.
26. Probably Frank's cousin Kate, wife of Erasmus Gower whose son was a PoW from November 1914 until 1918.
27. Pet name for Olivia Fell, who was to marry Frank in 1928, sister of Marian, daughter of Edward Nelson Fell.
28. Thought to be Lieutenant Edward Hugh Heath.
29. Lieutenant Leonard Arthur Carey, Regt. No. 1288, Private in 2nd KEH, commissioned Second Lieutenant 23 April 1916 2nd Battalion Devonshire Regiment, killed in action 1 July 1916.
30. Lieutenant Colonel John Vans Agnew of Barnbarroch (1855-1941), then head of the family and Frank's first cousin.
31. Thought to be Lance-Corporal Frederick J. Lucas, Regt. No. 648, of Australia.
32. Lieutenant George Henry Heasman, enlisted as a Private in the 19th Hussars and in 1915 he transferred to King Edward's Horse (Special Reserve) and went to France in May 1916. Appointed to the RFC in April 1917; on 4 January 1918 he was killed in an air crash while instructing a student pilot.
33. John Edward Bernard Seely, 1st Baron Mottistone CB, CMG, DSO, TD, PC, JP, DL (31 May 1868 – 7 November 1947) British soldier and politician, known as 'Galloper' Jack, subject of the play and film *War Horse*.

Chapter 2: Training and Guard Duty, October 1915–August 1916
1. Major General Henry Byron Jeffreys, Royal Artillery, Frank's cousin.

Chapter 3: At the Battle of the Somme, August–November 1916
1. Olivia Fell.
2. Deo volente – God willing.
3. Lieutenant later Major A.V. Monk, MC, 2nd King Edward's Horse and Tank Corps.

4. *Scribner's Magazine* was an American periodical; the issues of July and August 1916 carried articles by Frank about war in the trenches.
5. Lieutenant Raymond Asquith, son of the Premier, Herbert Asquith, killed in action 15 Sep 1916, commemorated Guillemont Road Cemetery.

Chapter 4: With the Tanks in Action, December 1916–November 1917

1. Thought to be Private Sidney Thomas, Regimental Number 1036, who survived the war and was discharged 19 November 1918.
2. J. Pennington Gardiner.
3. Patrick Alexander 'Minor' Vans Agnew, Frank's brother, a lawyer in Florida, married to Marian Fell, Olivia's sister.
4. Probably Frank's younger sister Gertrude.
5. Colonel later Brigadier General Anthony A. Courage, DSO, MC, commissioned in the 15th Hussars, 1896, CO of B Battalion, HBMGC from January 1917.
6. Frank's boat that he used to get to and from his home on Paradise Island, Florida.
7. Edward Nelson Fell; presumably Frank used to drive his car.
8. General Sir William Eliot Peyton, KCB, KCVO, DSO, Sir Douglas Haig's Military Secretary.
9. Captain Easton Brock Dudgeon, 1866-1944, 'an Edinburgh man', a member of the London Stock Exchange, two years older than Frank.
10. No.5 Section consisted of Second Lieutenants Simpson, Vans Agnew, Brockwell and Alex Crerar, born in Scotland ca 1893 who later emigrated to Australia.

Chapter 5: Battle of Messines, 5 June 1917

1. General, later Field Marshal, Sir Herbert Plumer.
2. Major Frank Tucker, MC, West Yorkshire Regiment and Tank Corps (born 1886).
3. Actually a tributary of the Douve, marked Steenebeek on Frank's map, running roughly south, close to the British frontline.
4. Corporal R.A. Tait, MM and Bar, captured at Fontaine, 23 November 1918, discharged 26 Aug. 1919, thought to be Reginald Arnan Tait (1879-1950) an engineer in civilian life.
5. Lieutenant William John Gordon Birnie, Gordon Highlanders and Tank Corps, killed at Fontaine 23 Nov. 1917, Cambrai Memorial, Louverval.
6. Thought to be Capt. Samuel Blackwell, DSO, E Battalion Tank Corps, died 20 Nov 1917, commemorated at Ribécourt Cemetery.
7. Lieutenant Geoffrey Arthur Henry Ley, Devonshire Regiment and Tank Corps, an insurance clerk before the war, killed July 30, 1917 aged 26, Soissons Memorial. His only brother was killed in the Battle of Arras in March 1917.

Chapter 6: Interval

1. Lieutenant J.E. Doyle.
2. Lieutenant Colonel R.C.R. Hill, DSO, Indian Army, Royal Engineers and Tank Corps, Colonel of B Battalion.

Chapter 7: The Third Battle of Ypres, 31 July 1917

1. The story of 'Sergeant Phillips' is mentioned in Steele and Hart's *Passchendaele, the Sacrificial Ground* but the authors tend to the view that it has no basis in fact.
2. Major later Lieutenant Colonel Edward Daniel Bryce, DSO and 3 Bars.
3. In Frank's typescript the tank's name is given as Bandit (which was B23); this may be a transcription error or even a lapse of memory. It appears from other records that he was actually in Brigand (B24), and that Brigand was also the tank he commanded at Messines. It seems possible that Frank originally wrote a shorthand note, perhaps simply the initial 'B' in his original manuscript and that the typist extrapolated from the later entries where Bandit appears correctly, Bandit II (B23) being the tank he was in at Cambrai. However Frank's account is consistent throughout and may be correct.
4. Lieutenant Lionel Salvin Henry 'Dickie' Bowlby, 2nd Dragoons (Royal Scots Greys), Frank's cousin, killed 4 June 1916, brother of Geoff Bowlby who was killed 16 May 1916.
5. Lieutenant Arthur Mitchell Williamson, Tank Corps, Regt. No. 200994 (1898-1917).
6. Lieutenant Sydney Alfred Brockwell, London Regiment, Tank Corps from 20 January 1917, born London, 1895, died Australia, 1975 where he had a son; his tombstone inscribed 'British Army Old Contemptible – 1914'.
7. Major Edward Daniel Bryce, later Colonel commanding B Battalion, Tank Corps.
8. Lieutenant Arthur Adams Dalby, MC, (1897-1965), West Yorkshire Regt. and Tank Corps. Son of the Rev. L.B. Dalby of Preston, awarded Military Cross for action of Nov 20, 1917 at Marcoing, badly wounded and made prisoner of war. Frank wrote in a note, 'Dalby came to the front in the Bantam battalion. He was one of the first Stokes mortar men before he joined tanks; he was terribly stout-hearted'.
9. Major Edward Lovelace Vans Agnew, Yorkshire Regiment, Frank's cousin.
10. Captain George Edward Porter MC and Bar, Devonshire Regiment and Tank Corps.
11. Not identified.
12. Captain G. Kelson, 1st King Edward's Horse, died 27 Dec 1919, commemorated South Africa.
13. The Battle of La Malmaison was one of the first notable actions of the French under General Pétain; it culminated on 24 October 1917 in the capture of La Malmaison and control of the ridge of Chemin des Dâmes.

Chapter 8: The First Battle of Cambrai, 19–22 November 1917

1. Bundles of wood wired together and rolled into a cylinder 10 feet long.
2. Second Lieutenant, later Major Nathaniel John 'Neil' Gordon-Clark, (1898-1985), Devonshire Regiment and Tank Corps, writer on economic planning; served in Intelligence in World War Two as a member of London Controlling Section specializing in deception operations.
3. Major later Lieutenant Colonel Louis Sydney Henshall, DSO, (1889-1957), South Lancashire Regiment, commanding No. 5 Company Tank Corps, an architect before the war.

Chapter 9: The First Battle of Cambrai, 23 November 1917
1. Corporal Tait, gunner; Lance Corporal Thomas H. Hood 200323, gearsman; Privates Henry L. Bennett 200415, gunner, formerly RFA; Cyril Bazeley 75913, Royal Sussex Regiment, later Tank Corps, driver; W. Yeoman 75475, gunner; Coleman (see below) and J. Buckham 200267, gunner.
2. Private Frederick John Coleman 75849, gunner, enlisted Colchester 9 Dec. 1915 Essex Regiment, later Tank Corps, wounded and taken prisoner at Fontaine-Notre-Dâme, discharged as unfit for War Service, 13 Dec 1918.
3. Lieutenant Ralph Melville Law, Tank Corps, son of Professor Law of Toronto University.

Chapter 10: Prisoner of War
1. Captain Hugh Warren Victor Benjamin Broomhead Diamond, Tank Corps (1881–1966), actor.
2. Lieutenant General Sir Hugh Jamieson Elles, KCB, KCMG, KCVO, DSO (1880–1945), first commander of the Tank Corps. In his book *Tanks In The Great War 1914-1918* Colonel J.F.C. Fuller, DSO, an aide of General Elles, wrote 'The statement made in the daily press that General Elles' order ran – "England expects every tank to do its damnedest," was a pure journalistic invention and one in very bad taste.' Presumably that was taken to mean that they should fight to the death.

Chapter 11: Münster Lager
1. Lieutenant Colonel Neville Bowes Elliott-Cooper, VC, DSO, MC, died 11 Feb. 1918, Hanover.

Chapter 12: Hanover
1. Second Lieutenant Herbert Farmer Evans, RHA and RFC, missing 9 November 1916, interned 2 June 1918, born 1897, so a prisoner at the age of nineteen.
2. At an enquiry held in early 1918, after the German counter-attack had wiped out big British gains made in the first phases of the Battle of Cambrai, senior officers denied or justified failures at a strategic level and pinned the blame largely on the poor performance of junior officers and the men in the field. It is hard to imagine that Frank would have applauded the outcome.
3. Plasmon, a proprietary dried milk, was manufactured by the International Plasmon Co, and was added to a number of different products: Plasmon Oats, Cocoa and Biscuits.

Chapter 13: Karlsruhe
1. Cap comforters were worn during the First World War as a warm alternative to the service dress cap, the fabric often pulled low over the ears in the cold; it appears to be a short scarf but when turned partially inside out and fitted on the head it becomes a woollen hat.
2. Thought to be Lieutenant H.J. Davey, Machine Gun Corps, missing 30 November 1917.

3. Thought to be Second Lieutenant R. Reader, 11th Battalion, King's Royal Rifle Corps, missing 30 November 1917, repatriated 17 December 1918.

4. Lieutenant Colonel Lionel Holmes Wood Troughton, Rifle Brigade, Captain of the Surrey cricket team, died 31 August 1933.

5. Lieutenant Colonel Raymond Henry Baldwin, The East Surrey Regiment (1872-1949).

6. Thought to be Major E.N. Marris MC (not Morris), Lincolnshire Regt and D Battalion Tanks Corps, missing 20 November 1917, repatriated January 1919. Later Frank says he's of A. Battalion but this appears to be an error.

7. SMS *Wolf* (formerly the freighter *Wachtfels*) was an armed merchant raider or auxiliary cruiser of the German Imperial Navy.

8. Lieutenant Thomas Malcolm Dickinson, B Flight, No. 56 Squadron, RFC, missing 6 Jun 1917, repatriated 19 January 1919. A captain in the 16th Cavalry, Indian Army, he was attached to the 1st Grenadier Guards, wounded at Festubert 1915, attached RFC, died under operation to his wounds in Egypt 4th January 1921 aged 27.

9. Captain J.E. Johnston, 20 Squadron, RFC, missing 2 December 1917, repatriated December 1918.

10. Captain J.C.B. Tragett, South Wales Borderers.

11. Lieutenant Kenneth L. Golding, RFC.

Chapter 14: Heidelberg

1. Lieutenant Thomas Milbourn Mercer, King Edward's Horse and Tank Corps, born Lancashire 1892, killed at Fontaine commanding tank B30, Bally Hackle II.

2. Sub-Lieutenant J. Osborn Groves, Royal Naval Air Service, missing 5 July 1915, interned Switzerland, 22 May 1918.

3. Lieutenant Percy Gerald de Paravicini, 11th Battalion, King's Royal Rifle Corps, missing 30 November 1917, repatriated 25 December 1918, son of Percy John de Paravicini.

4. Commandant Richard of Brest, Finistère, perhaps the man who commanded the 1st Battalion the 2nd Régiment d'Infanterie Coloniale (which came from Brest) near the Belgian frontier in August 1914.

5. Apparently D. Fry, as this is how he signed an article about billiards in the Heidelberg camp newsletter; thought to be Second Lieutenant D.A.B. Fry, 8th Battalion, Royal Fusiliers, missing 30 November 1917, repatriated 25 December 1918. According to Frank he was the 'brother of the great C.B. Fry', but C.B. Fry appears to have had only one brother, Major Walter Burgess Fry who died in PoW camp on 17 March 1915.

6. Captain Erasmus Gower, taken prisoner at battle of Mons in September 1914, Frank's cousin.

7. Mesopotamia, modern–day Iraq.

8. Lieutenant John Beauchamp Harvey, RFC, born London, Ontario, 8 November 1892. Reported missing 24 May and prisoner 12 July 1917. He took part in the 1920 Canadian Chess Championship in which he tied for first place and was still alive and playing chess in 1957.

9. Second Lieutenant J.O. Evans, killed at Fontaine, 23 November 1917 commanding B28, Black Arrow II.

10. Second Lieutenant A. Simpson, killed at Fontaine, commander of B24, Brigand II, the 'unlucky thirteenth' tank.

11. Second Lieutenant H.W. Christmas, commander of B36, Bayardo II, wounded at Fontaine.

12. Second Lieutenant Arthur Mansfield Niall, 6th Inniskilling Dragoons, missing 1 Dec 1917, repatriated 21 Dec 1918, fl. 1930, New South Wales, Australia.

13. Captain C.W. Young, 20th Battalion, King's Royal Rifle Corps, missing 2 October 1918 repatriated 28 November 1918.

14. Lieutenant Maurice Richard Corneel Lacante (1883-1918), died of his wounds soon after his release after four years as a PoW.

15. Second Lieutenant S.A. Clark, 9th Battalion, Essex Regiment, missing 11 July 1917, interned 13 May 1918.

16. Nelson, son of Edward Nelson Fell, brother of Olivia and Marian.

17. Thought to be sous-Lieutenant Pierre Bayard of the Infantry whose name appeared in a list of those taken prisoner in the *Gazette des Ardennes* on 24 March 1916, a newspaper of the occupied territory.

18. Latin for 'at your pleasure' usually shortened to 'ad lib'.

19. Lieutenant Samuel George Montague Nathan, Royal Warwickshire Regt, (1897–1937), missing 3 May 1917. It is claimed that in 1921, as a member of the Auxiliary Division of the Royal Irish Constabulary, he carried out the murder of the Mayor and the ex-Mayor of Limerick. He re-joined the British Army but was court-martialed and discharged in 1926. He died in the Spanish Civil War fighting for the Republican cause.

20. Thought to be Lieutenant L. Goldstein, Royal Field Artillery, missing 30 November 1917, repatriated 18 December 1918.

21. Thought to be Second Lieutenant F.A. Mann, RFC, missing 7 July 1917, repatriated 18 December 1918.

22. Second Lieutenant D.F. Brundritt, C Battalion, Tank Corps, missing 20 Nov 1917, interned 23 Dec 1918.

23. Captain (or Major) F.C Walker, 14 Battalion, London Regiment (London Scots), missing 24 November 1917, repatriated 17 December 1918.

24. Estate in Leicestershire, requisitioned at the start of the war for use as a prisoner of war camp.

Chapter 15: Fürstenberg

1. Lieutenant W.O.H. Ellis, 9th Battalion, Royal Welsh Fusiliers, missing 24 March 1918, repatriated 17 December 1918, thought to be William Oldaker Ellis (1886-1961) Senior Assistant, (scientific), Farnborough in World War Two.

2. Captain Herbert Seppings Lidiard, MC, (1893-1981) 3rd Battalion, London Regiment, missing 26 November1917, repatriated 17 December 1918.

3. Of the Pioneers, not identified.

4. Lieutenant Colonel C.H. Howard-Bury, 9th Battalion, King's Royal Rifle Corps.

5. Lieutenant Colonel A.J.H. Sloggett, 7th Battalion, Rifle Brigade, missing 21 March 1918, repatriated 19 January 1919, son of the Chief Medical Officer, BEF.

6. Lieutenant Colonel Lord A.K. Farnham, 2nd Battalion, Royal Inniskilling Fusiliers, missing 21 March 1918, repatriated 17 December 1918.
7. Second Lieutenant Stanley Edmundson, Manchester Regiment and 21st Battalion, Machine Gun Corps, missing 22 March 1918, repatriated 17 December 1918.
8. Second Lieutenant Herbert Charles Howell, 6th Battalion, Durham Light Infantry, attached from Border Regiment, missing 27 May 1918, repatriated 31 December 1918.
9. Lieutenant Charles Albert Boraston, MC, (ca 1879-1950) missing 30 March 1918, repatriated 17 December 1918.
10. William Vett, successor of Emil Vett - co-founder in 1868 of Magasin du Nord in Copenhagen.
11. Thought to be Louise Baroness Wedell-Wedellsborg, (1869 – 1932) daughter of Baron Gustav Wedell-Wedellsborg.
12. Prince Valdemar of Denmark GCTE (1858–1939) youngest son of Christian IX of Denmark and his wife Louise of Hesse-Kassel.
13. Victor Alexander Sereld Hay, 21st Earl of Erroll and 4th Baron Kilmarnock, KCMG (1876–1928) was First Secretary in Copenhagen, 1918–19.

Index